OS/2 PROGRAMMING

Herbert Schildt and
Robert Goosey

Osborne **McGraw-Hill**

Berkeley New York St. Louis San Francisco
Auckland Bogotá Hamburg London Madrid
Mexico City Milan Montreal New Delhi Panama City
Paris São Paulo Singapore Sydney
Tokyo Toronto

Osborne **McGraw-Hill**
2600 Tenth Street
Berkeley, California 94710
U.S.A.

For information on translations or book distributors outside of the U.S.A.,
please write to Osborne **McGraw-Hill** at the above address.

OS/2 Programming

 234567890 DOC 99876543

ISBN 0-07-881910-5

Acquisitions Editor Emily Rader	**Copy Editors** Cynthia de Hay Joseph Ferrie	**Illustrator** Susie C. Kim
Technical Editor Bob Eidson	**Proofreaders** K. D. Sullivan Peter Vacek	**Computer Designer** Stefany Otis
Project Editors Judith Brown Claire Splan	**Indexer** Phil Roberts	**Cover Designer** Studio Silicon

C O N T E N T S

C O N T E N T S

C O N T E N T S

CHAPTER 11 FILE I/O

CHAPTER 12 CREATING AND USING DYNAMIC LINK LIBRARIES

C O N T E N T S

INTRODUCTION

The purpose of this book is to give you a "jump start" into the world of OS/2.*x* programming. OS/2 is a very complex operating system, and the ways that you, the programmer, can interact with OS/2 are numerous and varied. This book will help you understand quickly the essence of programming OS/2.

What makes OS/2 exciting is that it is a true preemptive multitasking operating system. OS/2 also takes full advantage of the capabilities and power of the 80386 microprocessors, including 32-bit processing. Although microcomputers have been able to run multitasking operating systems, such as UNIX, for several years, the results have not always been entirely satisfactory, partly because the porting of a multi-user, multitasking operating system to a single-user, highly interactive environment generally produced the worst of both worlds: slow response time combined with an old, TTY-based interface. OS/2 maintains the highly interactive nature of the personal computing environment, while allowing greater throughput by means of full 32-bit processing power and preemptive multitasking.

OS/2 opens the doors to a whole new world for programmers. Fully harnessing the capabilities of OS/2 will allow you to create highly efficient and powerful programs, the likes of which could have never been seen in previous operating systems offered for the personal computing environment.

ABOUT THIS BOOK

This book was written specifically for OS/2, versions 2.0 and above, which are radically different from their 1.0 to 1.3 predecessors. Very little time is spent in this book discussing how earlier releases of OS/2 worked. The reason for this is simple. If you are new to OS/2 programming, this book contains all the information you will need to understand the OS/2 programming philosophy and its underlying technical details. If you are migrating from an earlier release, this book will give you a thorough understanding of the differences and new capabilities of releases 2.0 and above so that you may begin to incorporate this added power into your applications as quickly as possible.

As you will see in this book, there is little in OS/2 that is difficult to grasp or use. However, OS/2 is so large that it is sometimes hard to see the larger view. As you begin to learn to program for OS/2, it may seem difficult to pull all the pieces together, but as you become more experienced, the logical design of OS/2 will become apparent. This book can help you achieve that "view from the top" of OS/2.

This book assumes that you have experience as a programmer and a basic understanding of how to use OS/2 in the PC environment. The examples are in C, so a basic understanding of the C programming language is necessary.

HOW THIS BOOK IS ORGANIZED

Part One of this book gives you an overview of OS/2, including a look at the 80386/80486 processors and some basic programming guidelines. If you are familiar with the 80386 processor, and the basic programming concepts of OS/2, this part may be skipped. However, if you have never programmed in a 32-bit environment, I suggest you review the 32-bit programming section in Chapter 2.

Part Two covers the Presentation Manager Application Programming Interface. Creating windows, interacting with your program through menus and dialogs, and using the mouse are some of the areas covered. A chapter on using graphics with the Presentation Manager is also contained in Part Two of this book.

Part Three covers the core services of OS/2. This section explains how to use multitasking in your programs to unleash the power of OS/2. It also explains how to control separate processes, how to communicate between processes, perform file I/O, and construct and utilize dynamic linked libraries.

CONVENTIONS USED IN THIS BOOK

In this book, functions and keywords are shown in boldface type along with variable names when referenced in text. General forms of variable names are shown in italics. Also, when referencing a function name in text, the name of the function is followed by parentheses. In this way you can easily distinguish a variable name from a function name.

DISK OFFER

If you're like most busy programmers, you would probably like to use the many programs presented in this book, but hate the thought of typing them into the computer. For this reason the source code to all the functions and programs contained in this book are made available on disk. So, if you'd like to spend more time exploring the sample programs, and less time trying to get the hand keyed-in program to work, simply fill in the following order form and mail it, along with a check or money order, to the address shown.

Order Form

Please send me the programs listed in *OS/2 Programming* on a IBM compatible disk. Enclosed is a check or money order for $24.95. Foreign orders only: Checks must be drawn on a U.S. bank, and please add $5 for shipping and handling.

Name _____

Address _____

City _____ State _____ Zip _____

Telephone _____

Disk size (check one): 5 1/4 _____   3 1/2_____
Send to:
Robert Goosey
OS/2 Programming Disk
2464 El Camino Real, Suite 537
Santa Clara, CA 95051
This offer is good through January 1995.

Please allow 3 to 6 weeks for delivery. Osborne/McGraw-Hill assumes NO responsibility for this offer. This is solely an offer of Robert Goosey, and not of Osborne/McGraw-Hill.

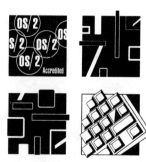

PART

ONE

INTRODUCTION TO OS/2 PROGRAMMING

Part One presents some necessary background information on OS/2 and discusses the special 80386 features that OS/2 exploits. You will learn about OS/2's design philosophy, and you will be introduced to the basics of OS/2 programming.

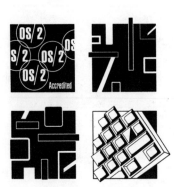

OS/2: AN OVERVIEW

OS/2 is a very large program, consisting of many subsystems. Although no single piece of OS/2 is difficult to understand or use, what can be difficult is grasping the totality of it. To help alleviate this problem, this chapter presents an overview of the OS/2 operating system, including its design philosophy, operation, and its basis in the 80386 processor. Most of the topics discussed in this chapter will be fully explored in subsequent chapters.

This chapter begins with a brief description of the origins of OS/2, followed by a discussion of the 80386 CPU, an understanding of which is so essential to an understanding of OS/2 programming. The chapter concludes with a brief tour of the OS/2 programming environment. Along the way, several new terms that have been coined or popularized as a result of OS/2 are introduced. If you already have a good basic understanding of the 80386 and of OS/2's operation, you can skip to Chapter 2.

THE HERITAGE OF OS/2

Although OS/2 was created new from the ground up, it owes much to the operating systems that preceded it. To understand why certain things in OS/2 are the way they are requires that you understand OS/2's heritage. Those of you that participated in the microcomputer revolution of the late seventies already know much of the story. However, if you are new to microcomputers, many of the bits and pieces of OS/2 make the most sense when you understand where they came from. Real microcomputer operating systems began with Digital Research's CP/M, which was designed for the Intel 8080 CPU, an 8-bit processor. (The 8080 was the forerunner to the 8086.) In the early days of microcomputing, each computer manufacturer supplied its own "operating system," which usually consisted of little more than a primitive set of disk file I/O functions. In addition to being very crude, these operating systems also suffered from the fact that they were different from one another. The differences between the systems prevented software developers from developing programs which could be mass marketed to the full range of microcomputers. When Gary Kildahl, the founder of Digital Research, created CP/M, it was with the goal of providing a common operating system for all microcomputers. To a very great extent he succeeded in this goal. CP/M is a compact, yet highly adaptive single-tasking operating system that was nothing short of perfect for the first 8-bit microcomputers.

What makes CP/M so important is that it made all the various microcomputers, manufactured by the then numerous manufacturers, software-compatible. Compatibility was a crucial, necessary ingredient to the future success of the microcomputer, because it allowed software developers to invest large amounts of time and money into creating products that ran under CP/M. Without the unifying force of CP/M, the software market would have been fragmented, thus preventing the cost-effective development of excellent software. As you will soon see, the issue of compatibility plays an important role in the development of OS/2.

When IBM began development of its first personal computer, they chose to base its architecture on the next generation of Intel microprocessors. These processors included the 16-bit 8086 and its close relative, the 8088. (IBM actually used the 8088 because it provided a cost-effective way to access a 16-bit processor using 8-bit interface chips. From here on, any reference in this book to the 8086 includes both the 8086 and the 8088.) Before the PC was released, experts speculated that it would use a new version of CP/M as its operating system. However, for reasons that are still unclear, Digital Research and IBM did not come to an agreement to use CP/M. Instead, IBM asked Microsoft, which was already working on languages for the PC, to develop a new operating system. The operating system was called PC-DOS when first released. Now, it is generally referred to simply as DOS.

Because IBM and Microsoft knew that literally thousands of programs originally written for CP/M would be converted to run under DOS, DOS was designed to be highly compatible with the original CP/M. In fact, the basis for the file system and for its system interface was CP/M. Like CP/M, DOS is a single-tasking, highly adaptive operating system that could fully control the new 16-bit microcomputers. Since its release in 1981, DOS has become the world's most popular operating system with well over 10,000,000 users worldwide. Some analysts suggest that DOS will still be in common use into the 21st century.

As good as DOS is, it does suffer from two major maladies. First, because it was originally designed for use with the 8086, it can only directly access 1 megabyte of RAM. Within this megabyte, only 640K can effectively be used because of the way the ROM and video RAM of the original PC was located. Although 640K of program memory space still sounds like a lot when viewed from the perspective of many existing DOS applications, it is far too small for the next generation of "smart" (AI-based) software or for large database or spreadsheet programs. Also, 640K is not a lot of memory when it is used in a multitasking environment. The second drawback to DOS is that it is single-tasking. Without multitasking capabilities, it is impossible to make the most efficient use of the computer. As you will see later in this chapter, much of the CPU's time is spent waiting for things to happen. During these "dead" moments, a multitasking operating system can perform another task. However, in a single-tasking system this time is simply lost.

The memory restriction found in DOS is based in the architecture of the 8086 processor and is not easily removed. Although it is possible to multitask the 8086, it is not a good idea, because the 8086 provides no way to protect one task from another. That is, if two programs were executed simultaneously using an 8086 processor, it would be possible for one program to adversely affect the execution of the second. Because of this, DOS continues to limit application memory to 640K and to remain single-tasking. It was clear that any efforts to remove these restrictions would come about because of an advance in CPU design.

The next processor released by Intel was the 80186, which was really just a faster 8086 and not important otherwise. However, in 1983 Intel released the 80286. The 80286 CPU could run all programs written for the 8086/88, but included several new instructions and a second mode of operation. When the 80286 was running in this second mode, it could address 16 megabytes of RAM and it had the ability to isolate concurrently executing programs from each other. The reason that the 80286 included two modes of operation was for the sake of compatibility with software written for the 8086/88. However, the two modes of operation are, more or less, mutually incompatible with each other. As you will come to understand, these two modes were the cause of numerous problems in the creation of the first version of OS/2.

The 80286 is the processor that IBM chose to use in the PC AT, introduced in 1984. However, because no software existed to make use of the 80286's second mode of operation, it was run by DOS simply as a faster 8086 with all of the 8086's limitations.

The newest Intel processors in common use are the 80386 and 80486. The 80386 is a vastly improved version of the 80286 and supports four basic modes of operation: 8086 "real" mode, 80286 emulation, virtual 8086, and its own 80386 operation mode. Actually, because of the way the 80386 is designed it does not have an 80286 emulation mode as such. The virtual 8086 mode is what gives OS/2 the power to multitask DOS applications. More accurately, the 80386 automatically acts like an 80286 when presented with 80286 instructions. The 80486 is similar to the 80386, but the 80486 has a math coprocessor built into the microprocessor. This and the inclusion of an on-board cache and other speed increasing enhancements, allows the 80486 to outperform the 80386 in many ways. OS/2 2.0 requires the 80386 or the 80486 to run.

In 1987 IBM released its PS/2 line of personal computers. Although the low-end PS/2 models are based upon the older 8086 processor, the models 50 and 60 use Intel 80286 and the model 80 uses the 80386 processor. To take full advantage of these machines required a new operating system. Three of the most important goals of this new operating system were to eliminate the 640K memory barrier, to support multitasking, and, for better or worse, to provide an upward compatibility path from DOS. To this end, Microsoft and IBM launched a joint development project, headed by Gordon Letwin on the Microsoft side and Ed Iacobucci on the IBM side. The result of their efforts was OS/2 1.0.

Following the release of 1.0 through 1.3, and partway into the development of 2.0, IBM and Microsoft continued to work together on OS/2. In 1991, IBM and Microsoft had a parting of ways. Since that time, IBM alone has carried out the development of OS/2.

From this historical perspective, let's see what OS/2 2.0 is all about.

THE 80386 AND OS/2: A FAMILY AFFAIR

First and foremost, OS/2 2.0 and later versions are 80386-based operating systems, but will also run on the 80486. In many ways, OS/2 is the actualization of the imaginary operating system for which the 80386 was originally designed. The Intel designers created the 80386 for a multitasking environment. Its ability to emulate its forerunners, the 8086 through the 80286, was necessary, but uninteresting. What the designers created was a processor that could serve as a solid base for the next generation of microcomputer operating systems. With this goal in mind, they implemented several important and necessary features that essentially defined what that operating system would be like. In fact, many of OS/2's features are closely linked with related features of the 80386. Hence, the understanding of OS/2 from a programmer's point of view really begins with an understanding of the 80386 processor.

Because of its heritage and its attempts to maintain software compatibility with its ancestors, the 80386 is a somewhat "quirky" chip. In fact, the 80386 actually has four separate modes of operation! In this section we will discuss some aspects of the 80386 that relate specifically to OS/2 programming.

 Note: Nothing in the sections that follow assume that you have significant familiarity with 80386 assembly language programming. However, implicit to OS/2 programming are the concepts of subroutines (both calling and returning from them), the stack, and stack operations. Simply put, you should have, minimally, some general understanding of how a computer goes about its business.

THE ARCHITECTURE OF THE 80386

The 80386 contains five classes of registers, into which information is placed for processing or program control. The registers fall into the following categories:

▶ Ten general purpose registers

▶ Six segment registers

▶ Four protection registers

▶ Four control registers

▶ Eight debug and two test registers

The *general purpose registers* are the "workhorse" registers of the CPU. These registers are 32 bits wide. It is in these registers that values are placed for processing various operations, including: arithmetic operations, such as adding or multiplying; comparisons, such as equality, less than, greater than, and the like; and branch (jump) instructions. The first four of the general purpose registers, EAX, EBX, ECX, and EDX, can be accessed in three ways: as one 32-bit register, as two 16-bit registers, or the lower 16 bits of each register can be accessed as two 8-bit registers. These various methods of access exist in order to maintain compatibility with previous generations of the 8086 microprocessor family. The next four registers, EBP, ESI, EDI, and ESP, can be accessed as either a single 16-bit or 32-bit register. The remaining two registers, EFLAGS and EIP, are called status registers. These registers can also be accessed as single 16-bit or 32-bit registers.

The first four *segment registers* are the same as in any of the 8086 family of processors. The CS, DS, ES, and the SS registers hold current segment values, or selector values when running in protected mode. Selectors will be discussed later in this chapter, but for now just think of them as a special form of a segment value. Two new segment registers were introduced by the 80386. The FS and the GS are additional registers added to hold extra selectors. All of the segment registers are 16-bit. Hidden from view is a descriptor cache associated with each of the segment registers. When operating in protected mode, this cache holds additional information about the memory the segment register points to, but these are not directly accessible to the programmer and they will not be discussed here.

The *protection registers* are designed to support the protection feature of the 80386 family. These four registers, GDTR, IDTR, LDTR, and TR, were introduced by the 80386 family, and hold information specific to the 80386 protected mode operation.

The *control registers* manage the paging and numeric processor mechanism, and on the 80486 processors, control the cache operations. The CR0, CR1, CR2, and CR3 are 32-bit registers, each bit representing a specific state within the microprocessor.

The *debug* and *test registers* are not generally used by application programmers and will not be discussed in detail in this book. These registers would be used by emulators and real-time embedded applications of the 80386 family of microprocessors.

Figure 1-1 shows the layout of the 80386 registers.

SEGMENTED AND VIRTUAL MEMORY MODELS

The entire Intel CPU line is based on the original 8086, which views the memory of the system as if it were organized into 64K chunks called *segments*. This is also how the 80386 views memory when operating in real mode. However, we are going to be concentrating on the 80386 protected mode of operation. This is the mode OS/2 2.0 runs in, and the mode all programs written for OS/2 2.0 will use. While operating in protected mode, the 80386 has basically two modes of operation: *segmented* and *virtual* (flat) mode. The first mode uses the segment registers to hold a "pointer" into a table of addresses. This "pointer" is what is known as a *selector*. Although this is similar to how the 8086 family of processors operate, the way in which the actual linear address is calculated is quite different. Loosely speaking, the contents of a segment register is used to look up a base address, and this value is then combined with that of another register (or immediate value). This second value is called the *offset*. Segments or offsets on the 80386 can be as large as the entire address space, 4 gigabytes.

Like most things in life, the segment/offset memory model has its good and bad points. In the plus column, the segmented scheme makes it easy to write relocatable code. It also makes it easier to develop virtual memory techniques. In the minus column, the segmented approach tends to complicate what is essentially a nearly intuitive concept: memory. Most programmers think of memory as strictly linear. That is the most natural view. However, the segmentation model requires that we think of memory abstractly, as disjointed pieces—a somewhat unnatural concept. The debate over the segmentation memory model has raged for years and will probably continue to rage.

The second mode of operation, the flat model, is the one OS/2 uses, and it is the model most programs developed for OS/2 2.*x* will use. The flat model simply means that the address space is linear. The segment address is always set to zero, and the offset contains the entire 32-bit address. This is often referred to as the *0:32* mode of addressing. Programs execute very quickly in this mode, because the segment registers can be loaded once, and thereafter only the offset values need to be loaded in order to access memory, saving the time it takes to repeatedly load a

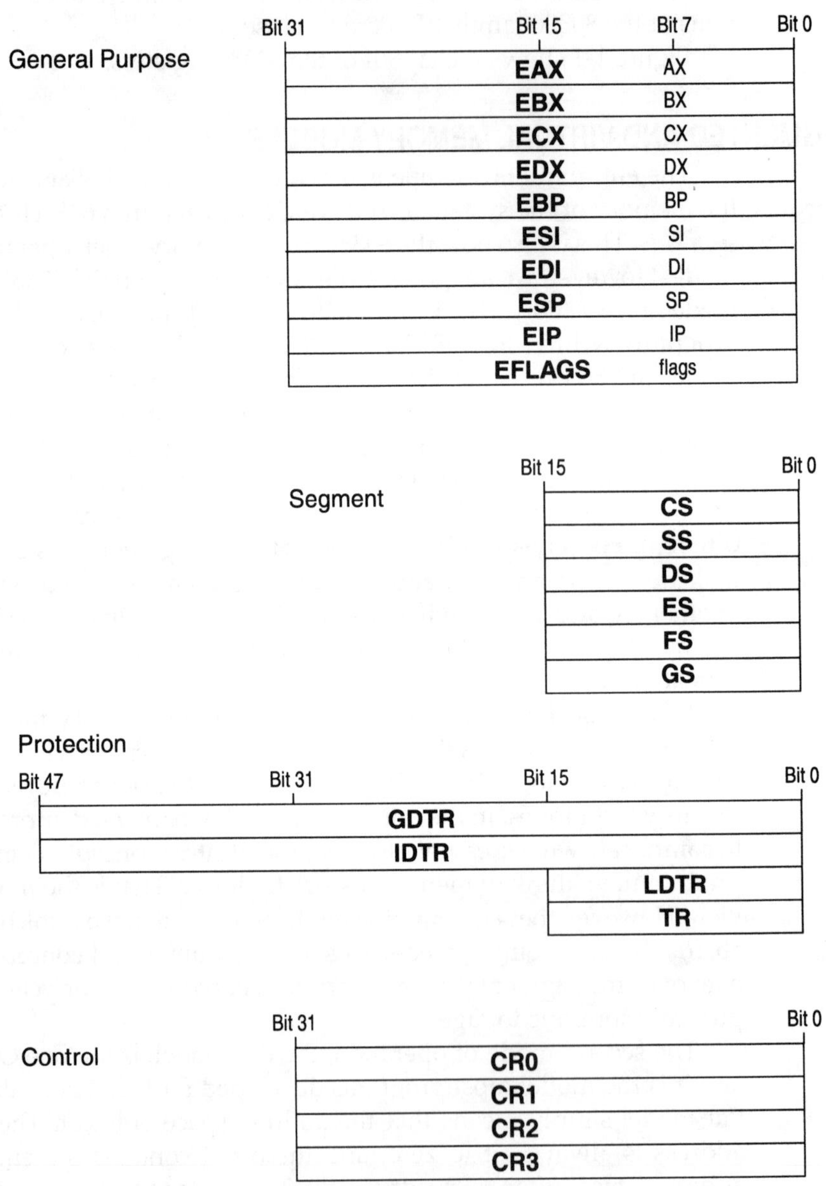

General Purpose

Bit 31	Bit 15	Bit 7	Bit 0
	EAX	AX	
	EBX	BX	
	ECX	CX	
	EDX	DX	
	EBP	BP	
	ESI	SI	
	EDI	DI	
	ESP	SP	
	EIP	IP	
	EFLAGS	flags	

Segment

Bit 15	Bit 0
CS	
SS	
DS	
ES	
FS	
GS	

Protection

Bit 47	Bit 31	Bit 15	Bit 0
	GDTR		
	IDTR		
		LDTR	
		TR	

Control

Bit 31	Bit 0
CR0	
CR1	
CR2	
CR3	

FIGURE 1-1

The 80386 CPU Registers

segment register. All of this information on how the memory is organized and accessed is interesting, but actually, because OS/2 does the work for you, you do not need to worry too much about where your programs execute in memory or how that memory is organized.

REAL VERSES PROTECTED MODE

As you might already know, in order to maintain software compatibility with its ancestors, the 80386 has to be able to execute 8086 programs. To provide for this, the 80386 CPU can operate in either *real* or *protected* mode. These modes of operation are so different in some respects that it may be easier to think of the 80386 as two CPUs in one package. Fortunately, beginning with release 2.0 of OS/2, the processor can be switched into protected mode shortly after startup, and thereafter remain in protected mode. Earlier versions of OS/2 required switching into real mode when running DOS programs. As you will see later in this chapter, OS/2 2.0 and later versions can run DOS programs in protected mode by using the virtual real mode of the 80386 processor.

When the 80386 is running in protected mode, several new instructions become available, and the way the system memory and resources are accessed changes. Perhaps the most significant differences are the way physical memory is protected and the way addresses are calculated. The 80386 can directly access up to 4 gigabytes of system RAM. In protected mode, programs are assigned a privilege level. Only the most privileged programs have access to certain instructions, such as interrupt and I/O instructions. Also, in protected mode it is possible for the CPU to prevent one program from accidentally interfering with another that is concurrently executing. In fact, it is this feature which gave protected mode its name. Finally, protected mode operation allows the 80386 to use some special instructions that make multitasking easier to implement.

PROTECTED MODE ADDRESS CALCULATION

To access 4 gigabytes of RAM requires at least a 32-bit address. This is one of the reasons why the registers on the 80386 have been increased in size to 32 bits. The location of any byte in memory is known as the *offset*. In the segmented model, the segment is used to determine which section of memory the offset refers to; but in the flat memory model, the offset is the complete address, and the segment register no longer holds a useful value. Actually, the segment register is still used to calculate the address, but the physical address is obtained through the use of the memory paging unit.

The flat model employs what is known as a *virtual memory system*. The address stored in the register is a virtual address organized into equal sized chunks of memory known as *pages*. The physical address of a virtual page is set at load time and is not relocatable thereafter. Because the memory is set up in pages, these pages can be swapped in and out of memory as the operating system sees fit.

When the 80386 calculates an address in protected mode (whether in the flat or the segmented model), it uses the value of a segment register as an index into a descriptor table. It then adds the base segment address to the offset to calculate the complete address. As the address is being calculated, the various access information is being checked. If your program attempts to reference memory that it shouldn't, a general protection fault will be generated. When the paging unit is enabled for the flat memory scheme, additional checking is done by the memory paging unit when the virtual address is converted into a physical address.

The CPU maintains three types of descriptor tables: the *global descriptor table* (GDT), the *local descriptor table* (LDT), and the *interrupt descriptor table* (IDT). Loosely speaking, the GDT holds address information that is available to all tasks in the system. The LDT holds address information that is local to each task. The IDT holds address information related to the interrupt service routines. As stated, these tables are maintained automatically by OS/2 for you, so that in general you will not need to worry about them while programming. However, understanding them is important in order to get a clear grasp of how OS/2 handles multiple tasks.

THE ADVANTAGES OF PROTECTED MODE ADDRESSING

Aside from the fact that a larger amount of memory can be accessed in protected mode operation, the use of descriptor tables and the memory paging unit change the meaning of the address registers and have several positive effects, which OS/2 exploits to provide a stable and efficient multitasking environment. First, because the register holds an index rather than an address, the operating system is able to move segments in memory at will by changing the base segment address in the descriptor table entry. When the memory paging unit is enabled, the pages are freely swapped in and out as the operating system services the many tasks running on the system. All of this is accomplished in a way that is completely transparent to the application program, because the program does not "know" what part of memory it is using, or which pages are currently in physical memory. Thus, even while the program is executing, it can be moved about in memory. This feature is important, because it allows tasks to be swapped in and out of memory. It is possible for OS/2 to overcommit memory by moving tasks in and out of RAM, storing them temporarily on disk. This means that you can run programs that require more RAM than is in the system, or to run more programs simultaneously than would normally fit in the system RAM.

The fact that various access rights, including privilege levels, are now linked with a memory location allows OS/2 to control access both to itself and to other system resources. Essentially, for code to access memory, it must have equal or higher memory access privileges.

I/O PRIVILEGES

Another feature of the 80386 is its I/O protection. Because the protected mode operation of the 80386 was designed for a multitasking environment, it had to have some way of controlling access to certain instructions, including input and output instructions. Without this control, several different applications could—and probably would—write to the same devices at the same time, resulting in chaos. Control is achieved via a program's *I/O privilege level* (IOPL for short). Although the details are not important as they relate to this book, the basic IOPL concept works like this: the only routines that have access to IN and OUT instructions—and to the various interrupt instructions—are those routines that have been granted I/O access.

OS/2 AND THE TWO 80386 OPERATIONAL MODES

As has been stated frequently in the foregoing discussion, the 80386 mode of operation designed for a multitasking environment is the protected mode. Hence, OS/2 uses this mode and requires all programs that execute under its control to do likewise.

Although OS/2 is a protected mode operating system, the OS/2 designers needed to provide what is sometimes referred to as a *compatibility path* from the older DOS to OS/2. To this end, a DOS emulator needed to be created that ran under the control of OS/2. However, as you know, DOS is a real mode operating system, and real mode and protected mode are mutually exclusive: they can't both be active at the same time. Here is the solution the OS/2 developers chose: when running a DOS program, use the virtual 86 mode of the 80386 processors. The virtual 86 mode of the

80386 processor allows the operating system to run one or more real mode programs without actually switching to real mode. With this scheme, all of the memory protection of the protected mode can be utilized.

The big problem is that real mode programs like to take full control of the system, bypassing any operating system that is present in the system. As you will soon see, OS/2 must control all system devices if it is to keep multiple tasks from trying to use the same device at the same time. This control is achieved largely through the use of the protected mode's privilege and I/O protection levels, which do not exist in real mode. Although OS/2 can prevent some types of device-request collisions, it cannot stop them all. Some real mode programs will simply not run at all under the OS/2 DOS emulator. Programs which must take over the hardware may have problems running, based on how they were designed. OS/2 seems capable of running most DOS programs, but stay away from programs that directly manipulate the disk or file systems.

OS/2 ESSENTIALS

From a programming perspective, multitasking capabilities are the most important attribute of OS/2. Virtually all the differences between DOS and OS/2 are due, either directly or indirectly, to OS/2's support of multitasking. Because it is such an important topic, let's begin with it.

THREADS, PROCESSES, AND TASKS

The OS/2 design team did multitasking right! OS/2's tasking model is based upon the simultaneous execution of pieces of code, rather than on the simultaneous execution of programs. In OS/2 terminology, the smallest unit of execution is called a *thread*. All programs consist of at least one thread, but they may contain several. Hence, it is possible for a single program to have two or more parts of itself executing at the same time. This means that not only can OS/2 execute two or more programs at the same time, but it can also execute two or more parts of a single program concurrently.

In OS/2 terminology a *process* and a *task* are the same, and they are very loosely synonymous to *program*. A process owns various resources, including such things as memory, files, and threads.

THE OS/2 MULTITASKING MODEL

As OS/2 is currently implemented, it is designed to share a single CPU between several threads. It does this by granting each thread a short amount of CPU time called a *time slice*. Although, technically speaking, only one thread is actually executing at any single point in time, the time slicing is so rapid that the threads in the system appear to be running at the same time.

Multitasking is controlled in OS/2 through the use of a preemptive, priority-based scheduler. OS/2 associates a priority with each thread. Higher priority threads are granted access to the CPU before lower priority ones. There are four main priority categories. In order of highest to lowest, they are

▶ Time-critical

▶ Foreground

▶ Regular

▶ Idle

Time-critical tasks are those that must respond immediately to some event, such as communication programs. Within the time-critical category there are 32 priority levels.

The foreground and regular priorities are really two flavors of regular tasks. When a program is on the screen, OS/2 gives its threads a foreground priority, which is the highest priority that regular tasks can have. This is done to insure that interactive sessions always take place without jerky or sluggish responses. Other regular threads in the system will be given background priority when they are not displayed on the screen. Within this level there are 32 priority levels. OS/2 dynamically changes the priority of non-foreground threads at this level to provide for the most efficient use of the CPU.

Finally, the lowest priority tasks are given idle priority. This level executes only when there are no higher priority tasks capable of executing. Within this group, 32 priority levels are available.

OS/2 always runs the highest priority thread capable of executing. When two or more threads share the same priority level, they are granted CPU time slices in a round-robin fashion. At first you may think that a high priority thread would dominate the CPU, but this is not the case, because most programs, even time-critical ones, spend much of their time waiting for an event to occur. When a thread is waiting, OS/2 stops executing it and runs another. Also, OS/2 has certain parameters that determine the longest amount of time a process can be suspended, which help eliminate this sort of problem.

A thread inside a process is in one of three mutually exclusive states: *blocked, ready-to-run,* or *running.* Any time a thread is waiting for something, its execution is said to be blocked. For example, a thread that is part of an interactive program may be waiting for keyboard input. Until that input is received, the thread can execute no further, which causes the execution of that thread to become blocked. Blocked threads are not given CPU time until the event they are waiting for occurs. Once this happens, the thread is in a ready-to-run state, but it is still not executing. It only resumes execution when OS/2's scheduler grants it a slice of CPU time. If the unblocked thread is of higher priority than the thread(s) currently being executed, then the currently executing thread(s) is preempted and the unblocked thread is allowed to run. Otherwise, it must wait until all higher priority tasks are blocked.

The single most advantageous attribute of a thread-based multitasking system is that it allows greater throughput by permitting independent pieces of your program to execute concurrently. For example, a word processing program could be simultaneously formatting text for output and taking input from the user.

INTERPROCESS COMMUNICATION

OS/2 supports several forms of interprocess communication (IPC). These include pipes, queues, semaphores, and signals. Many devices are sequential in nature. That is, they cannot be used by two or more threads at the same time. Whenever two or more threads need to use one of these devices, they must coordinate their activity. The part of a program that accesses such a device is called a *critical section.* Before entering a critical section, a thread must make sure that the device accessed by that section is not already in use by another thread. This is accomplished using IPC, and the process is referred to as *synchronization*. You will see several examples of this in Chapter 10.

OS/2'S PROTECTION STRATEGY

As was mentioned during the discussion of the 80386, for a multitasking operating system to be successful, it must prevent programs running under it from adversely affecting each other or the operating system itself. In essence, the operating system must protect programs and itself from harm. OS/2 achieves this protection by utilizing the 80386's privilege level mechanism and protected mode addressing scheme.

As you may recall, the 80386 supports four privilege levels, numbered 0 through 3. Level 0 is the most trusted, and level 3 is the least trusted. In OS/2, the core routines, usually called the *kernel*, are at level 0. Level 1 is unused by OS/2 at this time. Application programs run at levels 2 and 3. The only way to access routines at a more trusted level is through a *call gate*. This is the method used by OS/2 to allow your programs access to the various OS/2 services. Using this scheme, OS/2 is able to prevent a program from accessing any part of OS/2 in an uncontrolled manner.

If a program attempts to access memory outside its currently defined limits, a general protection fault is generated. OS/2 intercepts this fault and terminates the process that caused it. In this way one program cannot destroy another's code or data areas. (Keep in mind that it is possible for two or more programs to share memory when it is desirable that they do so.)

Because OS/2 controls the page and descriptor tables, it can mark certain areas as read-only, which means that programs can read the data in that area but not change it.

Finally, OS/2 has control of all I/O devices. This means that, in general, an application program cannot execute an IN or OUT instruction or turn interrupts on or off. (In a multitasking operating system all I/O is interrupt driven; hence a program cannot be allowed to alter the state of the interrupts.) By denying the use of I/O instructions, OS/2 is able to prevent two or more programs from accessing the same device at the same time. (It is possible for OS/2 to grant a program the ability to perform I/O in some special situations. This feature will be discussed later in this book.)

VIRTUAL MEMORY

OS/2 takes advantage of the 80386's virtual memory capabilities. OS/2 is able to overcommit the memory of the system by swapping unused pages to disk until they are needed. Although excess swapping can slow a multitasking system to a crawl, a small amount of swapping is hardly noticeable. This is because most programs contain code that is seldom executed. When a request for memory is made and none is available, OS/2 examines each page and swaps to disk the one least recently used. Should this page be needed, a memory fault is generated and OS/2 swaps the page back in, perhaps swapping a different page out in the process. What is particularly nice about OS/2's virtual memory capabilities is that they are performed automatically and do not require any additional effort on your part.

THE APPLICATION PROGRAM INTERFACE

A program accesses OS/2's system services via the *Application Program Interface* (API). OS/2 does not use a software interrupt scheme to utilize a system service. Instead, the API is a *call-based interface.* In this approach, each OS/2 service has a name associated with it, and this name is used to call it. To use this method, the necessary parameters (if any) are pushed onto the stack and the appropriate OS/2 function is called. Most OS/2 functions return 0 (in the EAX register) if successful.

If you are programming in a high-level language, such as C, then the work of putting the parameters to a call on the stack is done for you by the compiler. However, if you are programming in assembler, then your programs must do this explicitly. For example, the OS/2 function **DosSleep()** is used to suspend the execution of the thread that calls it for a specified number of milliseconds. Shown in pseudoassembly, this is how **DosSleep()** is called so that the calling thread suspends for 100 milliseconds:

```
PUSH 100
CALL DosSleep
```

We will look more closely at how the API functions are called in the next chapter.

DYNAMIC LINKING

The API is implemented in OS/2 using a procedure called *dynamic linking.* Here is how it works. All the functions in the API are stored in a relocatable format called a *dynamic link library* (DLL). When your program calls an API function, the linker does *not* add the function's code into the executable version of your program. Instead, it adds loading instructions for that function, such as what DLL it resides in. When your program is executed, the necessary API routines are also loaded by the OS/2 loader. (It is also possible to load routines after the program has started execution.) A dynamic link routine is called a *dynlink.*

Dynlinks have some very important benefits. First, because virtually all programs designed for use with OS/2 will use OS/2 functions, the use of dynlinks prevents disk space from being wasted by the significant amount of duplicated object code that would be created if the OS/2 function code was actually added to each program's executable file. Second, updates and enhancements to OS/2 can be accomplished by changing the dynlink libraries. Thus existing programs will automatically make use of the improved or expanded functions. Finally, it is possible for you to create your own dynlink libraries and let your programs profit from the advantages of dynamic linking.

THE PRESENTATION MANAGER

Although not included in OS/2 before version 1.1, the Presentation Manager is a standard part of OS/2. The Presentation Manager is a top-level graphical interface. Applications which use the Presentation

Chapter 1

Manager run under the OS/2 Workplace Shell. The Workplace Shell supports such things as multiple, overlapping windows, character fonts, menus, and the mouse. The Presentation Manager is covered in significant detail in section two of this book.

THE OS/2 PHILOSOPHY

Embodied in the functional aspects of OS/2 is the OS/2 philosophy, which is essentially this: OS/2 should provide a stable multitasking environment that is both flexible and extensible. As you have seen, the 80386 family of microprocessors supply the raw materials to support a stable multitasking environment in which one program cannot destroy another. Also, its protected mode addressing scheme allows OS/2 to support dynamic linking, which allows easy modification to most of the code that comprises OS/2. It also allows new OS/2 system services to be added, either by IBM, or by a third party.

From the programmer's point of view, OS/2 is a giant toolkit. In the rest of this book you will learn how to access those tools to create OS/2 programs.

FUNDAMENTALS OF OS/2 PROGRAMMING

In this chapter we will examine in significant technical detail several key points relating to the use of OS/2's API (Application Program Interface) services. Before you can begin to write programs that run under OS/2, you need to understand exactly how to interface to the API. Remember, the API services are your program's gateway to OS/2.

This chapter begins with a discussion of the OS/2 call-based interface, and describes how to compile and link OS/2 programs. Along the way, some sample programs are developed that illustrate several important OS/2 interfacing concepts. The chapter treats in some detail the different categories of API functions and how they are accessed. It concludes with a discussion of some general OS/2 and 32-bit programming practices, including the use of function prototypes, and it points out some mistakes commonly made by programmers migrating from a 16-bit programming environment.

THE OS/2 CALL-BASED INTERFACE

Your program interacts with OS/2 by using the API functions, which are kept in dynlink (dynamically linked) libraries. Dynlink libraries are discussed in Chapter 12, but for now you can think of them much as you do the statically linked libraries you already have used in other operating systems, such as DOS. The big difference is that the library functions are not actually loaded into memory until they are needed. In Chapter 1 it was mentioned that OS/2 API functions are accessed via a CALL instruction, and a very general explanation of the procedure was given. Here, you will learn in detail the procedures used to call the API routines.

THE CALL FORMAT

Routines in the API (or in any dynlink library, for that matter) must be reached by issuing a CALL instruction. Prior to issuing the CALL instruction, however, your program must push onto the stack, in the proper order, the parameters used by the API service that you will be calling. In a high-level language like C, the compiler does the job of pushing the parameters onto the stack. The OS/2 API interface supports four basic types of parameters:

▶ byte (8 bits)

▶ word (16 bits)

▶ double word (32 bits)

▶ pointer (32 bits)

Before discussing these further, let's take a short detour and review the difference between call-by-reference and call-by-value parameter passing conventions.

Call-by-Value

There are essentially two ways in which a subroutine may be passed its parameters. The first is *call-by-value*. Using this method, the subroutine is passed copies of the actual information (values) that it needs. Any modifications the subroutine makes to a parameter's value will not affect the calling routine's copy of the parameter. The subroutine is always operating on a copy of the original value, and therefore it cannot modify the original value.

Call-by-Reference

The second way parameters can be passed to a subroutine is *call-by-reference.* In this approach, the calling routine passes the address of, or in

C terms, a pointer to the parameter of the subroutine. When this method is used, the subroutine indirectly accesses and manipulates the original data found in the calling routine. Changes to the parameter affect the caller's copy, because the subroutine is actually operating on the caller's data.

The OS/2 API services require the use of both call-by-value and call-by-reference. If the API service does not need to return information to the caller via the parameters, then call-by-value is used; otherwise, the parameters will need to be passed by reference. Finally, any complex data or variable length data structures must be passed by reference. Several of the API services operate on conglomerate data types that are the equivalent of a C structure. OS/2 does not pass these on the stack. Instead, only a pointer is passed.

Many API services require a parameter type called an *ASCIIZ* string, which is simply a zero terminated string. When a string of this sort is required, its address is passed—not the entire string.

ERROR RETURN

As stated in the preceding section, the OS/2 API functions return information to the calling routine through call-by-reference parameters. However, all of the API services return a success/error code in the EAX register. When an API service is called from a C program, the value returned in the EAX register automatically becomes the return value of the API routine. In general, all the functions return 0 when successful. A non-zero return implies an error. Many of the examples presented in this book do not check for errors, but this is because these are small sample programs, not because error checking shouldn't be done. In actual programming practice, it is strongly recommended that all API return values be checked for an error condition.

A SAMPLE C PROGRAM

The C program that follows is an example using the **DosBeep()** API function. To compile this program you must have a C compiler that runs under OS/2. This book uses the IBM C compiler ICC. This book also uses some of the tools found in the OS/2 Toolkit, also supplied by IBM.

Assuming you name the sample program WHOOP.C, compile the program using this command:

```
ICC WHOOP.C
```

This will cause the sample program to be compiled and linked, including the necessary dynlink libraries.

In this simple program, the function **DosBeep()** is assumed to be successful and its error return code is not examined:

```
/* C language demonstration program using DosBeep() */

#include <os2.h>
#include <stdio.h>

main()
{
  int i;

    for(i=100; i<2500; i+=50)
    DosBeep(i, 1);   /* sound the speaker */

    puts("Press ENTER to quit");
  getchar();  /* read and discard the keypress */
}
```

As you will see, many of the API services will either always work or will always work if you supply correct input. For this reason, the error code will often be ignored in the sample programs in the interest of conserving time and space. However, as you will see in subsequent examples, certain API services should always have their return codes examined. The API function **DosBeep()** is found in a dynlink library. This book will explain the concepts behind dynlink libraries, and it will show you how to create your own dynlink libraries.

As you probably noticed, the API service **DosBeep()** is shown in mixed case in the C program. In the C environment, the API services are called using their mixed case version, such as **DosBeep()**. All OS/2 functions use this naming convention, and you will soon get used to it. This is how the functions appear in the header file, and this is how the prototypes are accessed. In actuality, all API functions are known to the system in upper case only. When you are accessing the API functions from assembly language programs, the API functions need to appear in upper case.

Also notice that C's standard functions, like **puts()** and **getchar()**, can be used in OS/2 programs. These functions in turn access the necessary API services.

Keep in mind that in many cases, functionally similar C programs can be written using C's standard library functions, rather than calling the API directly. This will be the case with many of the API services. In something as simple as the preceding program, using **puts()** in preference to an API call that writes to the screen is probably a good idea, because of ease of use. API services often overlap parallel standard library functions. However, there is an important reason why you might want to access an API service directly, even if a similar C standard library function exists: efficiency.

As part of the quest for greater performance, high-performance software designed for DOS traditionally bypassed the C standard library functions as well as DOS itself. A similar situation will exist for OS/2 programs. You will find that in several areas you will want to bypass C's standard library functions in favor of calling the API routines directly, in order to achieve faster runtime execution.

Understand that when you call a standard C function that is paralleled by OS/2, your call to the standard function is generally passed along to the corresponding API service. This means that instead of generating one call, you generate two calls (one to the standard function and one to the API). However, when you call the API directly, only the one call to the API service routine is generated. As you probably know, each time you call a routine, time is consumed. For the fastest possible programs, you should call the API directly. Keep in mind, however, that if several sections of your programs are not time-critical, it makes more sense to call the standard functions, because they are more portable between operating systems and are occasionally easier to use.

All the examples in this book are in C, because programs in C provide a better means of presenting and illustrating the API services than do assembly programs. Also, most programmers will use C to develop OS/2 applications, so it makes sense to show examples in the language that will be used more frequently.

USING STANDARD HEADER FILES

The header file OS2.H must be included with every C program or module that uses any of the OS/2 constructs, definitions, or functions. This file causes the information required to use the API services to be added to your program.

Because there are a large number of API services, the header files that contain their definitions are quite large, and it can take the compiler quite a long time to read and process them. For this reason, OS/2 has organized the header files into logical groups. By default, the compiler does not include all parts of the header files. Instead, a series of **#ifdef** statements prior to including OS2.H are used to conditionally include or exclude large parts of the API service declarations. Many of the common symbols used in the **#ifdef** statement are listed in Table 2-1.

Except for a few of the symbols in Table 2-1 (listed at the beginning) that cause large sections of the OS/2 system declaration to be included, defining one of these symbols causes a specific (and smaller) subsection of the OS/2 header file declarations and defines to be included. You will see some of these defines being used in this book as sample programs are developed. The API function descriptions in the OS/2 technical reference library show exactly which of these defines to use for each of the API functions.

The reason that one of these defines was not needed before including OS2.H in the sample C program is that some services, including **DosBeep()**, are always included automatically. More information on these defines will follow in the chapters which discuss the use of the different API functions.

C AND THE API PARAMETERS

OS/2 defines and refers to data types in a way that is a little different from standard C. The standard types are renamed or redefined through the use of macro replacements or type define statements. IBM has also adopted a standard naming convention for both variables and functions, which may look strange to the first time OS/2 programmer. With a little

Symbol	Subsystem Accessed
INCL_PM	Include all the PM subsystems.
INCL_WIN	Include all window subsystems.
INCL_BASE	Include all the base API subsystems.
INCL_GPI	Include all of the graphics subsystems.
INCL_DOS	Include all the kernel subsystems.
INCL_DOSERRORS	Define all the OS/2 errors.
INCL_DOSSEMAPHORES	Access the semaphore subsystem.
INCL_DOSMEMMANAGER	Include the memory manager subsystem.
INCL_DOSDOSPROCESS	Thread and process manipulation.
INCL_DOSDOSNMPIPES	Include declarations to use pipes.
INCL_DOSFILEMGR	Include the file I/O declarations.
INCL_DOSQUEUES	Include declarations to use queues.
INCL_DOSMODULEMGR	Module level resource access.
INCL_DOSDATETIME	Include date and time declarations.
INCL_DOSEXCPTIONS	Exception handling services.
INCL_DOSNLS	National language support services.
INCL_DOSASYNCTIMER	Include declarations for timer services.
INCL_WINWINDOWMGR	Window management services.
INCL_WINMESSAGEMGR	Message management services.
INCL_WININPUT	Mouse and keyboard services.
INCL_WINDIALOGS	Dialog box declarations.
INCL_WINSTATICS	Static control declarations.
INCL_WINBUTTONS	Button control declarations.
INCL_WINENTRYFIELDS	Entry field declarations.
INCL_WINMLE	Multiple line entry fields.
INCL_WINLISTBOXES	List box control declarations.

TABLE 2-1

Conditional Include Symbols

Symbol	Subsystem Accessed
INCL_WINMENUS	Menu control declarations.
INCL_WINSTDDLGS	Include all PM dialog and controls.
INCL_WINSTDBOOK	Notebook control declarations.
INCL_WINSTDCNR	Container control declarations.
INCL_WINSTDSLIDER	Slider control declarations.
INCL_WINSTDSPIN	Spin button declarations.
INCL_WINSTDVALSET	Value set declarations.
INCL_WINSCROLLBARS	Scroll bar declarations.
INCL_WINFRAMEMGR	Frame manager declarations.
INCL_WINFRAMECTLS	Frame control declarations.
INCL_WINRECTANGLES	Include the rectangle routines.
INCL_WINSYS	Include the system values.
INCL_WINTIMER	Include the timer routines.

TABLE 2-1

Conditional Include Symbols (continued)

practice, some of these techniques will become natural to use and helpful in documenting your programs.

DATA TYPES

Many of the types presented in the following chapters will no doubt look strange to you. These types are simply OS/2 names for the data types you are quite used to using. OS/2 has defined these types in header files, and this book will use these type definitions in all of the prototype definitions, and in most of the examples presented. I suggest that you too adopt this convention for your programs. Some of the new data types are simple macro defines of the old ones; others are type defined to the new type.

A few of the more common OS/2 API types are listed here in Table 2-2.

OS/2 API	Standard C
CHAR	char
SHORT	short
INT	int
LONG	long
UCHAR	unsigned char
BYTE	unsigned char
UINT	unsigned int
USHORT	unsigned short
ULONG	unsigned long
PCHAR	char *
PINT	int *
PLONG	long *
BOOL	unsigned long
PSZ	char *
HWND	unsigned long
VOID	void

TABLE 2-2

API Data Types

As you probably noticed, all of the OS/2 types are simply fancy names for one of the standard C types. In general, placing a preceding "P" on most of the OS/2 types turns the type into a pointer to the type. As you use these definitions, you will get quite comfortable with most of them. Other seldom used ones may require reference to a manual or header file to figure out what sort of value is stored in the type. I have found them to be useful in that they are a little more self-documenting than the base type.

Although OS/2 has defined several new names for types, it is not absolutely necessary to use these type declarations. Their native C base types can be used in place of the OS/2 defined name. This will not cause any technical problems, and programs written in this way can be compiled

Chapter 2

successfully by any OS/2 compatible C compiler. This allows programs migrating from another operating system to work without the hassle of converting all the variable declarations to the OS/2 style of type naming.

NAMING CONVENTIONS

If you are new to OS/2 programming, several of the variable and function names used in this book and other OS/2 documentation will probably seem rather unusual. The reason for this is that they all follow a set of naming conventions. For functions, the name consists of a function class, followed by a verb, which is usually followed by a noun. The initial characters of the function class, the verb, and the noun are capitalized. The main function class prefixes and descriptions are presented in Table 2-3.

For variable names, IBM uses a rather complex system of indicating the type of data stored in the variable through the variable's name. To accomplish this, a lower case prefix is added to the beginning of the variable's name. The variable name proper begins with a capital letter. The prefix indicates the data type stored by the variable or the purpose of the

Prefix	Class Description
Dev	Device functions
Drg	Direct manipulation functions
Ddf	Dynamic data formatting
Gpi	Graphics functions
Prf	Profile functions
Spl	Spooler functions
Win	Window functions
Dos	Control program functions

TABLE 2-3
Function Class by Prefix

variable, which is not necessarily the same as the declared type of the variable. Some of the more common prefixes are shown in Table 2-4.

Prefixes can also be user or system defined types. This can make using and understanding prefixes more confusing. Frankly, the use of type prefixes is controversial and is not universally supported. Many OS/2 programmers use this method; many do not. This book, for the most part, will not use this method of naming variables. However, you are free to use any naming convention you like.

Prefix	Purpose or Type
b	A byte value
c	A count or size
clr	A variable that holds a color
f	Bitfield (flags) variable
h	A handle
hwnd	A window handle
id	An identity
l	Long integer
msg	A message
p	Pointer (may be added to any type)
rc	Return value
s	Short integer
us	Unsigned short integer
ul	Unsigned long integer
sz	A null terminated string
psz	Pointer to null terminated string

TABLE 2-4

Variable Prefix Characters

THE API SERVICES

The API services can be separated into two broad categories: the Presentation Manager services and the basic OS/2 kernel. The Presentation Manager category includes the windowing and graphics portion of the API, and includes services to access the mouse, keyboard, and other I/O devices. The basic kernel contains the services that manage multitasking capabilities, inter-process communication, and file I/O.

THE MAJOR API CATEGORIES

The second part of this book covers Presentation Manager API services. The third part covers the non-Presentation Manager services. These non-Presentation Manager API services comprise the core OS/2 functions. You cannot write programs that effectively use the power of OS/2 without them. Although the two types of services are presented separately, all of the core API services can and should be used when you are developing code for the Presentation Manager.

There are four basic types of applications that can run in the OS/2 environment:

▶ OS/2 windowable

▶ DOS Windows

▶ OS/2 full-screen

▶ Presentation Manager

OS/2 windowable applications do not use the Presentation Manager mouse or keyboard services, and they do not create a message queue, although a windowable application can be run in a Presentation Manager window. The full-screen application is similar, but runs in full-screen mode. The DOS Windows application can run in full screen or in a window, but runs in the virtual 8086 mode discussed in Chapter 1. The most exciting type of application, and the one that most OS/2 applications will belong to, is the Presentation Manager application.

The second part of this book will use Presentation Manager applications exclusively for sample programs, and the third part will use the windowable type of application for sample programs.

CONVENTIONS USED BY THE API SERVICES

A large portion of the remainder of this book is devoted to the description of the API services. Because most of the examples in this book are in C, the proper way to call an API service will be shown using C function prototype notation. In fact, from a C program, the API services actually resemble any other C library function. The proper way to call an API function can be illustrated by the following C prototype declaration:

APIRET APIENTRY DosBeep()(ULONG *freq*, ULONG *dur*);

This is, of course, the prototype for the **DosBeep()** API function used in the previous sample program. All such prototypes are followed by a description of the function's parameters. APIENTRY is defined as **_System**, and APIRET is simply a ULONG (**unsigned long**) return value. These declarations will be found on all API function prototypes, and they simply declare the return and linkage types.

As you will see in the examples that appear in subsequent chapters, some of the API services must be passed the address of a data structure. While the name of the structure and the names of the fields that comprise the structure are not important to OS/2 (it has no knowledge of them), they are very important to the C programmer. Because each C compiler that runs under OS/2 must declare the API services and define any structures required by them, it must assign names to both the structures and the fields. The trouble is that there is no reason why two different compiler manufacturers have to use the same names when describing the same structures. (Remember, the API services never "see" the names, only the data.) The question, as far as this book is concerned, is which compiler's naming conventions to follow. This book is written from the point of view of the IBM C compiler. By default, references to structure names and fields will follow the IBM naming conventions, as described earlier in this chapter.

USING C PROTOTYPES

In C, a function returning a value other than **int** must be declared prior to its use, so that the compiler can generate the proper return codes. In ANSI standard C, you can take this idea one step further by also declaring the number and types of the function's arguments. This expanded definition is called a *function prototype*. Function prototypes are not part of the original UNIX C, but were added by the ANSI standardization committee and are used by the IBM OS/2 compiler. They enable C to provide stronger type checking, somewhat similar to that provided by languages like Pascal. Function prototypes also provide a convenient means of documenting the calling syntax of a function.

The IBM OS/2 compiler issues errors if functions are called with arguments that cause illegal type conversions or with a different number of arguments. This error checking can only be accomplished if prototypes are used. Although C is designed to be very forgiving, some type conversions are simply not allowed. For example, it is an error to attempt to convert a pointer into a **float**. Function prototypes will catch, and thus prevent, this sort of error.

A user-defined function prototype takes the same general form as the API prototypes,

type function_name(*arg_type1, arg_type2,...,arg_typeN*);

where *type* is the type of value returned by the function, and *arg_type* is the type associated with each argument.

As an example, the following program will cause an error message to be issued, because there is an attempt to call **func()** with a pointer instead of the **float** required.

```
/* This program uses function prototypes to enforce
   strong type checking in the calls to func().
   The program will compile with errors because of
   the mismatch between the type of the arguments
   specified in the function's prototype and
   the type of arguments used to call the function. */

float func(int, float); /* the prototype */

main()
{
  int x, *y;

  x = 10;  y = 10;
  func(x, y);  /* type mismatch */
}

float func(int x, float y)
```

```
{
  float result;
  result = (float)x/y;
  printf("%f\n", result);
}
```

Not only does the use of function prototypes help you trap bugs before they occur, but it also helps verify that your program is working correctly by not allowing functions to be called with mismatched arguments or with an incorrect number of arguments. It is even more important to use prototypes in larger programs or in situations when several programmers are working on the same project.

On a related subject, it has been possible in C to declare parameters to a function in two different ways: the traditional (sometimes called *classic*) and modern methods. The traditional method is the only method allowed by the earlier C compilers, while the modern form defined by the ANSI standard is used by newer C compilers, including the OS/2 C compiler from IBM. Actually, either method will work in the newer compilers, but you cannot mix the two types of declarations when using the IBM OS/2 2.*x* compiler.

In the modern approach, both the type and the name of the variable are placed in the argument list, enclosed in parentheses, that follows the function's name. That is, the form of the function parameter declaration is similar to the form of the prototype declaration, except that the name of the parameter must be included. This is the method used throughout this book, and it is the recommended method.

In the traditional form, only the names of a function's parameters are placed between the parentheses following the function's name. Then, before the function's opening curly brace, the parameters are declared using a syntax identical to a variable declaration. The following example declares the previously used function **func()**, using the classic form of parameter declarations:

```
float func(x, y)
int x;
float y;
{
  float result;
  result = (float)x/y;
  printf("%f\n", result);
}
```

When porting older code to newer systems, the traditional form of function definitions can be used without going through all the work of converting to the modern form, but you will not get the benefits of the type checking that is performed when prototypes are used. In fact, starting with OS/2 release 2.0, the IBM compiler does not allow mixing the classic style with prototypes. If you have not already done so, I suggest taking the time to convert to the modern form.

PROGRAMMING IN A 32-BIT ENVIRONMENT

If you are used to programming on the PC, then there are a few things you should be aware of before starting to program in OS/2 2.*x*. First, there are no far and near pointers. Memory is a flat linear address space. Second, integers are now the same size as long integers: 32 bits. This was not the case when developing programs under DOS or a previous version of OS/2. Integers used to be the same size as shorts: 16 bits. This is a major cause of problems when porting existing code from any other operating system that has 16-bit integers.

DEFAULT DATA SIZES

The integer size for 32-bit programming environments, including OS/2 2.*x*, is 32 bits. This may seem too obvious to mention, but many hours have been spent tracking down problems related to just this difference. If you are developing new code, just keep aware of the new integer size. If you are moving code from an older DOS or OS/2 operating system, you will want to look out for some of the common coding problems associated with the length of integers.

Most problems come from tricky, or simply poor, programming practices. Operations that assume the rollover or truncation of a value at the 16-bit limit of integers will be the biggest problem. Other problem areas include assumptions about the number of bits in a structure or union that contains integers.

One of the harder bugs to find related to the change in integer sizes is when the parameters or return values of a function do not match between the function call and function definition. A function that by default used to return 16 bits, now returns 32 bits. The same problem occurs with parameters: if a mismatch occurs in the middle of the parameter list, the remaining parameters will act as if garbage was sent by the callee. For this reason alone I recommend using prototypes for all user-defined functions. Also insure that all the necessary header files are included by using the appropriate **#include** statements in your programs.

A SHORT WORD ABOUT .DEF FILES

If you already know something about OS/2 programming, then you may have heard about .DEF files. Essentially, a .DEF file is a text file that contains information about a source code file that you will be assembling or compiling. Its use with non-library code is optional, and no .DEF files are needed to compile and run the sample programs just shown, nor will .DEF files be necessary to compile most of the sample programs presented in this book. Its main use is to allow dynamic link libraries to be created, but you do not need a .DEF file to use an existing dynlink library. You will learn more about .DEF files in the following chapters. The construction of dynamic link libraries is discussed in Chapter 12.

Now that we have all this preliminary information out of the way, let's move on to some real OS/2 Presentation Manager programming.

PART

TWO

PROGRAMMING THE PRESENTATION MANAGER

Part Two of this book shows how to create Presentation Manager applications. Although not technically required, virtually all significant OS/2 programs will be written for the Presentation Manager interface. As you will see, writing a Presentation Manager application is not as easy as writing a DOS program. However, programming for the Presentation Manager is also not as difficult as you may have been lead to believe. In essence, to create a successful Presentation Manager program, you simply must follow a well-defined set of rules. If you follow these rules, you will have no trouble developing programs for the Presentation Manager.

While this section contains all information necessary for you to write the most common type of Presentation Manager application, it does not discuss all aspects of Presentation Manager programming. The Presentation Manager is simply too large a system. (In fact, several large books are required to fully document the Presentation Manager programming environment!) The purpose of this section is to introduce the basics of the Presentation Manager and provide a "fast track" to Presentation Manager programming. If you will be writing extensively for the Presentation Manager, you will absolutely need the *Presentation Manager Programming Reference* (a three-volume set), which details the hundreds of Presentation Manager API (Application Program Interface) functions. Because the Presentation Manager is a very large and complex environment, you will want to have available as much information as possible about how to use it.

PRESENTATION MANAGER PROGRAMMING OVERVIEW

This chapter introduces Presentation Manager programming. It has two main purposes. First, it discusses in a general way what the Presentation Manager is, how a program must interact with it, and what rules must be followed by every Presentation Manager application. Second, it develops an application skeleton that will be used as a basis for all other Presentation Manager programs. As you will see, all Presentation Manager programs share a few common traits. It is these shared attributes that will be contained in the application skeleton.

WHAT IS THE PRESENTATION MANAGER?

To an extent, what the Presentation Manager is depends upon whether you are an end user or a programmer. From the user's point of view, the Presentation Manager is a window with which to interact in order to run applications. From the programmer's point of view, the Presentation Manager is a specific application-designed philosophy. It is a collection of several hundred API functions that support a graphics-oriented windowing system that runs under a multitasking operating system. The Presentation Manager is one giant toolbox of inter-related services which, when used correctly, allow the creation of application programs that all share a common user interface.

The goal of a Presentation Manager-style program is to enable a person who has basic familiarity with the OS/2 operating system to sit down and run virtually any application without prior training. In theory, if you can run one Presentation Manager program, you can run them all. Of course, in actuality, most useful programs will still require some sort of training in order to be used effectively, but at least this instruction can be restricted to *what* the program *does*, not *how* the user must *interact* with it. In fact, much of the code in a Presentation Manager application is there just to support the user interface.

At this point it is very important for you to understand that not every program that runs under OS/2 will necessarily present the user with a Presentation Manager-style interface. Only those programs written to take advantage of the Presentation Manager common interface design will look and feel like all other Presentation Manager programs. While you can override the basic Presentation Manager design philosophy, you had better have a good reason to do so; otherwise, the users of your programs will, most likely, be very disturbed. Quite honestly, if you are writing application programs that use the Presentation Manager, they should conform to the accepted Presentation Manager programming philosophy.

As mentioned, a Presentation Manager program is graphics oriented, which means that it provides a Graphical User Interface (GUI). While graphics hardware and video modes are quite diverse, many of the differences are handled by the Presentation Manager. This means that, for the most part, your program does not need to worry about what type of graphics hardware or video mode is being used.

Let's look at a few of the more important features of the Presentation Manager.

THE DESKTOP MODEL

With few exceptions, the point of a window-based user interface is to provide on the screen the equivalent of a desktop. On a desk may be found several different pieces of paper, one on top of another, often with fragments of different pages visible beneath the top page. The equivalent of the desktop in OS/2 is the window. The equivalents of pieces of paper are windows on the screen. On a desk you may move pieces of paper about, maybe switching which piece of paper is on top or how much of another is exposed to view. OS/2 allows the same type of operations on its windows. By selecting a window you can make it current, which means putting it on top of all other windows. You can enlarge or shrink a window, or move it about on the screen. In short, OS/2 lets you control the surface of the screen the way you control the surface of your desk.

THE MOUSE

Unlike DOS, OS/2 allows the use of the mouse for almost all control, selection, and drawing operations. Of course, to say that it *allows* the use of the mouse is an understatement. The fact is that the Presentation Manager interface was *designed for the mouse*—it *allows* the use of the keyboard! Although it is certainly possible for an application program to ignore the mouse, it does so only in violation of a basic Presentation Manager design principle.

ICONS AND GRAPHICS IMAGES

OS/2 allows (but does not require) the use of icons and bitmapped graphics images. The theory behind the use of icons and graphics images is found in the old adage: a picture is worth a thousand words.

An icon is a small symbol used to represent some function or program that can be activated by moving the mouse to the icon and double-clicking on it. A graphics image is generally used to simply convey information quickly to the user.

MENUS AND DIALOG BOXES

Aside from standard windows, there are also special-purpose windows. The most common of these are the menu and dialog boxes. Briefly, a menu is, as you would expect, a special window that contains only a menu from which the user makes a selection. However, instead of having to provide the menu selection functions in your program, you simply create a standard menu window using the Presentation Manager functions.

A dialog box is a special window that allows more complex interaction with the application than that allowed by a menu. For example, your application might use a dialog box to input a filename. With few exceptions, non-menu input is accomplished by a Presentation Manager program via a dialog box.

HOW PRESENTATION MANAGER AND YOUR PROGRAM INTERACT

When you write a program for many operating systems, it is your program that initiates interaction with the operating system. For example, in a DOS program, it is the program that requests such things as input and output. Put differently, programs written in the "traditional way" call the operating system. The operating system does not call your program. However, in a large measure, OS/2 works in the opposite way. It is OS/2 that calls your program. The process works like this: a Presentation Manager program waits until it is sent a *message* by OS/2. The message is passed to your program through a special function that is called by OS/2. Once a message is received, your program is expected to take an appropriate action. While your program may call one or more Presentation Manager API functions when responding to a message, it is still OS/2 that initiates the activity. More than anything else, it is the message-based interaction with OS/2 that dictates the general form of all Presentation Manager programs.

There are many different types of messages that OS/2 may send your program. For example, each time the mouse is clicked on a window belonging to your program, a mouse-clicked message will be sent to your program. Another type of message is sent each time a window belonging to your program must be redrawn. Still another message is sent each time the user presses a key when your program is the focus of input. Keep one fact firmly in mind: as far as your program is concerned, messages arrive randomly. This is why Presentation Manager programs resemble interrupt-driven programs. You can't know what message will be next.

OS/2 IS MULTITASKING

As mentioned, OS/2 is a multitasking operating system. As a multitasking operating system, it uses *preemptive multitasking*. In this scheme, the operating system simply stops executing one program and moves on to the next in a round-robin fashion. This is not how all operating systems work. Some systems, such as Microsoft Windows 3.1, use *non-preemptive* multitasking which requires the program itself to relinquish the CPU after a given time.

THE API

As stated, the Presentation Manager environment is accessed through a call-based interface called the API (Application Program Interface). The API functions provide all the system services performed by OS/2.

There is a subsystem to the API called the GPI (Graphics Programming Interface), which is the part of OS/2 that provides device-independent graphics support. It is the GPI functions that make it possible for a Presentation Manager application to run on a variety of different hardware.

THE COMPONENTS OF A WINDOW

Before moving on to specific aspects of programming under the Presentation Manager, a few important terms need to be defined. Figure 3-1 shows a standard window with each of its elements pointed out.

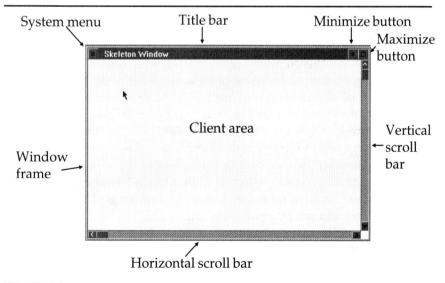

FIGURE 3-1

Elements of a standard window

All windows have a border that defines the limits of the window and that is used to move or resize the window. At the top of the window are several items. On the far left is the system menu icon (or box, as it is commonly called). Clicking on this box causes the system menu to be displayed. To the right of the system menu box is the window's title. At the far right are the minimize and maximize boxes. The client area is the part of the window in which your program activity takes place. Most windows also have horizontal and vertical scroll bars that are used to move text through the window.

SOME PRESENTATION MANAGER APPLICATION BASICS

Before developing the Presentation Manager application skeleton, some basic information needs to be stated.

THE MAIN FUNCTION

The **main()** function must define and create the windows used by your application. In addition, the **main()** function receives and dispatches messages sent by the Presentation Manager.

THE WINDOW FUNCTION

All Presentation Manager programs contain a window function. This function's purpose is to process messages from the Presentation Manager. Typically, the window function's body consists of a **switch** statement that links a specific response to each message the program will respond to. Your program need not respond to every message that OS/2 sends. For messages that your program doesn't care about, you can let the Presentation Manager provide default processing of them. Since there are hundreds of different messages that the Presentation Manager can generate, it is common for most messages to simply be processed by the Presentation Manager and not by your program.

All messages are 32-bit integer values. Further, all messages are linked with any additional information that the message requires.

WINDOW CLASSES

When your Presentation Manager program first begins execution, it will need to define and register a *window class*. (Here, the word *class* is not being used in its C++ sense. In this usage, it means *style* or *type*.) When you register the window class, you are telling Presentation Manager about the form and function of the window. However, registering the window class does not cause a window to come into existence. To actually create a window requires additional steps.

THE MESSAGE LOOP

As explained earlier, OS/2 communicates with your program by sending it messages. All Presentation Manager applications must establish a *message loop*, usually this is inside the **main()** function. This loop reads any pending message from the application's message queue, acts on messages, and dispatches messages back to OS/2. Any messages the application cares to ignore can be handled by the default message handler built into the Presentation Manager interface.

PRESENTATION MANAGER DATA TYPES

As you will soon see, the OS/2 API, including the Presentation Manager API, does not use standard C data types such as **int** or **char ***. Instead, all data types used by Presentation Manager have been defined by a **typedef** within the OS2DEF.H (or an associated) file. These files are supplied with your OS/2 development kit. Some of the most common types are HWND, LONG, ULONG, BOOL, INT, and PCHAR. HWND is a 32-bit unsigned **long** that is used as a handle. A *handle* is simply a value that identifies some resource. LONG is defined as a 32-bit **long**, and ULONG is defined as a 32-bit **unsigned long**. BOOL is also an **unsigned long**, and is used primarily to indicate values that are either true or false (Boolean). INT is a 32-bit integer and is simply another name for **int**. PCHAR is what is used for a **char** pointer. As you will see, adding a leading P to most any of the types turns the declaration into a pointer to that type.

In addition to the basic types described above, the API defines several structures. The one that is needed by the first skeleton program is MSG. The MSG structure holds a Presentation Manager message structure that is used by the message queue. These structures will be discussed later in this chapter.

A PRESENTATION MANAGER SKELETON

Now that the necessary background information has been covered, it is time to develop a minimal Presentation Manager application. As stated, all Presentation Manager programs have certain things in common. In this section a Presentation Manager skeleton is developed that provides these necessary features. In the world of Presentation Manager programming, application skeletons are commonly used because there is a substantial "price of admission" when creating a Presentation Manager program. Unlike DOS programs that you may have written, in which a minimal program is about 5 lines long, a minimal Presentation Manager program is approximately 50 lines long. Therefore, application skeletons are commonly used when developing Presentation Manager applications.

A minimal Presentation Manager program contains the **main()** function and a window function. The **main()** function must perform the following general steps:

1. Initialize the window system.

2. Initialize the message queue.

3. Register the window procedure class.

4. Display the window.

5. Begin running the message loop.

6. Close the application resources.

The program will respond to all relevant messages. Since the skeleton program does nothing but display its window, there are no messages it must respond to. The only message that is included in the application skeleton is one to tell the Presentation Manager to clear out the client area of the window whenever the window is created or moved.

The operation of the **main()** function is straightforward. It first initializes the link between the Presentation Manager and the program, registers a new window class, creates a window, and executes its message loop. As messages are received, they are dispatched to **window_func()** by calling **WinDispatchMsg()**. The message loop terminates when the WM_QUIT is received. This message is generated by choosing the Close option in the OS/2 system menu.

Before discussing the specifics, examine the following program, which is a minimal Presentation Manager skeleton. It creates a standard window. The window contains the system menu and is, therefore, capable of being minimized, maximized, moved, resized, and closed. It also contains the standard minimize and maximize icons. Before continuing, enter this program and compile it. If you are using the C Set/2 compiler, use the following command to compile the skeleton program:

```
ICC -B"/PM:PM" SKELETON.C
```

The -B"/PM:PM" flag tells the compiler to produce a Presentation Manager program.

```
/* A Presentation Manager application skeleton. */

#define INCL_WIN
#include <os2.h>

MRESULT EXPENTRY window_func(HWND, ULONG,
                             MPARAM, MPARAM);

main()
{
  HAB hand_ab;          /* Anchor Block */
  HMQ hand_mq;          /* message queue */
  HWND hand_frame;      /* Frame */
  QMSG q_mess;          /* message queue */
  ULONG flFlags;        /* Window frame definition */
  unsigned char class[] = "MyClass";  /* class name */

  /* define the frame contents */
  flFlags = FCF_TITLEBAR |    /* have a title bar */
            FCF_SIZEBORDER |  /* be a sizeable window */
            FCF_MINMAX |      /* have min and max buttons */
            FCF_SYSMENU |     /* include a system menu */
            FCF_VERTSCROLL |  /* vertical scroll bar */
            FCF_HORZSCROLL |  /* horizontal scroll bar */
            FCF_SHELLPOSITION; /* default size and location */

  hand_ab = WinInitialize(0);  /* Get the Anchor Block */

  hand_mq = WinCreateMsgQueue(hand_ab, 0); /* start a queue */

  if(!WinRegisterClass(   /* register this window class */
```

```
                              hand_ab,                /* anchor block */
                              (PSZ) class,            /* class name */
                              (PFNWP) window_func,    /* window function */
                              CS_SIZEREDRAW,          /* window style */
                              0))                     /* no storage */
        exit(1);

      hand_frame = WinCreateStdWindow(
                      HWND_DESKTOP,      /* window type */
                      WS_VISIBLE,        /* frame style */
                      &flFlags,          /* definitions */
                      (PSZ)class,        /* client class */
                      (PSZ)"Skeleton Window", /* title */
                      WS_VISIBLE,        /* client style */
                      0,                 /* resource modules */
                      0,                 /* resource identifier */
                      NULL);             /* pointer to client */
      /* message loop */
      while(WinGetMsg(hand_ab, &q_mess, 0L, 0, 0))
        WinDispatchMsg(hand_ab, &q_mess);

      /* Shut down the application window and queue */
      WinDestroyWindow(hand_frame);
      WinDestroyMsgQueue(hand_mq);
      WinTerminate(hand_ab);
}


/* This is the window function. */
MRESULT EXPENTRY window_func(
                      HWND handle, ULONG mess,
                      MPARAM parm1, MPARAM parm2)
{

  switch(mess) {

    case WM_ERASEBACKGROUND:
    /* By returning TRUE, the Presentation Manager
       automatically clears the window each time the window
       is resized or moved.
    */
      return (MRESULT)TRUE;

    default:
    /* All messages not handled by the window_func,
    must be passed along to the Presentation Manager for
```

```
    default processing.
     */
      return WinDefWindowProc(handle, mess, parm1, parm2);
  }
  return (MRESULT)FALSE;
}
```

UNDERSTANDING THE PRESENTATION MANAGER SKELETON

Now that you have seen a Presentation Manager program, let's walk through this skeleton program step-by-step.

First, all OS/2 programs, including Presentation Manager programs, must include the header OS2.H. This file contains the API function prototypes and various types and definitions used by the Presentation Manager. By defining a macro prior to including OS2.H, you can include just the subsection of the API you will be using. In this example, since we are using the window part of the API, we define INCL_WIN. The example program then goes through the various steps to define the message queue and window class and to create the application window.

OBTAINING AN ANCHOR BLOCK

One of the first things you will want your Presentation Manager application to do is obtain an anchor block handle by calling **WinInitialize()**, whose prototype is shown here:

HAB APIENTRY WinInitialize(ULONG *handle*);

Here, *handle* must be 0. Notice that the function returns HAB, which is a pointer that points to the region of memory used by the Presentation Manager to hold various bits of information about the window environment relative to the application program. This region of memory is called the *anchor block* and the pointer to it is called the *anchor block handle*. If the system cannot be initialized, a 0 is returned. The anchor block handle is required as a parameter by many Presentation Manager services.

Unlike the core API services, which return 0 for success, many of the Presentation Manager services return 0 on failure.

CREATING A MESSAGE QUEUE

After initializing the window system, all Presentation Manager applications must create a message queue using **WinCreateMsgQueue()**, which has this prototype:

HMQ APIENTRY WinCreateMsgQueue(HAB *anchor_block*, LONG *size*);

The *anchor_block* is the handle obtained using **WinInitialize()**. The size of the queue is determined by the value of *size*, or, if *size* is 0, the system default is used. Generally, the system default queue size is acceptable.

Each element in the message queue is contained in a structure called QMSG and defined like this:

```
struct {
        HWND hwnd; /* handle of the recipient window */
        ULONG msg; /* the message */
        MPARAM mp1; /* additional message info */
        MPARAM mp2; /* additional message info */
        ULONG time; /* time message was generated */
        POINTL ptl; /* position of mouse pointer */
        ULONG reserved;
        } QMSG;
```

The POINTL structure is defined like this:

```
struct {
        LONG x;
        LONG y;
        } POINTL;
```

WinCreateMsgQueue() returns a handle to the message queue or NULL if the request fails.

REGISTERING A WINDOW CLASS

Before you can actually create a window, you must register its class using **WinRegisterClass()**, whose prototype is shown here:

BOOL APIENTRY WinRegisterClass(HAB *anchor_block*,
                               PSZ *classname*,
                               PFNWP *window_func*,

ULONG *style*,
ULONG *storage_bytes*);

Here, *anchor_block* is a pointer to the anchor block. The string pointed to by *classname* is the name of the window class being registered. The address of the window function must be passed as the third parameter. The style of the window is specified by *style*. Finally, the number of bytes of additional storage beyond that needed by the window is specified by *storage_bytes*. Your program may use this extra storage for its own purposes. For the examples in this book, this field will be 0.

The sort of window being registered is described by the value of *style*. The only style we will be using in this book has the value 4L and is defined as CS_SIZEREDRAW. Using this style causes the Presentation Manager to inform your program each time the window is resized.

The **WinRegisterClass()** service returns non-zero if successful and NULL on failure.

CREATING A STANDARD WINDOW

Once you have initialized the window system relative to your application, created a message queue, and registered the class, it is time to create a window. The easiest way to create a standard window is to use the **WinCreateStdWindow()** API service. Its prototype is shown here:

HWND APIENTRY WinCreateStdWindow(HWND *parent_handle*,
                             ULONG *style*,
                             PSZ *classname*,
                             PSZ *title*,
                             ULONG *client_style*,
                             HMODULE *module*,
                             ULONG *resource*,
                             PHWND *client_handle*);

The *parent_handle* must be the handle of the parent window. When a program begins execution, its parent is the screen, which, for the examples in this book, has HWND_DESKTOP for its handle.

The value of *style* determines several features of the window. It can be a combination of several values. The most common, along with the macro names given to them, are shown in Table 3-1.

Macro Name	Value	Meaning
WS_VISIBLE	0x80000000L	Make window visible
WS_MINIMIZED	0x01000000L	Minimize window
WS_MAXIMIZED	0x00800000L	Maximize window
FCS_TITLEBAR	0x00000001L	Include title bar
FCS_SYSMENU	0x00000002L	Include system menu
FCS_VERTSCROLL	0x00000010L	Include vertical scroll bar
FCS_HORZSCROLL	0x00000020L	Include horizontal scroll bar
FCS_SIZEBORDER	0x00000040L	Include sizing border
FCS_BORDER	0x00000200L	Use thin border
FCS_MINBUTTON	0x00001000L	Include minimize icon
FCS_MAXBUTTON	0x00002000L	Include maximize icon
FCS_MINMAX	0x00003000L	Include both min and max icons

TABLE 3-1

Common Values for the **WinCreateStdWindow()** *Style Parameter*

The *classname* parameter points to the string that identifies the class. This should be the same string that was used in the call to **WinRegisterClass()**.

The string pointed to by *title* will be used as the title of the window for identification purposes.

For most purposes the *client_style* parameter should be 0L, indicating that the client window should be of the same style as the window class.

The *resource* and *module* parameters are used to identify a resource module. For the examples in this chapter, no resource modules are needed, so these parameters should be NULL and 0, respectively.

The **WinCreateStdWindow()** service returns a handle to the frame if successful and 0 on failure.

AN EXAMPLE OF THE MESSAGE LOOP

For your program to process messages, it will require the use of **WinGetMsg()**, whose prototype is shown here:

```
BOOL APIENTRY WinGetMsg(HAB anchor_block,
                        PQMSG message,
                        HWND window,
                        ULONG first,
                        ULONG last);
```

The message retrieved from the queue is put in the queue structure pointed to by *message*. If *window* is not 0, then it causes **WinGetMsg()** to retrieve messages directed to only the specified window. Most of the time your application will want to receive all messages. In this case, *window* should be 0. All messages are integers. The *first* and *last* parameters determine the range of messages that will be accepted by defining the end points of that range. If you wish to receive all messages, then *first* and *last* should both be 0. **WinGetMsg()** returns TRUE unless a termination message is received, in which case it returns FALSE.

In many situations, once a message has been received, it is simply dispatched to the correct window without further processing by your program within the message loop. The service that sends messages along their way is **WinDispatchMsg()**, whose prototype is shown here:

```
MRESULT APIENTRY WinDispatchMsg(HAB anchor_block,
                                PQMSG message);
```

By calling this function, the message will automatically be routed to the proper window function. **WinDispatchMsg()** returns the value returned by the window function.

PROGRAM TERMINATION

Before your program terminates it must do three things: close any active windows, close the message queue, and deactivate the window system interface created by the **WinInitialize()** service. To accomplish these things, the Presentation Manager provides the services **WinDestroyWindow()**, **WinDestroyMsgQueue()**, and **WinTerminate()**. Their prototypes are shown here:

BOOL APIENTRY WinDestroyWindow(HWND *handle_window*);
BOOL APIENTRY WinDestroyMsgQueue(HMQ *handle_msgQ*);
BOOL APIENTRY WinTerminate(HAB *anchor_block*);

Here, *handle_window* is the handle of the window to be closed. The *handle_msgQ* is the handle to the message queue to be destroyed. Finally, the window system is disconnected by calling **WinTerminate()** with the anchor block handle.

AN EXAMPLE OF THE WINDOW FUNCTION

As mentioned earlier, all programs that are compatible with the Presentation Manager must pass to the Presentation Manager the address of the window function that will receive messages. In a Presentation Manager application, the most important single function is the window function. It receives the messages sent by the Presentation Manager and takes appropriate action. This function must be declared as shown here:

```
MRESULT EXPENTRY window_func(HWND handle, ULONG mess,
                             MPARAM parm1, MPARAM parm2)
```

The window function receives the Presentation Manager messages in its parameters. In essence, the Presentation Manager sends your program a message by calling the window function. The value of *handle* is the handle of the window receiving the message. The message itself is contained in the integer *mess*. Finally, some messages require further information, which is put into the *parm1* and *parm2* parameters.

The sample window function presented earlier contains entries in the **switch** statement for only two of the several common messages that can be generated by the Presentation Manager. A more complete window function template is shown here. It can be inserted into the original skeleton program, replacing the existing window function. This window function recognizes many of the most used messages.

```
/* This is a much more complete window function template. */
```

```
MRESULT EXPENTRY window_func(HWND handle, ULONG mess,
                            MPARAM parm1, MPARAM parm2)
{

  switch(mess) {
   case WM_CREATE:
   /* Perform any necessary initializations here. */
     break;

    case WM_PAINT:
    /* Refresh the window each time the WM_PAINT message
       is received.
        */
      break;

    case WM_ERASEBACKGROUND:
    /* By returning TRUE, the PM automatically erases
       the old window each time the window is resized
       or moved. Without this, your program must
       manually handle erasing the window when it changes
       size or location.
        */
      return (MRESULT)TRUE;

    case WM_CHAR:
    /* Process keystrokes here. */
      break;

    case WM_HSCROLL:
    /* Process horizontal scroll request. */
      break;

    case WM_VSCROLL:
    /* Process vertical scroll request. */
      break;

    case WM_MOUSEMOVE:
    /*  Process a mouse motion message. */
      break;

    case WM_BUTTON1DOWN:
    /* 1st mouse button is pressed. */
      break;

    case WM_BUTTON2DOWN:
```

```
      /* 2nd mouse button is pressed. */
        break;

      case WM_BUTTON3DOWN:
      /* 3rd mouse button is pressed. */
        break;

      /* If required by your application, you may also need to
         process these additional mouse messages:

         WM_BUTTON1UP
         WM_BUTTON1DBLCLK
         WM_BUTTON2UP
         WM_BUTTON2DBLCLK
         WM_BUTTON3UP
         WM_BUTTON3DBLCLK
      */

      default:
        /* All messages not handled by the window_func,
        must be passed along to the PM for default
        processing.
        */
        return WinDefWindowProc(handle, mess, parm1, parm2);
  }
  return (MRESULT)FALSE;
}
```

Because this program is a skeleton for future applications, it does not do anything with the messages. However, you will soon see examples that do. Also keep in mind that when your program does not actually need to worry about a message, such as a program that does not have scroll bars, its message can be removed from the **switch** statement. In this case, the default processing will handle it.

The Presentation Manager can generate several different types of messages. Some of the more common ones are shown in Table 3-2. Some of these messages will be used in the sample programs developed in this chapter and Chapter 4.

Let's look at the meaning of some of these messages.

When a window is created, the WM_CREATE message is sent to the window function. This allows your program to initialize values or to perform other startup operations.

Macro Name	Value	Meaning
WM_BUTTON1DWN	0x0071	Button 1 down
WM_BUTTON1UP	0x0072	Button 1 up
WM_BUTTON1DBLCLK	0x0073	Double-click on button 1
WM_BUTTON2DWN	0x0074	Button 2 down
WM_BUTTON2UP	0x0075	Button 2 up
WM_BUTTON2DBLCLK	0x0076	Double-click on button 2
WM_BUTTON3DWN	0x0077	Button 3 down
WM_BUTTON3UP	0x0078	Button 3 up
WM_BUTTON3DBLCLK	0x0079	Double-click on button 3
WM_CHAR	0x007A	Keystroke occurred
WM_CREATE	0x0001	Window has been created
WM_DESTROY	0x0002	Window is being destroyed
WM_ERASEBACKGROUND	0x004F	OK to erase background request
WM_HSCROLL	0x0032	Horizontal scroll
WM_MOVE	0x0006	Window is being moved
WM_MOUSEMOVE	0x0070	Mouse has moved
WM_PAINT	0x0023	Refresh window display
WM_SHOW	0x0005	Window is shown or removed
WM_SIZE	0x0007	Window is being resized
WM_VSCROLL	0x0031	Vertical scroll
WM_QUIT	0x002A	Window being terminated

TABLE 3-2

Some Common Messages

As you know, the Presentation Manager allows the user to move and resize windows. It also allows the user to cover part of a window with another. These operations imply that all or part of the window must be redrawn at some point in time. The Presentation Manager generates the

WM_PAINT message whenever the contents of the window must be refreshed.

The WM_ERASEBACKGROUND message tells your program that the window needs to be erased, perhaps because the window is being moved. By having the window function return TRUE, you are allowing the Presentation Manager to do this for you. Otherwise, your program must do it.

Each time a key is pressed, the WM_CHAR message is generated. We will be looking more closely at this message later. Each time the user requests a vertical scroll the WM_VSCROLL message is generated. Each time a horizontal scroll is requested, the WM_HSCROLL is generated. The mouse messages are self-explanatory.

The window function does not need to explicitly process all the messages it receives. In fact, it is common for an application to process only a few types of messages. So what happens, then, to the rest of the messages received by the window function? The answer is that they are passed back to the Presentation Manager for default processing using the **WinDefWindowProc()** service. Its prototype is shown here:

MRESULT APIENTRY WinDefWindowProc(HWND *handle,*
                                  ULONG *message,*
                                  MPARAM *parm1,*
                                  MPARAM *parm2*);

As you can see, the **WinDefWindowProc()** simply passes back to the Presentation Manager the parameters it was called with. Any messages received, but not processed, by **window_func()** are passed along to the Presentation Manager via a call to **WinDefWindowProc()**. This step is necessary because all messages must be dealt with in one fashion or another.

USING A DEFINITION FILE

When you compiled the skeleton, you provided the necessary linker command directly to the compiler. Linker commands can be placed in a definition file, and then passed to the compiler or the linker. A *definition file* is simply a text file that specifies certain information and settings needed by your Presentation Manager program. As your programs grow in complexity, you will find uses for the definition file. However, when dealing with simple programs, a definition file is unnecessary.

All definition files use the extension .DEF. For example, the definition file for the skeleton program could be called SKELETON.DEF. The compiler recognizes the .DEF extension and automatically passes the file to the linker for processing. Here is a definition file that you can use to compile the skeleton program.

```
NAME WinSkel WINDOWAPI
DESCRIPTION 'Skeleton Program'
DATA MULTIPLE
HEAPSIZE 8192
STACKSIZE 8192E
```

This file specifies information that is used by the linker when creating the executable file. The last argument of NAME corresponds to the option passed to the linker when you originally compiled the skeleton program (-B"/PM:PM").

Once you have created the definition file, you can use it by simply including the file on the compiler command line.

```
ICC skeleton.c skeleton.def
```

For small programs, such as many of the examples in this book, it is not necessary to use the .DEF file. As we move on to more complex examples, the reasons for using a .DEF file will become more apparent.

Now that you know how to write a basic skeleton program, let's move on and explore more features of the Presentation Manager.

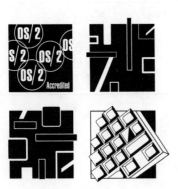

PROCESSING MESSAGES

As explained in Chapter 3, the Presentation Manager communicates with your application by sending it messages. For this reason, the processing of these messages is at the core of all Presentation Manager applications. In the previous chapter you learned how to create a Presentation Manager application skeleton. In this chapter, that skeleton will be expanded to receive and process several common Presentation Manager messages.

WHAT ARE PRESENTATION MANAGER MESSAGES?

There are hundreds of Presentation Manager messages. Each message is represented by a unique 32-bit integer value. In the header file PMWIN.H, there are standard names for these messages. Generally, you will use the defined name, not the actual integer value, when referring to a message. Here are some common Presentation Manager messages:

```
WM_CHAR
WM_PAINT
```

```
WM_MOVE
WM_BUTTON2UP
WM_BUTTON1DOWN
```

Two other values accompany each message and contain information related to the specific message. These 32-bit values are declared as VOID pointers (MPARAM), but they actually can be holding one of many different data items, including an integer, a set of flag bits, or a pointer to another data item such as a structure. They typically hold things like cursor or mouse coordinates, the value of a keypress, or a system-related value such as character size. As each message is discussed, the meaning of the values contained in these message values will be described.

As mentioned in Chapter 3, the function that actually processes Presentation Manager messages is your program's window function. As you should recall, this function is passed four parameters: the handle of the window that the message is for, the message itself, and two additional message parameters.

The information carried in the last two message parameters varies so much that the Presentation Manager defines a set of macros for passing and extracting the data from these items. A few of the popular ones are described in Tables 4-1 and 4-2.

You will see some of these macros in use later in this chapter.

Macro Name	Used for Passing
MPFROMP(p)	Pointers
MPFROMHWND(hwnd)	Window handles
MPFROMCHAR(ch)	CHAR, UCHAR, or BYTE
MPFROMSHORT(s)	SHORT, USHORT, or BOOL
MPFROMLONG(l)	LONG or ULONG

TABLE 4-1

Macros for Passing Data Through a MPARAM Variable

Macro Name	Used for Getting
PVOIDFROMMMP(mp)	Any pointer value
HWNDFROMMP(mp)	Window handles
CHAR1FROMMP(mp)	First char from a 32-bit value
CHAR2FROMMP(mp)	Second char from a 32-bit value
CHAR3FROMMP(mp)	Third char from a 32-bit value
CHAR4FROMMP(mp)	Fourth char from a 32-bit value
SHORT1FROMMP(mp)	Lower word from a 32-bit value
SHORT2FROMMP(mp)	Upper word from a 32-bit value
LONGFROMMP(mp)	Any LONG or ULONG

TABLE 4-2

Macros for Extracting Data from a MPARAM Variable

OUTPUTTING TEXT

Outputting text to a client window is not as easy as you might expect because none of the C runtime functions, such as **printf()**, can be used. The reason for this restriction has to do with the fact that the C standard output functions have no knowledge of a windowed environment. Beyond the fact that your programs must use special Presentation Manager output functions to display text in a window, outputting text is still not a trivial task. This is because the Presentation Manager maintains a level of abstraction between your program and the output device.

THE PRESENTATION SPACE AND THE DEVICE CONTEXT

When your program outputs something to the "screen," it is actually outputting information to a *presentation space* (PS). Think of a presentation space as being a data structure that contains several pieces of information about the size and form of the "screen." The reason that the word *screen* has been placed in quotes in the foregoing sentences is that a presentation space is not necessarily linked to the screen; it could be linked with the printer, for example. The device that the presentation space is actually linked to is called its *device context* (DC). For the rest of this discussion, the device context is assumed to be the screen.

There are three types of presentations spaces: the normal-PS, the micro-PS, and the cached micro-PS. The examples in this chapter will use only the cached micro-PS, but it is important that you understand the general concept behind all three.

The normal-PS is the most flexible of the three presentation spaces. Your program will want to use the normal-PS when it will be writing to devices other than the screen or when a screen display will be in existence a long time without a refresh. A micro-PS is similar to a normal-PS except that it requires less memory and has fewer capabilities. Finally, the cached micro-PS is the simplest presentation space to use and requires the least memory. However, the cached micro-PS operates only with the screen so it cannot be used to send output to any other device.

PROCESSING THE WM_PAINT MESSAGE

Each time a window is moved, resized, or uncovered, the WM_PAINT message is sent to the program's window function. Each time this message is received, your program must completely redisplay any output that was in the window. The process is often referred to as *refreshing* the window. Although it is possible to output to the window during the processing of other messages, the most common place for this to occur is when handling the WM_PAINT message. For this reason we will begin our discussion of text output as it relates to the processing of the WM_PAINT message.

Before you can output anything to the screen, you need to obtain a presentation space handle. There are several ways to do this. However, when processing the WM_PAINT message, the easiest way is to use the **WinBeginPaint()** service to return a micro-PS handle. The prototype for **WinBeginPaint()** is shown here,

HPS   APIENTRY WinBeginPaint(HWND *handle*,
                             HPS *p_space*,
                             PRECTL *region*);

where *handle* is the handle of the window that will be drawn to and *p_space* is the handle of the presentation space. If this value is 0, then a micro-PS will automatically be allocated and its handle returned by the service. The structure pointed to by *region* will contain the coordinates of the region that needs to be updated. This parameter may be 0 in cases where it is simply easier for the program to update the entire window rather than a portion.

The **WinBeginPaint()** function serves a second important function: it informs the Presentation Manager that a window refresh is beginning. For this reason, it is a good idea to call to **WinBeginPaint()** immediately after a WM_PAINT message is received.

The simplest way to write a line of text to a window is to use the **GpiCharStringAt()** service, whose prototype is shown here,

```
LONG APIENTRY GpiCharStringAt(HPS p_space,
                              PPOINTL loc,
                              LONG size,
                              PCH string);
```

where *p_space* is the presentation space handle. The structure pointed to by *loc* contains the coordinates of the location at which the string will be written. The *size* parameter holds the size and *string* points to the actual string.

The return value of **GpiCharStringAt()** is somewhat complex and is not required by the examples in this chapter.

The POINTL structure is defined like this:

```
struct POINTL {  LONG x;  LONG y; } ;
```

It is critical to keep in mind that the X,Y locations in the POINTL structure are specified in *pels*, not in characters.

Although in its default mode no cursor is seen in a window, each window does keep track of the position of an invisible "cursor." The position of this invisible cursor is called the *current position*. Many of the output services, including **GpiCharStringAt()**, affect the location of the current position. After the string has been displayed using **GpiCharStringAt()**, the current position is advanced to the pel immediately following the last character in the string.

The **GpiCharStringAt()** service does not process carriage returns or line feeds, so your program must manually advance to new lines when needed.

Before the code that processes the WM_PAINT message finishes, it must issue a call to **WinEndPaint()**, which has this prototype:

BOOL APIENTRY WinEndPaint(HPS *p_space*);

Here, *p_space* is the handle of the presentation space updated by the program. If **WinEndPaint()** is successful, it returns TRUE; otherwise, it returns FALSE.

Assuming the necessary variable declarations, the following fragment outputs "This is a test" on the screen, starting at the lower left corner.

```
case WM_PAINT:
  /* get a handle to the presentation space */
  p_space = WinBeginPaint(handle, 0, NULL);
  /* output a message that starts at the lower left corner */
  coords.x = 0;
  coords.y = 0;
  GpiCharStringAt(p_space, &coords, 14, "This is a test");
  /* close the presentation space */
  WinEndPaint(handle);   break;
```

Each time the window associated with this code fragment is moved, resized, or uncovered, the WM_PAINT message is received and the line of text will be redisplayed. An entire program that uses the code fragment is shown here:

```
/* Output a string. */

#define INCL_WIN
#include <os2.h>

MRESULT EXPENTRY window_func(HWND, ULONG, MPARAM, MPARAM);

main()
{
  HAB hand_ab;           /* anchor block */
  HMQ hand_mq;           /* message queue */
  HWND hand_frame;       /* Frame */
  QMSG q_mess;           /* message queue */
  ULONG flFlags;         /* Window frame definition */
  unsigned char class[] = "MyClass";  /* class name */

  /* define the frame contents */
  flFlags = FCF_TITLEBAR |        /* have a title bar */
```

```
            FCF_SIZEBORDER |    /* be a sizeable window */
            FCF_MINMAX |        /* have min and max buttons */
            FCF_SYSMENU |       /* include a system menu */
            FCF_VERTSCROLL |    /* vertical scroll bar */
            FCF_HORZSCROLL |    /* horizontal scroll bar */
            FCF_SHELLPOSITION;  /* default size and location*/

  hand_ab = WinInitialize(0);  /* Get the anchor block */

  hand_mq = WinCreateMsgQueue(hand_ab, 0); /* start a queue */

  if(!WinRegisterClass(   /* register this window class */
                  hand_ab,               /* anchor block */
                  (PSZ) class,           /* class name */
                  (PFNWP) window_func,   /* window function */
                  CS_SIZEREDRAW,         /* window style */
                  0))                    /* no storage */
     exit(1);

  hand_frame = WinCreateStdWindow(
                  HWND_DESKTOP, /* window type */
                  WS_VISIBLE,   /* frame style */
                  &flFlags,     /* definitions */
                  (PSZ)class,   /* client class */
                  (PSZ)"Skeleton Window", /* title */
                  WS_VISIBLE,   /* client style */
                  0,            /* resource modules */
                  0,            /* resource identifier */
                  NULL);        /* pointer to client */
   /* message loop */
  while(WinGetMsg(hand_ab, &q_mess, 0, 0, 0))
    WinDispatchMsg(hand_ab, &q_mess);

  /* Shut down the application window and queue */
  WinDestroyWindow(hand_frame);
  WinDestroyMsgQueue(hand_mq);
  WinTerminate(hand_ab);
}

/* This is the window function. */
MRESULT EXPENTRY window_func(HWND handle, ULONG mess,
                             MPARAM parm1, MPARAM parm2)
{
  HPS p_space;
  POINTL coords;
```

```
switch(mess) {
  case WM_PAINT:
    /* get a handle to the presentation space */
    p_space = WinBeginPaint(handle, 0, NULL);

    /* output a message, start at the lower left corner */
    coords.x = 0;
    coords.y = 0;
    GpiCharStringAt(p_space, &coords, 14, "This is a test");

    /* close the presentation space */
    WinEndPaint(handle);
    break;

  case WM_ERASEBACKGROUND:
    return (MRESULT)TRUE;

  default:
    return WinDefWindowProc(handle, mess, parm1, parm2);
}
  return (MRESULT)0;
}
```

To compile this program, be certain to use the method discussed in Chapter 3:

```
ICC -B"/PM:PM" prog_name
```

If you prefer, define and include a definition file. You can use the definition file we discussed in Chapter 3. The minimum .DEF file for this program is shown here:

```
NAME prog_name WINDOWAPI
```

DISPLAYING TEXT IN COLOR

You can change both the foreground and background colors used to display a character using **GpiSetColor()** and **GpiSetBackColor()**, respectively. The prototypes are shown here.

BOOL APIENTRY GpiSetColor(HPS *p_space*, LONG *color*);
BOOL APIENTRY GpiSetBackColor(HPS *p_space*, LONG *color*);

Here, *p_space* is the handle to the presentation space and *color* is the desired color, which can be one of the values shown in Table 4-3.

Keep in mind that once you set a foreground or background color, that color remains in effect until it is reset.

In the Presentation Manager's default mode of operation, once the foreground color is set, all subsequent screen output operations take place in that color. However, this is not the case for the background color

Macro Name	Value
CLR_DEFAULT	–3L
CLR_WHITE	–2L
CLR_BLACK	–1L
CLR_BACKGROUND	0L
CLR_BLUE	1L
CLR_RED	2L
CLR_PINK	3L
CLR_GREEN	4L
CLR_CYAN	5L
CLR_YELLOW	6L
CLR_NEUTRAL	7L
CLR_DARKGRAY	8L
CLR_DARKBLUE	9L
CLR_DARKRED	10L
CLR_DARKPINK	11L
CLR_DARKGREEN	12L
CLR_DARKCYAN	13L
CLR_BROWN	14L
CLR_PALEGREY	15L

TABLE 4-3

Macro Names for Color Settings

because, by default, the new background color is not "mixed" into the background color of the window. In order to mix the color in, you must call the **GpiSetBackMix()** service, whose prototype is shown here,

BOOL APIENTRY GpiSetBackMix(HPS *p_space*, LONG *mix*);

where *p_space* is the presentation space of the window and *mix* is the value that determines how the background color is mixed with the current screen color. The most common values are shown here:

Macro Name	Value	Meaning
BM_DEFAULT	0L	Use system default
BM_OVERPAINT	2L	Overwrite current color
BM_LEAVEALONE	5L	Leave current background color unchanged

To have the background color replace the current screen color, use BM_OVERPAINT.

Although not used by the sample programs in this chapter, **GpiSetMix()** can be used to set the mix of the foreground color. The prototype is shown here.

BOOL APIENTRY GpiSetMix(HPS *p_space*, LONG *mix*);

Here, *mix* specifies how the foreground color will be displayed. The most common values are shown here:

Name	Value	Meaning
FM_DEFAULT	0L	Use default
FM_OR	1L	OR text onto screen
FM_OVERPAINT	2L	Overwrite current screen color
FM_XOR	4L	XOR text onto screen
FM_LEAVEALONE	5L	Leave color attributes unchanged
FM_AND	6L	AND text onto screen

You may want to experiment with this service on your own.

The following program uses **GpiSetBackColor()**, **GpiSetColor()**, and **GpiSetBackMix()** to display a string using blue foreground and red background.

```
/* Output blue text on red background.
*/
#define INCL_WIN
#define INCL_GPI

#include <os2.h>

MRESULT EXPENTRY window_func(HWND, ULONG, MPARAM, MPARAM);

char class[] = "MyClass";


main()
{
  HAB hand_ab;            /* anchor block */
  HMQ hand_mq;            /* message queue */
  HWND hand_frame;        /* Frame */
  QMSG q_mess;            /* message queue */
  ULONG flFlags;          /* Window frame definition */
  unsigned char class[] = "MyClass";  /* class name */

  /* define the frame contents */
  flFlags = FCF_TITLEBAR |      /* have a title bar */
            FCF_SIZEBORDER |    /* be a sizeable window */
            FCF_MINMAX |        /* have min and max buttons */
            FCF_SYSMENU |       /* include a system menu */
            FCF_VERTSCROLL |    /* vertical scroll bar */
            FCF_HORZSCROLL |    /* horizontal scroll bar */
            FCF_SHELLPOSITION;  /* default size and location*/

  hand_ab = WinInitialize(0);  /* Get the anchor block */

  hand_mq = WinCreateMsgQueue(hand_ab, 0); /* start a queue */

  if(!WinRegisterClass(    /* register this window class */
                  hand_ab,               /* anchor block */
                  (PSZ) class,           /* class name */
                  (PFNWP) window_func,   /* window function */
                  CS_SIZEREDRAW,         /* window style */
                  0))                    /* no storage */
      exit(1);
```

```
      hand_frame = WinCreateStdWindow(
                      HWND_DESKTOP, /* window type */
                      WS_VISIBLE,   /* frame style */
                      &flFlags,     /* definitions */
                      (PSZ)class,   /* client class */
                      (PSZ)"Skeleton Window", /* title */
                      WS_VISIBLE,   /* client style */
                      0,            /* resource modules */
                      0,            /* resource identifier */
                      NULL);        /* pointer to client */
    /* message loop */
    while(WinGetMsg(hand_ab, &q_mess, 0, 0, 0))
      WinDispatchMsg(hand_ab, &q_mess);

    /* Shut down the application window and queue */
    WinDestroyWindow(hand_frame);
    WinDestroyMsgQueue(hand_mq);
    WinTerminate(hand_ab);
  }

/* This is the window function. */
MRESULT EXPENTRY window_func(HWND handle, ULONG mess,
                              MPARAM parm1, MPARAM parm2)
{
  HPS p_space;
  POINTL coords;

  switch(mess) {
    case WM_PAINT:
      /* get a handle to the presentation space */
      p_space = WinBeginPaint(handle, 0, NULL);

      /* use red background */
      GpiSetBackColor(p_space, CLR_RED);

      /* set mix to overwrite */
      GpiSetBackMix(p_space, BM_OVERPAINT);

      /* set foreground to blue */
      GpiSetColor(p_space, CLR_BLUE);

      coords.x = 0;
      coords.y = 0;
      GpiCharStringAt(p_space, &coords, 14, "This is a test");
```

```
      /* close the presentation space */
      WinEndPaint(handle);
      break;

    case WM_ERASEBACKGROUND:
      return (MRESULT)TRUE;

    default:
      return WinDefWindowProc(handle, mess, parm1, parm2);
  }
  return (MRESULT)0;
}
```

ACCESSING THE PRESENTATION SPACE

By using **WinGetPS()**, you can obtain a handle to a cached micro-PS without using **WinBeginPaint()**. The prototype for **WinGetPS()** is shown here:

HPS APIENTRY WinGetPS(HWND *win_handle*);

Here, *win_handle* is the handle of the window you will be outputting to. The handle to the presentation space is returned by the service.

Since you can only call **WinBeginPaint()** when the WM_PAINT message is received, the **WinGetPS()** service is useful when you want to output information during the processing of another message. (An example of this will be shown in the next section.)

When your routine is done outputting, it must call **WinReleasePS()**, which has this prototype,

BOOL APIENTRY WinReleasePS(HPS *p_space*);

where *p_space* is the presentation space handle obtained by a call to **WinGetPS()**.

RESPONDING TO A KEYPRESS

One of the most common Presentation Manager messages is generated when a key is pressed. As mentioned in passing earlier in this chapter, your

Presentation Manager programs cannot read keyboard input in the traditional fashion. For example, your programs may not call such standard library functions as **gets()** or **scanf()**. Instead, each time a key is pressed, a WM_CHAR message is sent to the active window.

The keystroke information is encoded into the two message parameters as follows: the first 16 bits of the first parameter contain several flags that tell you what type of key was pressed. These flags are shown in Table 4-4. It's time to use the macros described earlier in this chapter. The macro for extracting the first 16 bits of an MPARAM message parameter is SHORT1FROMMP(parm1).

The next 8 bits of the first parameter is a repetition count. This indicates how many times the key has been auto-repeated. The macro for getting this byte is CHAR3FROMMP(parm1). Generally, you will not need to worry about the auto-repeat information.

The high-order 8 bits of the first parameter holds the key's scan code. Certain keys, such as the arrow keys, do not have character codes, which

Macro Name	Value	Meaning When Set
KC_CHAR	1	Character
KC_VIRTUALKEY	2	Special key
KC_SCANCODE	4	Scan code
KC_SHIFT	8	Shift key
KC_CTRL	16	Control key
KC_ALT	32	ALT key
KC_KEYUP	64	Key is being released
KC_PREVDOWN	128	Key was down
KC_LONEKEY	256	Single key
KC_DEADKEY	512	Unused key
KC_COMPOSITE	1024	Key combination
KC_INVALIDCOMP	2048	Invalid combination
KC_TOGGLE	4096	Toggle key
KC_INVALIDCHAR	8192	Invalid key

TABLE 4-4

Keypress Flag Values

means that the scan code is used to identify them. The scan code is obtained by the macro CHAR4FROMMP(parm1).

The second parameter associated with the WM_CHAR message contains two items. The lower 16 bits contains the character code, assuming that a regular key has been pressed. That is, if the KC_CHAR flag is set in the first parameter, a valid character code will be found in the lower 16 bits of the second parameter. However, if a special key is pressed, the KC_CHAR flag will not be set and the character code of the second parameter will be 0. For U.S. style keyboards, only the first 8 bits is of interest, but for foreign systems, the full 16 bits may be needed. To get the character code, use the SHORT1FROMMP(parm2) macro.

The high-order 16 bits of the second parameter holds the virtual key code for the key that was pressed. All keystrokes are assigned a virtual code. However, for normal keys this code is 0. To obtain the virtual key code, you can use the SHORT2FROMMP(parm2) macro. The virtual key codes, along with their corresponding macro names, are shown in Table 4-5. As you can see, some virtual key codes are not able to be generated by the keyboard, but, instead, are generated by the Presentation Manager itself.

Macro Name	Value	Key
VK_CANCEL	04	CANCEL
VK_BACK	05	BACKSPACE
VK_TAB	06	TAB
VK_CLEAR	07	
VK_RETURN	08	ENTER
VK_SHIFT	09	SHIFT
VK_CONTROL	10	CTRL
VK_ALT	11	ALT
VK_ALTGRAF	12	
VK_PAUSE	13	PAUSE
VK_CAPITAL	14	CAPS LOCK

TABLE 4-5
Virtual Key Codes

Macro Name	Value	Key
VK_ESCAPE	15	ESC
VK_SPACE	16	SPACEBAR
VK_PGUP	17	PGUP
VK_PGDN	18	PGDN
VK_END	19	END
VK_HOME	20	HOME
VK_LEFT	21	LEFT ARROW
VK_UP	22	UP ARROW
VK_RIGHT	23	RIGHT ARROW
VK_DOWN	24	DOWN ARROW
VK_SELECT	25	
VK_PRINT	26	
VK_EXECUTE	27	
VK_INSERT	28	INS
VK_DELETE	29	DEL
VK_SCRLLOCK	30	SCROLL LOCK
VK_NUMLOCK	31	NUM LOCK
VK_NUMPAD0	32	Number pad 0
VK_NUMPAD1	33	Number pad 1
VK_NUMPAD2	34	Number pad 2
VK_NUMPAD3	35	Number pad 3
VK_NUMPAD4	36	Number pad 4
VK_NUMPAD5	37	Number pad 5
VK_NUMPAD6	38	Number pad 6
VK_NUMPAD7	39	Number pad 7
VK_NUMPAD8	40	Number pad 8
VK_NUMPAD9	41	Number pad 9

TABLE 4-5

Virtual Key Codes (continued)

Macro Name	Value	Key
VK_ADD	42	Number pad +
VK_SUBTRACT	43	Number pad –
VK_MULTIPLY	44	Number pad *
VK_DIVIDE	45	Number pad /
VK_DECIMAL	46	Number pad .
VK_ENTER	47	Number pad ENTER
VK_F1	48	F1
VK_F2	49	F2
VK_F3	50	F3
VK_F4	51	F4
VK_F5	52	F5
VK_F6	53	F6
VK_F7	54	F7
VK_F8	55	F8
VK_F9	56	F9
VK_F10	57	F10
VK_F11	58	F11
VK_F12	59	F12
VK_F13	60	F13
VK_F14	61	F14
VK_F15	62	F15
VK_F16	63	F16
VK_HELP	64	
VK_SYSREQ	65	SYSRQ
VK_MENU	11	Same as VK_ALT
VK_INS	28	Same as VK_INSERT
VK_DEL	29	Same as VK_DELETE

TABLE 4-5
Virtual Key Codes (continued)

Each time you press a key, a *make* signal is generated. Each time you release the key, a *break* signal is sent. When processing the WM_CHAR message, it is important to understand that your program will be receiving both these signals. Most of the time you will only want to take an action on keypress, not key release. To check for this, you must examine the state of the KC_KEYUP flag in the first parameter. If it is 0, then the key is being pressed. If it is 1, then the key is being released.

The following program reads keys from the keyboard and displays normal characters on the screen. It processes the *make* and skips the *break* signal. Keep in mind that before the window created by this program can receive input, you must click on the window to make it active. (Only when the window is active does it become the focus of the keyboard.) Notice that this program uses the **WinGetPS()** and **WinReleasePS()** functions.

```
/* This program reads keystrokes. */

#define INCL_WIN
#define INCL_GPI

#include <os2.h>

MRESULT EXPENTRY window_func(HWND, ULONG, MPARAM, MPARAM);

char class[] = "MyClass";


main()
{
  HAB hand_ab;                /* anchor block */
  HMQ hand_mq;                /* message queue */
  HWND hand_frame;            /* Frame */
  QMSG q_mess;                /* message queue */
  ULONG flFlags;              /* Window frame definition */
  unsigned char class[] = "MyClass";  /* class name */

  /* define the frame contents */
  flFlags = FCF_TITLEBAR |        /* have a title bar */
            FCF_SIZEBORDER |      /* be a sizeable window */
            FCF_MINMAX |          /* have min and max buttons */
            FCF_SYSMENU |         /* include a system menu */
            FCF_VERTSCROLL |      /* vertical scroll bar */
            FCF_HORZSCROLL |      /* horizontal scroll bar */
            FCF_SHELLPOSITION;    /* default size and location*/
```

```
    hand_ab = WinInitialize(0);   /* Get the anchor block */

    hand_mq = WinCreateMsgQueue(hand_ab, 0);   /* start a queue
*/

    if(!WinRegisterClass(   /* register this window class */
                    hand_ab,                /* anchor block */
                    (PSZ) class,            /* class name */
                    (PFNWP) window_func,  /* window function */
                    CS_SIZEREDRAW,          /* window style */
                    0))                     /* no storage */
        exit(1);

    hand_frame = WinCreateStdWindow(
                    HWND_DESKTOP, /* window type */
                    WS_VISIBLE,   /* frame style */
                    &flFlags,     /* definitions */
                    (PSZ)class,   /* client class */
                    (PSZ)"Skeleton Window", /* title */
                    WS_VISIBLE,   /* client style */
                    0,            /* resource modules */
                    0,            /* resource identifier */
                    NULL);        /* pointer to client */
      /* message loop */
    while(WinGetMsg(hand_ab, &q_mess, 0, 0, 0))
      WinDispatchMsg(hand_ab, &q_mess);

    /* Shut down the application window and queue */
    WinDestroyWindow(hand_frame);
    WinDestroyMsgQueue(hand_mq);
    WinTerminate(hand_ab);
}

/* This is the window function. */
MRESULT EXPENTRY window_func(HWND handle, ULONG mess,
                            MPARAM parm1, MPARAM parm2)
{
  HPS p_space;
  POINTL coords;
  CHAR ch;

  switch(mess) {

      case WM_CHAR: /* Process keystrokes here. */
```

```
                 /* process only keypresses, not key releases */
                 if(SHORT1FROMMP(parm1) & KC_KEYUP)
                   break;

                 if(SHORT1FROMMP(parm1) & KC_CHAR)
                   {
                   p_space = WinGetPS(handle);

                   /* use overwrite mode */
                   GpiSetBackMix(p_space, BM_OVERPAINT);

                   coords.x = 20;
                   coords.y = 20;

                   /* extract the character */
                   ch = SHORT1FROMMP(parm2);

                   /* display the character */
                   GpiCharStringAt(p_space, &coords, 1, &ch);

                   WinReleasePS(p_space);
                   }
                 break;

            case WM_ERASEBACKGROUND:
              return (MRESULT)TRUE;

            default:
              return WinDefWindowProc(handle, mess, parm1, parm2);
          }
        return (MRESULT)0;
      }
```

Keep in mind that the virtual key code and the scan code are two separate pieces of information. The scan code more or less relates to a specific keyboard implementation. However, the virtual key code is completely under the control of OS/2 and the Presentation Manager, which means it can map different keys into the virtual codes to accommodate changing situations, such as foreign languages. To see the difference between the virtual and scan codes, substitute this window function into the foregoing program. This version displays the scan and virtual codes for each key pressed.

```
/* Window function to display scan and virtual key codes. */
MRESULT EXPENTRY window_func(HWND handle, ULONG mess,
                             MPARAM parm1, MPARAM parm2)
{
  HPS p_space;
  POINTL coords;
  CHAR ch;
  CHAR str[80];
  SHORT i;

  switch(mess) {

     case WM_CHAR: /* Process keystrokes here. */
      /* process only keypresses, not key releases */
      if(SHORT1FROMMP(parm1) & KC_KEYUP)
        break;

     else /* display any keypress */
       {
        p_space = WinGetPS(handle);

        /* use overwrite mode */
        GpiSetBackMix(p_space, BM_OVERPAINT);
        coords.x = 20;
        coords.y = 20;

        /* extract the scan code */
        ch = CHAR4FROMMP(parm1);

        /* display the scan code */
        sprintf(str, "scan code %3d", ch);
        GpiCharStringAt(p_space, &coords, strlen(str), str);
        coords.x = 20;
        coords.y = 0;

        /* extract virtual code */
        i = SHORT2FROMMP(parm2);

        /* display the virtual code */
        sprintf(str, "virtual code %3d", i);
        GpiCharStringAt(p_space, &coords, strlen(str), str);
        WinReleasePS(p_space);
       }
     break;
```

Chapter 4

```
      case WM_ERASEBACKGROUND:
        return (MRESULT)TRUE;

      default:
        return WinDefWindowProc(handle, mess, parm1, parm2);
    }
    return (MRESULT)0;
}
```

A BETTER APPROACH TO SCREEN OUTPUT

As stated, often the best time for your Presentation Manager compatible programs to output information to the screen is when a WM_PAINT message is received. (Keep in mind that it is not technically wrong to output information to the screen during the processing of other messages, as was done in the previous two examples.) The reason for this is the Presentation Manager assumes that it is your program's job, in general, to maintain and update the screen whenever all or part of the window becomes invalid. A window is invalidated when it becomes uncovered, resized, or moved. Put another way, when a window's size or position is changed, or if a previously covered window is uncovered, then all or part of the information that was displayed in that window will need to be redrawn. This is the entire purpose of the WM_PAINT message. Output performed during the processing of another message will be lost if the window is moved or changed (unless, of course, the routine that processes the WM_PAINT message can refresh this output as well).

In order to fully redraw the window each time a WM_PAINT message is received implies that the WM_PAINT code must be capable of completely reconstructing the screen. To get a taste of what this entails, the following program is a rewrite of the one that reads a keystroke and displays the key. In this version, the code associated with the WM_CHAR message simply loads the variable **ch**. It is the code associated with the WM_PAINT message that actually outputs the character.

```
/* A second approach to displaying keystrokes on
   the screen.
*/

#define INCL_WIN
#define INCL_GPI

#include <os2.h>
```

```
MRESULT EXPENTRY window_func(HWND, ULONG, MPARAM, MPARAM);

char class[] = "MyClass";


main()
{
  HAB hand_ab;            /* anchor block */
  HMQ hand_mq;            /* message queue */
  HWND hand_frame;        /* Frame */
  QMSG q_mess;            /* message queue */
  ULONG flFlags;          /* Window frame definition */
  unsigned char class[] = "MyClass";  /* class name */

  /* define the frame contents */
  flFlags = FCF_TITLEBAR |      /* have a title bar */
            FCF_SIZEBORDER |    /* be a sizeable window */
            FCF_MINMAX |        /* have min and max buttons */
            FCF_SYSMENU |       /* include a system menu */
            FCF_VERTSCROLL |    /* vertical scroll bar */
            FCF_HORZSCROLL |    /* horizontal scroll bar */
            FCF_SHELLPOSITION;  /* default size and location */

  hand_ab = WinInitialize(0);  /* Get the anchor block */

  hand_mq = WinCreateMsgQueue(hand_ab, 0);  /* start a queue */

  if(!WinRegisterClass(   /* register this window class */
                  hand_ab,              /* anchor block */
                  (PSZ) class,          /* class name */
                  (PFNWP) window_func,  /* window function */
                  CS_SIZEREDRAW,        /* window style */
                  0))                   /* no storage */
      exit(1);

  hand_frame = WinCreateStdWindow(
                  HWND_DESKTOP, /* window type */
                  WS_VISIBLE,   /* frame style */
                  &flFlags,     /* definitions */
                  (PSZ)class,   /* client class */
                  (PSZ)"Skeleton Window", /* title */
                  WS_VISIBLE,   /* client style */
                  0,            /* resource modules */
                  0,            /* resource identifier */
```

```
                        NULL);           /* pointer to client */
   /* message loop */
  while(WinGetMsg(hand_ab, &q_mess, 0, 0, 0))
    WinDispatchMsg(hand_ab, &q_mess);

  /* Shut down the application window and queue */
  WinDestroyWindow(hand_frame);
  WinDestroyMsgQueue(hand_mq);
  WinTerminate(hand_ab);
}

/* This is the window function. */
MRESULT EXPENTRY window_func(HWND handle, ULONG mess,
                              MPARAM parm1, MPARAM parm2)
{
  HPS p_space;
  POINTL coords;
  static char ch='\0';

  switch(mess) {
    case WM_PAINT:
      /* Refresh the window each time the WM_PAINT message
      is received.
      */
      p_space = WinGetPS(handle);

      /* use overwrite mode */
      GpiSetBackMix(p_space, BM_OVERPAINT);

      coords.x = 20;
      coords.y = 20;

      /* display the character */
      GpiCharStringAt(p_space, &coords, 1, &ch);

      WinReleasePS(p_space);

      break;

    case WM_CHAR: /* Process keystrokes here. */
      /* process only keypresses, not key releases */
      if(SHORT1FROMMP(parm1) & KC_KEYUP)
        break;
```

```
      if(SHORT1FROMMP(parm1) & KC_CHAR)
        {
        ch = SHORT1FROMMP(parm2);

        /* update the window each time a key is pressed */
        WinUpdateWindow(handle);
        }
      break;

    case WM_ERASEBACKGROUND:
      return (MRESULT)TRUE;

    default:
      return WinDefWindowProc(handle, mess, parm1, parm2);
  }
  return (MRESULT)0;
}
```

This approach to screen output is very common in Presentation Manager compatible programs. In this method, all output is essentially directed to internal buffers that are written to the screen when the WM_PAINT message is received.

While handling the WM_PAINT message in the skeleton is quite simple, it must be emphasized that most real world versions of this program will be more complex because most windows contain considerably more output.

Since it is your program's responsibility to restore the window if it is resized or overwritten, you must always provide some mechanism to accomplish this. In real world programs, this is usually accomplished in one of three ways. First, your program can simply regenerate the output by computational means. This is most feasible when no user input is used. Second, your program can maintain a virtual screen that you simply copy to the window each time it must be redrawn. Finally, in some instances, you can keep a record of events and replay the events when the window needs to be redrawn. Which approach is best depends completely upon the application. Most of the examples in this book won't bother to redraw the window because doing so typically involves substantial additional code that often just muddies the point of an example. However, your programs will need to restore their windows in order to be valid Presentation Manager applications.

RESPONDING TO MOUSE MESSAGES

Since the Presentation Manager is, to a great extent, a mouse-based operating system, all Presentation Manager programs should respond to mouse input. Because the mouse is so important, there are several types of mouse messages. This section examines the two most common. These are WM_BUTTON1DOWN and WM_BUTTON2DOWN, which are generated when the left button and right button are pressed, respectively. Like all other messages, mouse messages not processed by the window function are passed to the **WinDefWindowProc()** function.

Let's begin with an example. Add the responses to the two mouse messages to the **switch** statement in the window function, as shown here:

```
case WM_BUTTON2DOWN: /* process right button */
  /* get a handle to the presentation space */
  p_space = WinGetPS(handle);

  /* use overwrite mode */
  GpiSetBackMix(p_space, BM_OVERPAINT);

  /* output a message */
  coords.x = SHORT1FROMMP(parm1);
  coords.y = SHORT2FROMMP(parm1);
  GpiCharStringAt(p_space, &coords, 14, "Right Button");

  WinReleasePS(p_space);
break;

case WM_BUTTON1DOWN: /* process left button */
  /* get a handle to the presentation space */
  p_space = WinGetPS(handle);

  /* use overwrite mode */
  GpiSetBackMix(p_space, BM_OVERPAINT);

  /* output a message */
  coords.x = SHORT1FROMMP(parm1);
  coords.y = SHORT2FROMMP(parm1);
  GpiCharStringAt(p_space, &coords, 14, "Left Button");

  WinReleasePS(p_space);
break;
```

When either button is pressed, the mouse's current X,Y location is specified in the second message parameter passed to the window function. The location can be accessed by using the OS/2 built-in macros: SHORT1FROMMP(parm1) for the X location and SHORT2FROMMP(parm1) for the Y location. The mouse-message response functions use these coordinates as the location to display their output. That is, each time you press a mouse button, a message will be displayed at the mouse pointer's location.

Here is the complete skeleton that responds to the two mouse messages discussed.

```
/* This example displays a message when either of the
   mouse buttons is pressed.
*/

#define INCL_WIN
#define INCL_GPI

#include <os2.h>

MRESULT EXPENTRY window_func(HWND, ULONG, MPARAM, MPARAM);

char class[] = "MyClass";


main()
{
  HAB hand_ab;              /* anchor block */
  HMQ hand_mq;              /* message queue */
  HWND hand_frame;          /* Frame */
  QMSG q_mess;              /* message queue */
  ULONG flFlags;            /* Window frame definition */
  unsigned char class[] = "MyClass";  /* class name */

  /* define the frame contents */
  flFlags = FCF_TITLEBAR |       /* have a title bar */
            FCF_SIZEBORDER |     /* be a sizeable window */
            FCF_MINMAX |         /* have min and max buttons */
            FCF_SYSMENU |        /* include a system menu */
            FCF_VERTSCROLL |     /* vertical scroll bar */
            FCF_HORZSCROLL |     /* horizontal scroll bar */
            FCF_SHELLPOSITION;   /* default size and location*/

  hand_ab = WinInitialize(0);  /* Get the anchor block */
```

```
    hand_mq = WinCreateMsgQueue(hand_ab, 0);   /* start a queue
*/

    if(!WinRegisterClass(    /* register this window class */
                    hand_ab,                    /* anchor block */
                    (PSZ) class,                /* class name */
                    (PFNWP) window_func,    /* window function */
                    CS_SIZEREDRAW,              /* window style */
                    0))                         /* no storage */
        exit(1);

    hand_frame = WinCreateStdWindow(
                    HWND_DESKTOP, /* window type */
                    WS_VISIBLE,    /* frame style */
                    &flFlags,      /* definitions */
                    (PSZ)class,    /* client class */
                    (PSZ)"Skeleton Window", /* title */
                    WS_VISIBLE,    /* client style */
                    0,             /* resource modules */
                    0,             /* resource identifier */
                    NULL);         /* pointer to client */
     /* message loop */
    while(WinGetMsg(hand_ab, &q_mess, 0, 0, 0))
      WinDispatchMsg(hand_ab, &q_mess);

    /* Shut down the application window and queue */
    WinDestroyWindow(hand_frame);
    WinDestroyMsgQueue(hand_mq);
    WinTerminate(hand_ab);
}

/* This is the window function. */
MRESULT EXPENTRY window_func(HWND handle, ULONG mess,
                            MPARAM parm1, MPARAM parm2)
{
  HPS p_space;
  POINTL coords;
  static char ch='\0';

  switch(mess) {
    case WM_BUTTON2DOWN: /* process right button */
      /* get a handle to the presentation space */
      p_space = WinGetPS(handle);

      /* use overwrite mode */
```

```
            GpiSetBackMix(p_space, BM_OVERPAINT);

            /* output a message */
            coords.x = SHORT1FROMMP(parm1);
            coords.y = SHORT2FROMMP(parm1);
            GpiCharStringAt(p_space, &coords, 14, "Right Button");

            WinReleasePS(p_space);
            break;

         case WM_BUTTON1DOWN: /* process left button */
            /* get a handle to the presentation space */
            p_space = WinGetPS(handle);

            /* use overwrite mode */
            GpiSetBackMix(p_space, BM_OVERPAINT);

            /* output a message */
            coords.x = SHORT1FROMMP(parm1);
            coords.y = SHORT2FROMMP(parm1);
            GpiCharStringAt(p_space, &coords, 14, "Left Button");

            WinReleasePS(p_space);
            break;

         case WM_ERASEBACKGROUND:
            return (MRESULT)TRUE;

         default:
            return WinDefWindowProc(handle, mess, parm1, parm2);
      }
      return (MRESULT)0;
}
```

Figure 4-1 shows sample output from this program.

GENERATING PRESENTATION MANAGER MESSAGES

It is possible for your application to post Presentation Manager messages. At first, you might wonder why your program would need to
generate a message, but actually you will find that there are many times

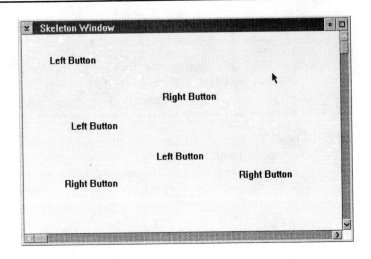

FIGURE 4-1

Sample output from the application skeleton

when it is handy to generate a message based on other messages your application has received. After all, Presentation Manager applications are based on processing messages.

DEFINING AND GENERATING MESSAGES

Not only can your application generate system messages, but it also can define and generate your own custom messages. To illustrate this, let's modify the previous program to respond to the WM_BUTTON1UP message. A good response might be to erase the line just printed to the window. To accomplish this, we will generate our own message, and respond to that message by erasing the previous screen output.

To define your own message, you simply assign your custom message its own unique ID number. Since the Presentation Manager reserves the first 4096 messages, simply choose a number greater than 4096 for your ID number. To post a Presentation Manager message to the system, your program will call the **WinPostMsg()** API function. Its prototype is shown here:

BOOL APIENTRY WinPostMsg(HWND *hwnd*,
ULONG *msg*,
MPARAM *mp1*,
MPARAM *mp2*);

Here, *hwnd* is the handle of the window that you want to send the message to. The parameter *msg* is the message being sent. The last two parameters are filled with the appropriate information relating to the message.

Here is a reworked version of the previous example that still responds to the same two mouse messages as before, but also responds to the WM_BUTTON1UP message. The action taken by the WM_BUTTON1UP message is to simply post the custom message MY_MESSAGE using the **WinPostMsg()** function.

In the following example, when either mouse button is pressed, the X,Y coordinates of the current mouse position are displayed. When the left mouse button is released, a custom message called "MY_MESSAGE" will be generated. As you will see, "MY_MESSAGE" simply prints a blank string right over the top of the previous printed string, effectively erasing the previously displayed coordinates. If the right mouse button is pressed, the coordinates remain displayed in the window.

```
/* This example processes the WM_BUTTONxUP and
   the WM_BUTTONxDOWN mouse messages.
*/

#define INCL_WIN
#define INCL_GPI

#include <os2.h>
#define MY_MESSAGE 4097

MRESULT EXPENTRY window_func(HWND, ULONG, MPARAM, MPARAM);

char class[] = "MyClass";


main()
{
  HAB hand_ab;          /* anchor block */
  HMQ hand_mq;          /* message queue */
```

```
HWND hand_frame;        /* Frame */
QMSG q_mess;            /* message queue */
ULONG flFlags;          /* Window frame definition */
unsigned char class[] = "MyClass";  /* class name */

/* define the frame contents */
flFlags = FCF_TITLEBAR |     /* have a title bar */
          FCF_SIZEBORDER |   /* be a sizeable window */
          FCF_MINMAX |       /* have min and max buttons */
          FCF_SYSMENU |      /* include a system menu */
          FCF_VERTSCROLL |   /* vertical scroll bar */
          FCF_HORZSCROLL |   /* horizontal scroll bar */
          FCF_SHELLPOSITION; /* default size and location */

hand_ab = WinInitialize(0);  /* Get the anchor block */

hand_mq = WinCreateMsgQueue(hand_ab, 0);  /* start a queue */

if(!WinRegisterClass(   /* register this window class */
                hand_ab,               /* anchor block */
                (PSZ) class,           /* class name */
                (PFNWP) window_func,   /* window function */
                CS_SIZEREDRAW,         /* window style */
                0))                    /* no storage */
    exit(1);

hand_frame = WinCreateStdWindow(
                HWND_DESKTOP, /* window type */
                WS_VISIBLE,   /* frame style */
                &flFlags,     /* definitions */
                (PSZ)class,   /* client class */
                (PSZ)"Skeleton Window", /* title */
                WS_VISIBLE,   /* client style */
                0,            /* resource modules */
                0,            /* resource identifier */
                NULL);        /* pointer to client */
  /* message loop */
while(WinGetMsg(hand_ab, &q_mess, 0, 0, 0))
  WinDispatchMsg(hand_ab, &q_mess);

/* Shut down the application window and queue */
WinDestroyWindow(hand_frame);
WinDestroyMsgQueue(hand_mq);
WinTerminate(hand_ab);
```

```
}

/* This is the window function. */
MRESULT EXPENTRY window_func(HWND handle, ULONG mess,
                            MPARAM parm1, MPARAM parm2)
{
  HPS p_space;
  static POINTL coords;
  CHAR str[16];

  switch(mess)
    {
      case WM_BUTTON2DOWN: /* process right button press */
        /* get a handle to the presentation space */
        p_space = WinGetPS(handle);

        /* use overwrite mode */
        GpiSetBackMix(p_space, BM_OVERPAINT);

        /* output a message */
        coords.x = SHORT1FROMMP(parm1);
        coords.y = SHORT2FROMMP(parm1);
        sprintf(str, "(%d,%d)", coords.x, coords.y);
        GpiCharStringAt(p_space, &coords, strlen(str), str);

        WinReleasePS(p_space);
        break;

      case WM_BUTTON1DOWN: /* process left button press */
        /* get a handle to the presentation space */
        p_space = WinGetPS(handle);

        /* use overwrite mode */
        GpiSetBackMix(p_space, BM_OVERPAINT);

        /* output a message */
        coords.x = SHORT1FROMMP(parm1);
        coords.y = SHORT2FROMMP(parm1);
        sprintf(str, "(%d,%d)", coords.x, coords.y);
        GpiCharStringAt(p_space, &coords, strlen(str), str);

        WinReleasePS(p_space);
        break;

      case WM_BUTTON2UP: /* process RIGHT button release */
```

```
        break;

    case WM_BUTTON1UP: /* process LEFT button release */
        /* post a user-defined message */
        WinPostMsg(handle, MY_MESSAGE, (MPARAM)0, (MPARAM)0);
        break;

    case MY_MESSAGE: /* Process custom message. */
        {
            PCHAR blank = "                    ";
            p_space = WinGetPS(handle);

            /* use overwrite mode */
            GpiSetBackMix(p_space, BM_OVERPAINT);

            /* overwrite last display, use same coords */
            GpiCharStringAt(p_space, &coords,
                            strlen(blank), blank);

            WinReleasePS(p_space);
        }
        break;

    case WM_ERASEBACKGROUND:
        return (MRESULT)TRUE;

    default:
        return WinDefWindowProc(handle, mess, parm1, parm2);
    }
    return (MRESULT)0;
}
```

Now that you have learned how to create, generate, and process the basic Presentation Manager messages, you can move on to creating message boxes and menus, which are the subject of Chapter 5.

MESSAGE BOXES AND MENUS

Now that you know how to construct a basic Presentation Manager skeleton that receives and processes messages, it is time to explore the Presentation Manager's user interface components. Although you can write a Presentation Manager application that appears just like a DOS application, doing so is not in the spirit of Presentation Manager programming. In order for your Presentation Manager applications to conform to Presentation Manager general design principles, you will need to communicate with the user using several different types of special windows. There are three basic types of user interface windows: message boxes, menus, and dialog boxes. This chapter discusses message boxes and menus. (The next chapter examines dialog boxes). As you will see, the basic style of each of these windows is predefined by the Presentation Manager. You need supply only the specific information that relates to your application.

Keep in mind that message boxes and menus are *child windows* of your original application windows. This means they are owned by your application and are dependent upon it. They cannot exist by themselves. Your application must always create a main window.

MESSAGE BOXES

By far the simplest interface window is the message box. A message box simply displays a message to the user and waits for an acknowledgment. It is possible to construct message boxes that allow the user to select among a few basic alternatives, but, in general, the purpose of a message box is simply to inform the user that some event has taken place.

To create a message box, use the **WinMessageBox()** API function. Its prototype is shown here:

```
ULONG APIENTRY WinMessageBox(HWND parent,
                             HWND owner,
                             PSZ text,
                             PSZ caption,
                             USHORT winid,
                             ULONG style);
```

Here, *parent* is the handle of the parent window and *owner* is the handle of the owner of the message box. The *text* parameter is a pointer to a string that will appear inside the message box. The string pointed to by *caption* is used as the caption for the box. The value of *winid* is the ID of the message box, and the value of *style* determines the exact nature of the message box, including what type of buttons will be present. Some of the most common values for *style* are shown in Table 5-1. These macros are defined in PMWIN.H and you can OR together two or more of these macros so long as they are not mutually exclusive.

WinMessageBox() returns either the user's response to the box or MBID_ERROR if an error occurred. The possible return values for the buttons are shown here:

Button Pressed	Return Value
Abort	MBID_ABORT
Retry	MBID_RETRY
Ignore	MBID_IGNORE
Cancel	MBID_CANCEL
No	MBID_NO
Yes	MBID_YES
OK	MBID_OK
Enter	MBID_ENTER

Value	Effect
MB_ABORTRETRYIGNORE	Displays Abort, Retry, and Ignore pushbuttons
MB_ICONEXCLAMATION	Displays exclamation point icon
MB_ICONHAND	Displays a stop sign icon
MB_ICONINFORMATION	Displays an information icon
MB_ICONQUESTION	Displays a question mark icon
MB_OKCANCEL	Displays OK and Cancel pushbuttons
MB_RETRYCANCEL	Displays Retry and Cancel pushbuttons
MB_YESNO	Displays Yes and No pushbuttons
MB_YESNOCANCEL	Displays Yes, No, and Cancel pushbuttons

TABLE 5-1

Some Common Message Box Types

To display a message box, simply call the **WinMessageBox()** function. The Presentation Manager will display it at its first opportunity. You do not need to obtain a device context or generate a WM_PAINT message. **WinMessageBox()** handles all of these details for you.

Here is a simple example that displays a message box when you press one of the mouse buttons:

```
/* A minimal Presentation Manager skeleton that
   demonstrates message boxes
*/
#define INCL_WIN
#define INCL_GPI

#include <os2.h>

MRESULT EXPENTRY window_func(HWND, ULONG, MPARAM, MPARAM);
```

```
char class[] = "MyClass";


main()
{
  HAB hand_ab;              /* anchor block */
  HMQ hand_mq;             /* message queue */
  HWND hand_frame;         /* frame */
  QMSG q_mess;             /* message queue */
  ULONG flFlags;           /* window frame definition */
  unsigned char class[] = "MyClass";   /* class name */

  /* define the frame contents */
  flFlags = FCF_TITLEBAR |      /* have a title bar */
            FCF_SIZEBORDER |    /* be a sizeable window */
            FCF_MINMAX |        /* have min and max buttons */
            FCF_SYSMENU |       /* include a system menu */
            FCF_VERTSCROLL |    /* vertical scroll bar */
            FCF_HORZSCROLL |    /* horizontal scroll bar */
            FCF_SHELLPOSITION;  /* default size and location */

  hand_ab = WinInitialize(0);  /* get the anchor block */

  hand_mq = WinCreateMsgQueue(hand_ab, 0); /* start a queue */

  if(!WinRegisterClass(   /* register this window class */
                    hand_ab,              /* anchor block */
                    (PSZ) class,          /* class name */
                    (PFNWP) window_func,  /* window function */
                    CS_SIZEREDRAW,        /* window style */
                    0))                   /* no storage */
       exit(1);

  hand_frame = WinCreateStdWindow(
                    HWND_DESKTOP,/* window type */
                    WS_VISIBLE,  /* frame style */
                    &flFlags,    /* definitions */
                    (PSZ)class,  /* client class */
                    (PSZ)"Skeleton Window", /* title */
                    WS_VISIBLE,  /* client style */
                    0,           /* resource modules */
                    0,           /* resource identifier */
                    NULL);       /* pointer to client handle */
    /* message loop */
  while(WinGetMsg(hand_ab, &q_mess, 0, 0, 0))
```

```
   WinDispatchMsg(hand_ab, &q_mess);

  /* Shut down the application window and queue */
  WinDestroyWindow(hand_frame);
  WinDestroyMsgQueue(hand_mq);
  WinTerminate(hand_ab);
}

/* This is the window function. */
MRESULT EXPENTRY window_func(HWND handle, ULONG mess,
                            MPARAM parm1, MPARAM parm2)
{
   ULONG response;

  switch(mess) {
    case WM_BUTTON2DOWN: /* process right button */
      response = WinMessageBox(HWND_DESKTOP,
                               handle,
                               "Press One:",
                               "Right Button",
                               0,
                               MB_ABORTRETRYIGNORE);

       switch(response) {
         case MBID_ABORT:
           WinMessageBox(HWND_DESKTOP, handle,
                       "", "Abort", 0, MB_OK);
           break;

         case MBID_RETRY:
           WinMessageBox(HWND_DESKTOP, handle,
                       "", "Retry", 0, MB_OK);
           break;

         case MBID_IGNORE:
           WinMessageBox(HWND_DESKTOP, handle,
                       "", "Ignore", 0, MB_OK);
           break;
         }
       break;

    case WM_BUTTON1DOWN: /* process left button */
      response = WinMessageBox(HWND_DESKTOP,
                                 handle,
                                 "Continue?",
```

```
                              "Left Button",
                              0,
                              MB_ICONHAND | MB_YESNO);

        switch(response) {
          case MBID_YES:
            WinMessageBox(HWND_DESKTOP, handle,
                          "", "Yes Selected", 0, MB_OK);
            break;

          case MBID_NO:
            WinMessageBox(HWND_DESKTOP, handle,
                          "", "No Selected", 0, MB_OK);
            break;
          }
        break;

      case WM_ERASEBACKGROUND:
        return (MRESULT)TRUE;

      default:
        return WinDefWindowProc(handle, mess, parm1, parm2);
    }
    return (MRESULT)0;
}
```

Each time a mouse button is pressed, a message box is displayed. For example, pressing the right button displays the message box shown in Figure 5-1.

As you will see, when you press the right button, a message box displays the buttons Abort, Retry, and Ignore. Depending upon your response, a second message box will be displayed that indicates which button you pressed. Pressing the left mouse button causes a message box to be displayed that contains a stop sign. This box allows a Yes or a No response.

Before continuing, it might be a good idea to experiment with message boxes, trying different types.

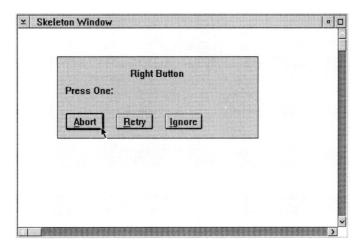

FIGURE 5-1
Sample message box

INTRODUCING MENUS

As you know, in the Presentation Manager the most common element of control is the menu. Virtually all OS/2 programs have some type of menu associated with them. Because menus are so common and important in Presentation Manager applications, the Presentation Manager API provides substantial built-in support for them. As you will see, adding a menu to a window involves these relatively few steps:

1. Define the form of the menu in a resource file.

2. Load the menu when your program creates its main window.

3. Process menu selections.

In the Presentation Manager, the top level of a menu is displayed across the top of the window. (You should be accustomed to this approach because it is used by virtually all OS/2 programs.)

Before beginning, it is necessary to explain what Presentation Manager resources and resource files are.

USING RESOURCES

The Presentation Manager defines several common types of objects as *resources*. Resources include things such as menus, icons, dialog boxes, and bitmapped graphics. Since a menu is a resource, you need to understand resources before you can add a menu to your program.

A resource is created separately from your program, but is added to the .EXE when your program is linked. Resources are contained in *resource files*, which have the extension .RC. In general, the filename should be the same as that of your program's .EXE file. For example, if your program is called PROG.EXE, then its resource file should be called PROG.RC.

Resource files will be generated differently, depending on what they contain. Some are text files that you create using a standard text editor. Others, such as icons, are most easily generated using one of the available icon editing tools, such as the Icon Editor supplied with the Presentation Manager Development Toolkit. The example resource files in this chapter are simply text files.

Resource files are not C programs, and therefore not compiled with the standard compiler. Instead, they must be compiled using a *resource compiler*. The resource compiler converts an .RC file into a .RES file, which may then be linked with your program.

COMPILING .RC FILES

Once you have created an .RC file, you can compile it into a .RES file using the IBM resource compiler called RC.EXE. You then link the .RES file with your program. If you are using the command line compiler, the process works like this: First, compile your program. Next, invoke the resource compiler as shown here:

```
RC filename
```

You don't need to specify an extension. This will cause the resource compiler to compile the resource file and automatically link it to your program. (This assumes that the name of the resource file is the same as the name of the executable file.)

To compile a resource file if you are using the IBM WorkFrame/2, simply add the name of the .RC file to your program's project file. This causes the resource compiler to automatically execute.

CREATING A SIMPLE MENU

Before a menu can be included, you must define its content in a resource file. All menu definitions have this general form:

```
MENU MenuID [options]
BEGIN
 SUBMENU Title, EntryID
  BEGIN
   MENUITEM

    .

    .

    .

  END
 SUBMENU Title, EntryID
  BEGIN
   MENUITEM

    .

    .

    .

  END
END
```

Here, *MenuID* is the ID of the menu, a unique number used to identify the menu. The keyword **MENU** tells the resource compiler that a menu is being created. There are several *options* that can be specified when creating the menu; you may use any nonconflicting combination. The macros used for *option* are shown in the following table. (Again, these macros are defined in PMWIN.H.)

Option	Meaning
DISCARDABLE	Menu may be removed from memory when no longer needed
FIXED	Menu is fixed in memory
LOADONCALL	Menu is loaded when used (default)
MOVEABLE	Menu may be moved in memory (default)
PRELOAD	Menu is loaded when your program begins execution

Following the **MENU** keyword are one or more **SUBMENU** key-words. Associated with a **SUBMENU** is the *Title*, which is the string to be displayed in the menu border. Following the *Title* is the *EntryID*, which, like the *MenuID*, is a unique number identifying this menu. Inside a **SUBMENU** are the **MENUITEM**s. The general form for these statements is shown here:

MENUITEM "*ItemText*", *ItemID* [, *ItemStyle*] [, *Attrib*]

Here, *ItemText* is the name of the menu selection, such as "Help" or "File." *ItemID* is a unique integer associated with a **MENUITEM** that will be sent to your Presentation Manager application when a selection is made. Typically, these values are defined as macros inside a header file that is included in both your application code and in the .RC resource file. The final two optional fields are the style and attributes of the **MENUITEM**. By default, the **MENUITEM** *ItemStyle* is MIS_TEXT, and all the attribute bits are off, which means the menu item is active and enabled.

The values for *ItemStyle* (defined in PMWIN.H) are shown in Table 5-2. When selected, most definitions of **MENUITEM** post a WM_COMMAND message. Exceptions to this are described in the table.

The values for the *Attrib* option of the **MENUITEM** (also defined in PMWIN.H) are shown in Table 5-3, along with the descriptions of their meaning.

INCLUDING A MENU IN YOUR PROGRAM

In order for a menu resource to be displayed in a window, it must be added to the window using the **WinCreateStdWindow()** service. First, you must add the FCF_MENU to the list of styles appearing in the second parameter, which is **flFlags** in the example programs. This lets OS/2 know that you will be using a menu resource. Second, you must pass the Presentation Manager the identifier of the menu, that is, the menu ID. This

Option	Meaning
MIS_TEXT	Default, normal text
MIS_BITMAP	Item display is a bitmap
MIS_SEPARATOR	Item is divided by a horizontal line. An item of this type cannot be checked, disabled, highlighted, or selected
MIS_OWNERDRAW	This item is drawn by the owner and posts WM_DRAWITEM and WM_MEASUREITEM messages
MIS_SUBMENU	Item is a submenu
MIS_MULTMENU	Multiple choice submenu
MIS_SYSCOMMAND	This item generates a WM_SYSCOMMAND message
MIS_HELP	A WM_HELP message is generated when an item of this style is selected
MIS_STATIC	This item is used to display information only
MIS_BUTTONSEPARATOR	Item is a button, pointer selectable
MIS_BREAK	This item begins a new row or column
MIS_BREAKSEPARATOR	Used in submenus only, same as MIS_BREAK, but also draws a dividing line
MIS_GROUP	Starts a multiple choice group
MIS_SINGLE	Used in MIS_GROUPs to denote radio buttons

TABLE 5-2
Types of Menu Styles

is done using the resources parameter. For example, this sample call uses resource identifier MENU1, which identifies menu number 1 as it is defined in the resource file.

```
/* define the frame contents */
flFlags = FCF_MENU |          /* use a resource menu */
          FCF_TITLEBAR |      /* have a title bar */
          FCF_SIZEBORDER |    /* be a sizeable window */
          FCF_MINMAX |        /* have min and max buttons */
          FCF_SYSMENU |       /* include a system menu */
          FCF_VERTSCROLL |    /* vertical scroll bar */
          FCF_HORZSCROLL |    /* horizontal scroll bar */
          FCF_SHELLPOSITION;  /* default size and location */

hand_frame = WinCreateStdWindow(
             HWND_DESKTOP,/* window type */
             WS_VISIBLE,  /* frame style */
             &flFlags,    /* definitions */
             (PSZ)class,  /* client class */
             (PSZ)"Menu Example Window", /* title */
             WS_VISIBLE,  /* client style */
             0,           /* resource modules */
             MENU1,       /* resource identifier */
             NULL);       /* pointer to client handle */
```

When the window is created, a menu bar will be displayed beneath the title bar. In this example, the menu bar will contain the selections Sample and Test.

Keep one thing firmly in mind: a resource file can contain resources for several different windows. However, all the resources for a specific window must all use the same resource identifier.

Option	Meaning
MIA_NODISMISS	Don't close menu after selection of item
MIA_FRAMED	Draw a frame around the item
MIA_CHECKED	Draw a check mark next to the item
MIA_DISABLED	Item cannot be selected
MIA_HILITED	Attribute is true when the item is selected

TABLE 5-3
Attributes of Menu Styles

RECEIVING MENU MESSAGES

Each time a menu selection is made, the Presentation Manager passes a message to your program. For most menu selections, this will be the WM_COMMAND message. The low-order word of the first parameter contains the identifier associated with the item selected. For our purposes, we can ignore the other information passed with the WM_COMMAND message.

SAMPLE MENU PROGRAM

Here is a program that demonstrates the use of a menu resource created in the previous section. Enter it at this time. To see a menu in action, first create this resource file and name it MENU.RC:

```
; Sample menu resource file

#include "menu.h"

MENU MENU1 PRELOAD
  BEGIN
    SUBMENU "Test", SUB1
      BEGIN
        MENUITEM "Option 1", ONE
        MENUITEM "Option 2", TWO
      END
    SUBMENU "Sample", SUB2
      BEGIN
        MENUITEM "Option 1", THREE
        MENUITEM "Option 2", FOUR
      END
  END
```

Now, create a header file to include in both the resource file and example program which defines the constants used to identify the resources defined in the resource file. Enter the following into a file named MENU.H:

```
/* define macro constants for menu example. */
```

```
#define MENU1    1
#define SUB1    10
#define SUB2    20
#define ONE    101
#define TWO    102
#define THREE  103
#define FOUR   104
```

Next, enter this program. Be sure to name your program and your menu resource file the same, except for the extension. Use .RC for your resource file, and .C for your program.

```
/* A menu example. */
#define INCL_WIN
#define INCL_GPI

#include <os2.h>
#include "menu.h"

MRESULT EXPENTRY window_func(HWND, ULONG, MPARAM, MPARAM);

char class[] = "MyClass";



main()
{
  HAB hand_ab;           /* anchor block */
  HMQ hand_mq;           /* message queue */
  HWND hand_frame;       /* frame */
  QMSG q_mess;           /* message queue */
  ULONG flFlags;         /* window frame definition */
  unsigned char class[] = "MyClass";  /* class name */

  /* define the frame contents */
  flFlags = FCF_MENU |          /* use a resource menu */
            FCF_TITLEBAR |      /* have a title bar */
            FCF_SIZEBORDER |    /* be a sizeable window */
            FCF_MINMAX |        /* have min and max buttons */
            FCF_SYSMENU |       /* include a system menu */
            FCF_VERTSCROLL |    /* vertical scroll bar */
            FCF_HORZSCROLL |    /* horizontal scroll bar */
            FCF_SHELLPOSITION;  /* default size and location */


  hand_ab = WinInitialize(0);  /* Get the Anchor Block */
```

```
hand_mq = WinCreateMsgQueue(hand_ab, 0); /* start a queue */

if(!WinRegisterClass(   /* register this window class */
                hand_ab,             /* anchor block */
                (PSZ) class,         /* class name */
                (PFNWP) window_func,/* window function */
                CS_SIZEREDRAW,       /* window style */
                0))                  /* no storage */
    exit(1);

hand_frame = WinCreateStdWindow(
                HWND_DESKTOP,/* window type */
                WS_VISIBLE,  /* frame style */
                &flFlags,    /* definitions */
                (PSZ)class,  /* client class */
                (PSZ)"Menu Example Window",
                WS_VISIBLE, /* client style */
                0,       /* resource modules */
                MENU1,   /* resource identifier */
                NULL);   /* pointer to client handle */

  /* message loop */
  while(WinGetMsg(hand_ab, &q_mess, 0, 0, 0))
    WinDispatchMsg(hand_ab, &q_mess);

  /* Shut down the application window and queue */
  WinDestroyWindow(hand_frame);
  WinDestroyMsgQueue(hand_mq);
  WinTerminate(hand_ab);
}

/* This is the window function */
MRESULT EXPENTRY window_func(HWND handle, ULONG mess,
                             MPARAM parm1, MPARAM parm2)

{
  HPS p_space;
  POINTL coords;
  static char ch='\0';

  switch(mess) {
      case WM_CREATE:
        /* Perform any necessary initializations here */
```

```
            break;

          case WM_COMMAND:
            p_space = WinGetPS(handle);

            /* use overwrite mode */
            GpiSetBackMix(p_space, BM_OVERPAINT);

            /* see what item selected */
            switch(SHORT1FROMMP(parm1)) {
              case ONE:
                coords.x = 20;
                coords.y = 60;
                GpiCharStringAt(p_space, &coords,
                               8, "test one");
                break;
              case TWO:
                coords.x = 20;
                coords.y = 40;
                GpiCharStringAt(p_space, &coords,
                               8, "test two");
                break;
              case THREE:
                coords.x = 110;
                coords.y = 60;
                GpiCharStringAt(p_space, &coords,
                               10, "sample one");
                break;
              case FOUR:
                coords.x = 110;
                coords.y = 40;
                GpiCharStringAt(p_space, &coords,
                               10, "sample two");
                break;

            }
          WinReleasePS(p_space);
          break;

          case WM_ERASEBACKGROUND:
            return (MRESULT)TRUE;

          default:
            return WinDefWindowProc(handle, mess, parm1, parm2);
      }
```

```
   return (MRESULT)0;
}
```

Compile the program just as you have compiled the previous examples. After compiling the program, invoke the resource compiler, which will compile your menu resource and link it with your executable program. If you forget to do the second step, your window will not appear and you will need to hit CTRL+C to kill your program. The following two commands will build a correct and complete program using the example resource file and example program (assuming you name your example files MENU.C and MENU.RC):

```
ICC -B"/PM:PM" MENU.C
RC MENU
```

As you can see when you try this program, each menu selection produces a unique response from the program. When you run it, your screen will look like that shown in Figure 5-2.

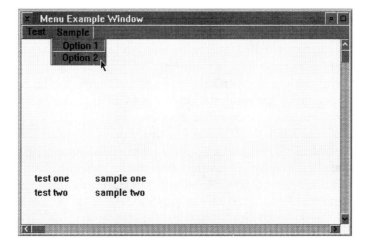

FIGURE 5-2

Sample output from the menu example

ADDING MENU ACCELERATOR KEYS

Before leaving menus, we will discuss one more feature relating to them. This feature is the accelerator key. *Accelerator keys* are special keystrokes that you define which, when pressed, automatically select a menu option even though the menu in which that option resides is not displayed. Put differently, you can select an item directly by pressing an accelerator key, bypassing the menu entirely. The term *accelerator keys* is an accurate description because pressing one is generally a faster way to select a menu item than by first activating its menu and then selecting the item.

To define accelerator keys relative to a menu, you must add an accelerator key table to your resource file. All accelerator table definitions have this general form:

```
ACCELTABLE MenuID [option]
BEGIN
 Key, subID1, type [,type] ...
 Key, subID2, type [,type] ...
 Key, subID3, type [,type] ...

  .
  .
  .

 Key, subIDn, type [,type] ...
END
```

Here, *MenuID* is the ID of the menu that the accelerators will be applied to and is also the ID of the accelerator table. The option field specifies one of the memory loading options. *Key* is the keystroke that selects the item, and *subIDn* is the ID value associated with the desired item. The *type* specifies what combination of keys will activate the accelerator. The *type* options may be one of the following: ALT, SHIFT, CONTROL, CHAR, SCANCODE, VIRTUALKEY, HELP, or SYSCOMMAND.

ALT, SHIFT, or CONTROL selects which keys will need to be pressed along with *Key* to activate the menu. CHAR specifies the ASCII representation of *Key*; this is the default. VIRTUALKEY is its counterpart, specifying that *Key* is a virtual key. If SCANCODE is specified, then the scancode for *Key* is used. Specifying the HELP style causes a WM_HELP message to be generated instead of the usual WM_COMMAND, and SYS-COMMAND causes a WM_SYSCOMMAND to be generated instead of the WM_COMMAND message.

The value of *Key* will be a quoted character, an ASCII integer value corresponding to a key, or a virtual key code. If a quoted character is used, then it is assumed to be an ASCII character. If it is a virtual key, then *type* must be VIRTUALKEY.

If the key is an uppercase quoted character, then its corresponding menu item will be selected if it is pressed while the CAPS LOCK function is active. If it is a lowercase character, then its menu item will be selected if the key is pressed by itself.

A *virtual key* is a system-independent code for a variety of keys. Virtual keys include the function keys F1 through F12, the arrow keys, and various non-ASCII keys. They are defined by macros in the header file PMWIN.H. All virtual key macros begin with VK_. The function keys are VK_F1 through VK_F12, for example. You should refer to PMWIN.H for the other virtual key code macros. To use a virtual key as an accelerator, simply include OS2.H in your .RC file, and then specify its macro for the *Key* and specify VIRTUALKEY for its *type*. You may also specify ALT, SHIFT, or CONTROL to achieve the desired key combination.

Here are some examples:

```
"a",   44, CONTROL,ALT ; select by pressing CTRL+ALT+A
"a",   13  CHAR        ; select by pressing A
"a",   86, CONTROL     ; select by pressing CTRL+A
"a",   11, ALT         ; select by pressing ALT+A
VK_F2,16  VIRTUALKEY   ; select by pressing F2
```

Here is the MENU.RC resource file from the previous example. It also contains accelerator key definitions for the menu items specified.

```
; Sample menu resource file

#include <os2.h>
#include "menu.h"

MENU MENU1 PRELOAD
  BEGIN
    SUBMENU "Test", SUB1
      BEGIN
        MENUITEM "Option 1 \tCTRL+a", ONE
        MENUITEM "Option 2 \tCTRL+b", TWO
      END
    SUBMENU "Sample", SUB2
      BEGIN
```

```
        MENUITEM "Option 1 \tALT+a", THREE
        MENUITEM "Option 2 \tALT+b", FOUR
    END
END

; Define menu accelerators
ACCELTABLE MENU1 PRELOAD
BEGIN
  "a", ONE, CONTROL
  "b", TWO, CONTROL
  "a", THREE, ALT
  "b", FOUR, ALT
END
```

Notice that the menu definition has been enhanced to display which accelerator key selects which option. Each accelerator key description in the menu is separated from its text string using a tab.

LOADING THE ACCELERATOR TABLE

Even though the accelerators are contained in the same resource file as the menu, they are not automatically loaded. In order to load the accelerator table, the FCF_ACCELTABLE flag must be specified along with the other window definition flags in the API function call to **WinCreateStdWindow()**. For example, the following fragment shows the appropriate flags to set in order to load an accelerator window along with all the options used so far in this book:

```
/* define the frame contents */
flFlags = FCF_MENU |            /* use a resource menu */
          FCF_ACCELTABLE |      /* use an accelerator table */
          FCF_TITLEBAR |        /* have a title bar */
          FCF_SIZEBORDER |      /* be a sizeable window */
          FCF_MINMAX |          /* have min and max buttons */
          FCF_SYSMENU |         /* include a system menu */
          FCF_VERTSCROLL |      /* vertical scroll bar */
          FCF_HORZSCROLL |      /* horizontal scroll bar */
          FCF_SHELLPOSITION;    /* default size and location */
```

To try using accelerators, substitute the following version of **main()** into the preceding application and add the accelerator table to your resource file.

```
/* A menu example */
#define INCL_WIN
#define INCL_GPI

#include <os2.h>
#include "menu.h"

MRESULT EXPENTRY window_func(HWND, ULONG, MPARAM, MPARAM);

char class[] = "MyClass";


main()
{
  HAB hand_ab;            /* anchor block */
  HMQ hand_mq;            /* message queue */
  HWND hand_frame;        /* frame */
  QMSG q_mess;            /* message queue */
  ULONG flFlags;          /* window frame definition */
  unsigned char class[] = "MyClass";  /* class name */

  /* define the frame contents */
  flFlags = FCF_MENU |           /* use a resource menu */
            FCF_ACCELTABLE |     /* use an accelerator table */
            FCF_TITLEBAR |       /* have a title bar */
            FCF_SIZEBORDER |     /* be a sizeable window */
            FCF_MINMAX |         /* have min and max buttons */
            FCF_SYSMENU |        /* include a system menu */
            FCF_VERTSCROLL |     /* vertical scroll bar */
            FCF_HORZSCROLL |     /* horizontal scroll bar */
            FCF_SHELLPOSITION;   /* default size and location */


  hand_ab = WinInitialize(0);   /* get the anchor block */

  hand_mq = WinCreateMsgQueue(hand_ab, 0); /* start a queue */

  if(!WinRegisterClass(   /* register this window class */
                  hand_ab,              /* anchor block */
                  (PSZ) class,          /* class name */
                  (PFNWP) window_func,  /* window function */
                  CS_SIZEREDRAW,        /* window style */
                  0))                   /* no storage */
      exit(1);
```

```
hand_frame = WinCreateStdWindow(
                HWND_DESKTOP,/* window type */
                WS_VISIBLE, /* frame style */
                &flFlags,   /* definitions */
                (PSZ)class, /* client class */
                (PSZ)"Menu with Accelerators",
                WS_VISIBLE, /* client style */
                0,       /* resource modules */
                MENU1,   /* resource identifier */
                NULL);   /* pointer to client handle */

  /* message loop */
 while(WinGetMsg(hand_ab, &q_mess, 0, 0, 0))
   WinDispatchMsg(hand_ab, &q_mess);

 /* Shut down the application window and queue */
 WinDestroyWindow(hand_frame);
 WinDestroyMsgQueue(hand_mq);
 WinTerminate(hand_ab);
}
```

Compile your program using the same two steps as described earlier, and run the program. You will see that when the key sequence is hit, the same action is taken as if you had selected the menu option.

Before moving on to the next chapter, you should experiment on your own using message boxes, menus, and accelerators. Try the various options and see what they do.

6

DIALOG BOXES

After menus, there is no more important Presentation Manager interface element than the dialog box. A dialog box is a type of window that provides a more flexible means by which the user can interact with your application. In general, dialog boxes allow the user to select or enter information that would be difficult or impossible using a menu.

It is important to understand that dialog boxes both generate messages (when accessed by the user) and receive messages (from your application). A message generated by a dialog box indicates what type of interaction the user has had with the dialog box. A message sent to the dialog box is essentially an instruction to which the dialog box must respond by performing the appropriate action. You will see examples of this type of message passing later in this chapter.

HOW DIALOG BOXES INTERACT WITH THE USER

A dialog box interacts with the user through one or more *control windows.* A control window is a specific type of input or output window. A control window is owned by its parent window, which, for the examples presented in this chapter, is the dialog box.

CONTROLS

The Presentation Manager supports many controls, including: buttons, list boxes, entry boxes, combination boxes, spin lists, notebooks, containers, value sets, and sliders. Along with these fancy controls, there are also the many standard frame controls, such as the title bar and scroll bar. There are other controls besides the ones listed here. Some controls are a combination of the functionality of two or more other controls.

In the course of explaining how to use dialog boxes, the examples in this chapter will illustrate the use of the pushbutton. The pushbutton is by far one of the most used window controls, and knowledge of its use will help provide a basic understanding of dialog boxes. Chapter 7 is dedicated to exploring the use of the other more complex controls available for use inside dialog boxes.

A pushbutton is one button in a "class" of buttons. A button is a control that the user "pushes" (by clicking the mouse or by tabbing to it and then pressing ENTER) to activate some response. You have already been using pushbuttons in message boxes. For example, the OK button that we have been using in most message boxes is a pushbutton. There can be one or more pushbuttons in a dialog box. Each button carries its own message back to the program that displayed the dialog box.

MODAL VERSUS MODELESS DIALOG BOXES

There are two types of dialog boxes: *modal* and *modeless.* The most common dialog boxes are modal. A modal dialog box demands a response before the parent program will continue. That is, a modal dialog box will not allow you to refocus input to another part of the parent window without first responding to the dialog box.

A modeless dialog box does not prevent the parent program from running. That is, it does not demand a response before input can be focused to another part of the parent window. When using modeless dialog boxes, it is important to consider the asynchronous operation this type of dialog box will create. However, this is not really a problem since Presentation Manager programs are all message based.

Since the modal dialog box is the most common, it is the type of dialog box examined in this chapter.

RECEIVING DIALOG BOX MESSAGES

A dialog box is a window (albeit, a special kind of window). Events that occur within it are sent to your program using the same message-passing mechanism the main window uses. However, dialog box messages are not sent to your program's main window function. Instead, each dialog box that you define will need its own function. This function must have the following prototype. (Of course, the name of the function may be anything that you like.)

```
MRESULT EXPENTRY dialog_func(HWND handle,
                            ULONG mess,
                            MPARAM parm1,
                            MPARAM parm2);
```

As you can see, this function receives the same parameters as the main window function. However, it differs from the main window function in that it returns a true or false result. This function is often referred to as the *dialog procedure*. Like your program's main window function, the dialog procedure will receive many messages. If it processes a message, then it must return TRUE. If it does not respond to a message, it must call **WinDefDlgProc()**, the default dialog procedure. The prototype for the default dialog procedure is shown here:

```
MRESULT APIENTRYWinDefDlgProc( HWND handle,
                            ULONG msg,
                            MPARAM mp1,
                            MPARAM mp2);
```

As you can see, the prototype for the default dialog procedure parallels the prototype for the user-defined dialog procedure.

In general, each control within a dialog box will be given its own resource ID. Each time that control is accessed by the user, a message will be sent to the dialog procedure, indicating the ID of the control and the type of action the user has taken. That function will then decode the message and take appropriate actions. This process is equivalent to the way messages are decoded by your program's main window function.

ACTIVATING A DIALOG BOX

To activate a dialog box, you must call the **WinDlgBox()** API function, whose prototype is shown here:

```
ULONG  APIENTRY WinDlgBox(HWND parent,
                          HWND owner,
                          PFNWP Dialog_func,
                          HMODULE rc,
                          ULONG id,
                          PVOID params);
```

Here, *parent* is a handle to the parent window and is often set to HWND_DESKTOP. After the call, *owner* will contain the handle of the window that controls the dialog. The *Dialog_func* parameter contains a pointer to the dialog procedure for this dialog box. If the resource definitions are not contained in the executable file, you supply the resource file handle in the *rc* parameter. The *id* parameter should contain the ID number for the dialog as defined in the resource file. The *params* parameter is used for application-defined data. This information is passed to the dialog procedure.

After a dialog box terminates, you must release the procedure by calling the API function **WinDismissDlg()**. It has this prototype:

```
BOOL APIENTRY WinDismissDlg(HWND handle,
                            ULONG result);
```

Here, *handle* is the parent window handle, and *result* is the answer received from the dialog box control.

The following code fragment of a window function and dialog function example illustrates how to activate and terminate a dialog box.

```
/* this is the window function */
MRESULT EXPENTRY window_func(HWND handle, ULONG mess,
                            MPARAM parm1, MPARAM parm2)
{
  switch(mess) {
        .
        .
        .
        WinDlgBox(HWND_DESKTOP, handle, dialog_func, 0, DLG1, 0);
        .
        .
        .
}

/* this is the dialog procedure */
MRESULT EXPENTRY dialog_func(HWND handle, ULONG mess,
                            MPARAM parm1, MPARAM parm2)
{
  switch(mess) {
        .
        .
        .
        WinDismissDlg(handle, OK);
        .
        .
        .
}
```

CREATING A SIMPLE DIALOG BOX

For the first dialog box, a simple example will be created. This dialog box will contain one pushbutton that, when pressed, will simply cause the dialog box to be removed from the screen. The dialog box will also contain the system menu and a title bar.

While this and other examples in this chapter don't do much with the information provided by the dialog box, they illustrate the central features that you will use in your own applications.

THE DIALOG BOX RESOURCE FILE

A dialog box is another resource that is contained in your program's resource file. Before developing a program that uses a dialog box, you will need a resource file that specifies one. Although it is possible to specify the contents of a dialog box using a text editor, entering its specifications as you do when creating a menu, this is seldom done. Instead, most programmers use the dialog editor supplied with the IBM WorkSet/2 Toolkit. The main reasons for this are that dialog box definitions involve relatively complex specifications and the placement of the various items inside the dialog box is best done interactively. For these reasons, the resource files in this chapter were created using the dialog editor. However, since the complete resource files for the examples in this chapter are supplied in their text form, you can simply enter them as text. Just remember that when creating your own dialog boxes, you will want to use the dialog editor.

 Note: Since most dialog boxes are created using the dialog editor, no explanation of the dialog box definition in the resource file is given in this chapter. However, the IBM *Presentation Manager Programming Reference* includes such a description if you are interested.

The following resource file defines the necessary information to display a simple dialog box. Included in this definition are a title, a system menu, and one pushbutton. Take the time to enter it into your computer now, and call it DIALOG.RC.

```
; Sample dialog box resource file.
#include <os2.h>
#include "dialog.h"

DLGTEMPLATE DLG1 LOADONCALL MOVEABLE DISCARDABLE
BEGIN
        DIALOG  "Dialog", DLG1, 69, 9, 148, 84,
                WS_VISIBLE, FCF_SYSMENU | FCF_TITLEBAR
        BEGIN
            PUSHBUTTON      "Push", ONE, 56, 36, 40, 14
```

```
        END
END
```

Also enter the following definitions for the resource identifiers into a header file called DIALOG.H:

```
/* macro constants for dialog box example */
#define DLG1 100
#define ONE 101
```

THE DIALOG BOX WINDOW FUNCTION

Each dialog box has a dialog procedure that is called when the dialog box generates messages. The following dialog function responds to the events that can occur within the example dialog box DIALOG:

```
/* this is the dialog procedure */
MRESULT EXPENTRY dialog_func(HWND handle, ULONG mess,
                             MPARAM parm1, MPARAM parm2)
{

  switch(mess) {
    case WM_COMMAND:
      switch (SHORT1FROMMP(parm1)) {
        case OK:
          WinDismissDlg(handle, OK);
          break;
        }
    default:
      return WinDefDlgProc(handle, mess, parm1, parm2);
    }
  return (MRESULT)0;
}
```

Each time a control within the dialog box is accessed, a WM_COM-MAND message is sent to **dialog_func()**, and the ID of the affected control is placed in *parm1*.

The dialog procedure, **dialog_func()**, processes the messages that can be generated by the box. In this first example, of course, there is only one button to push. When the user presses the button, the dialog box is terminated by a call to the API function **WinDismissDlg()**.

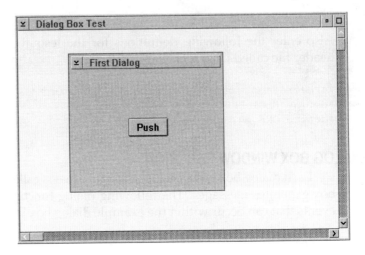

FIGURE 6-1

Sample output from the first dialog box program

THE FIRST DIALOG BOX SAMPLE PROGRAM

Here is the entire dialog box example. When the program begins execution, only the system level menu is displayed on the menu bar. The title "Dialog Box Test" appears in the menu bar. By pressing the left mouse button, the user causes the dialog box to be displayed. Once the dialog box is displayed, selecting the pushbutton causes the dialog box to close. A sample screen is shown in Figure 6-1.

```
/* a simple dialog box example */
#define INCL_WIN
#define INCL_GPI

#include <os2.h>
#include "dialog.h"

MRESULT EXPENTRY window_func(HWND, ULONG, MPARAM, MPARAM);
MRESULT EXPENTRY dialog_func(HWND, ULONG, MPARAM, MPARAM);
```

```
char class[] = "MyClass";


main()
{
  HAB hand_ab;            /* anchor block */
  HMQ hand_mq;            /* message queue */
  HWND hand_frame;        /* frame */
  QMSG q_mess;            /* message queue */
  ULONG flFlags;          /* window frame definition */
  unsigned char class[] = "MyClass";  /* class name */

  /* define the frame contents */
  flFlags = FCF_TITLEBAR |     /* have a title bar */
            FCF_SIZEBORDER |   /* be a sizeable window */
            FCF_MINMAX |       /* have min and max buttons */
            FCF_SYSMENU |      /* include a system menu */
            FCF_VERTSCROLL |   /* vertical scroll bar */
            FCF_HORZSCROLL |   /* horizontal scroll bar */
            FCF_SHELLPOSITION; /* default size and location */


  hand_ab = WinInitialize(0);  /* get the anchor block */

  hand_mq = WinCreateMsgQueue(hand_ab, 0); /* start a queue */

  if(!WinRegisterClass(   /* register this window class */
                  hand_ab,            /* anchor block */
                  (PSZ) class,        /* class name */
                  (PFNWP) window_func,/* window function */
                  CS_SIZEREDRAW,      /* window style */
                  0))                 /* no storage */
      exit(1);

  hand_frame = WinCreateStdWindow(
                  HWND_DESKTOP,/* window type */
                  WS_VISIBLE,  /* frame style */
                  &flFlags,    /* definitions */
                  (PSZ)class,  /* client class */
                  (PSZ)"Dialog Box Test",
                  WS_VISIBLE,  /* client style */
                  0,       /* resource modules */
                  0,       /* resource identifier */
                  NULL); /* pointer to client handle */
```

```
  /* message loop */
 while(WinGetMsg(hand_ab, &q_mess, 0, 0, 0))
   WinDispatchMsg(hand_ab, &q_mess);

 /* shut down the application window and queue */
 WinDestroyWindow(hand_frame);
 WinDestroyMsgQueue(hand_mq);
 WinTerminate(hand_ab);
}

/* this is the window function */
MRESULT EXPENTRY window_func(HWND handle, ULONG mess,
                                MPARAM parm1, MPARAM parm2)
{

  switch(mess) {

    case WM_BUTTON1DOWN:    /* left mouse button */
      WinDlgBox(HWND_DESKTOP, handle, dialog_func, 0, DLG1, 0);
      break;

    case WM_ERASEBACKGROUND:
      return (MRESULT)TRUE;

    default:
      return WinDefWindowProc(handle, mess, parm1, parm2);
  }

  return (MRESULT)0;
}

/* this is the dialog procedure */
MRESULT EXPENTRY dialog_func(HWND handle, ULONG mess,
                                MPARAM parm1, MPARAM parm2)
{

  switch(mess) {

    case WM_COMMAND:
      switch (SHORT1FROMMP(parm1)) {

        case ONE:
          WinDismissDlg(handle, ONE);
          return (MRESULT) TRUE;
```

```
        }

    default:
      return WinDefDlgProc(handle, mess, parm1, parm2);
    }

  return (MRESULT)0;
}
```

You can compile this program by using the same method used in Chapter 5. First compile the C program. Next compile and combine the resource file using the resource compiler:

```
ICC -B"/PM:PM" DIALOG.C

RC DIALOG
```

RESPONDING TO MULTIPLE DIALOG BOX MESSAGES

You have seen how easy it is to create dialog boxes, but the first example only handles one message. Before heading into Chapter 7, which explores many of the controls available through the dialog box, you need to see how to recognize and process multiple messages from dialog boxes.

The following example resource file defines three pushbuttons. Each of the three buttons will cause a different response. The dialog function will perform a different function based on the response from the dialog box. Also included in this example are the menus and accelerator tables discussed in Chapter 5. We will use the menu selections to call the dialog boxes.

Here is a resource file created using the dialog editor and containing three pushbuttons named Red, Green, and Cancel:

```
DLGTEMPLATE DLG1 LOADONCALL MOVEABLE DISCARDABLE
BEGIN
    DIALOG   "Three Buttons", DLG1, 73, 5, 148, 84,
             WS_VISIBLE, FCF_SYSMENU | FCF_TITLEBAR
    BEGIN
        PUSHBUTTON       "Red", FIVE, 15, 48, 40, 14
        PUSHBUTTON       "Green", SIX, 83, 48, 40, 14
        PUSHBUTTON       "Cancel", SEVEN, 33, 12, 71, 14
```

```
        END
END
```

If you combine this with the menu and accelerator example from Chapter 5, you get the resulting complete resource file, which will be used in the next example. Take a minute and enter the additional lines to your menu resource file. Name the file DIALOG2.RC.

```
; Sample menu resource file

#include <os2.h>
#include "menu.h"

MENU MENU 1 PRELOAD
   BEGIN
     SUBMENU "Test", SUB1
       BEGIN
         MENUITEM "Option 1 \tCTRL+a", ONE
         MENUITEM "Option 2 \tCTRL+b", TWO
       END
     SUBMENU "Sample", SUB2
       BEGIN
         MENUITEM "Option 1 \tALT+a", THREE
         MENUITEM "Option 2 \tALT+b", FOUR
       END
   END

; Define menu accelerators
ACCELTABLE MENU1 PRELOAD
BEGIN
   "a", ONE, CONTROL
   "b", TWO, CONTROL
   "a", THREE, ALT
   "b", FOUR, ALT
END

DLGTEMPLATE DLG1 LOADONCALL MOVEABLE DISCARDABLE
BEGIN
     DIALOG  "Three Buttons", 100, 73, 5, 148, 84,
             WS_VISIBLE, FCF_SYSMENU | FCF_TITLEBAR
     BEGIN
         PUSHBUTTON       "Red",   FIVE, 15, 48, 40, 14
         PUSHBUTTON       "Green", SIX, 83, 48, 40, 14
         PUSHBUTTON       "Cancel", SEVEN, 33, 12, 71, 14
```

```
      END
END
```

You will also need to add these additional lines to the MENU.H header file:

```
#define DLG1 100
#define FIVE 105
#define SIX 106
#define SEVEN 107
```

Each time a control window button within the dialog box is pressed, a WM_COMMAND message is sent to **dialog_func()**, and the ID of the selected control button is placed in *parm1*.

The dialog procedure, **dialog_func()**, processes the three messages that can be generated by the controls inside the dialog box. If the user presses Cancel, then the dialog box will be closed by using a call to the API function **WinDismissDlg()**. Pressing either of the other two buttons causes a message box to be displayed that confirms the selection.

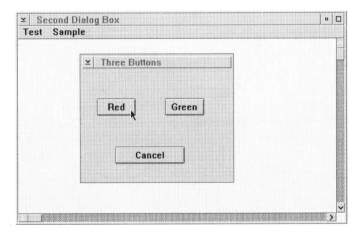

FIGURE 6-2

Sample output from the second dialog box program

THE SECOND DIALOG BOX SAMPLE PROGRAM

Here is the entire dialog box example that contains three buttons. When the program begins execution, only the top-level menu is displayed on the menu bar. By selecting Option 1 or Option 2 under the Test or Sample menus, the user causes the dialog box to be displayed. Once the dialog box is displayed, selecting a pushbutton causes a message box to be displayed that echoes the appropriate response. Type this program into your computer and call it DIALOG2.C. Again, you can compile this example using the same method described earlier in this chapter and in Chapter 5. A sample screen is shown in Figure 6-2.

```c
/* a second dialog box example */

#define INCL_WIN
#define INCL_GPI

#include <os2.h>
#include "menu.h"

MRESULT EXPENTRY window_func(HWND, ULONG, MPARAM, MPARAM);
MRESULT EXPENTRY dialog_func(HWND, ULONG, MPARAM, MPARAM);

char class[] = "MyClass";


main()
{
  HAB hand_ab;              /* anchor block */
  HMQ hand_mq;              /* message queue */
  HWND hand_frame;          /* frame */
  QMSG q_mess;              /* message queue */
  ULONG flFlags;            /* window frame definition */
  unsigned char class[] = "MyClass";  /* class name */

  /* define the frame contents */
  flFlags = FCF_MENU |            /* use a resource menu */
            FCF_ACCELTABLE |    /* use an accelerator table */
            FCF_TITLEBAR |      /* have a title bar */
            FCF_SIZEBORDER |    /* be a sizeable window */
            FCF_MINMAX |        /* have min and max buttons */
            FCF_SYSMENU |       /* include a system menu */
            FCF_VERTSCROLL |    /* vertical scroll bar */
```

```
            FCF_HORZSCROLL |   /* horizontal scroll bar */
            FCF_SHELLPOSITION; /* default size and location */


  hand_ab = WinInitialize(0);   /* get the anchor block */

  hand_mq = WinCreateMsgQueue(hand_ab, 0); /* start a queue */

  if(!WinRegisterClass(   /* register this window class */
                 hand_ab,                /* anchor block */
                 (PSZ) class,            /* class name */
                 (PFNWP) window_func,/* window function */
                 CS_SIZEREDRAW,          /* window style */
                 0))                     /* no storage */
  exit(1);

  hand_frame = WinCreateStdWindow(
                 HWND_DESKTOP,/* window type */
                 WS_VISIBLE,  /* frame style */
                 &flFlags,    /* definitions */
                 (PSZ)class,  /* client class */
                 (PSZ)"Second Dialog Box",
                 WS_VISIBLE,  /* client style */
                 0,       /* resource modules */
                 MENU1,      /* resource identifier */
                 NULL);      /* pointer to client handle */
  /* message loop */
  while(WinGetMsg(hand_ab, &q_mess, 0, 0, 0))
    WinDispatchMsg(hand_ab, &q_mess);

  /* shut down the application window and queue */
  WinDestroyWindow(hand_frame);
  WinDestroyMsgQueue(hand_mq);
  WinTerminate(hand_ab);
}

/* this is the window function */
MRESULT EXPENTRY window_func(HWND handle, ULONG mess,
                              MPARAM parm1, MPARAM parm2)
{

  switch(mess) {
    case WM_CREATE:
        /* perform any necessary initializations here */
```

```
            break;

        case WM_COMMAND:
          switch(SHORT1FROMMP(parm1)) {

            case ONE:
              WinDlgBox(HWND_DESKTOP, handle,
                        dialog_func, 0, DLG1, 0); break;

            case TWO:
              WinDlgBox(HWND_DESKTOP, handle,
                        dialog_func, 0, DLG1, 0); break;

            case THREE:
              WinDlgBox(HWND_DESKTOP, handle,
                        dialog_func, 0, DLG1, 0); break;

            case FOUR:
              WinDlgBox(HWND_DESKTOP, handle,
                        dialog_func, 0, DLG1, 0); break;
            }
            break;

        case WM_ERASEBACKGROUND:
          return (MRESULT)TRUE;

        default:
          return WinDefWindowProc(handle, mess, parm1, parm2);
    }
    return (MRESULT)0;
}

/* this is the dialog procedure */
MRESULT EXPENTRY dialog_func(HWND handle, ULONG mess,
                              MPARAM parm1, MPARAM parm2)

{

  switch(mess) {
    case WM_COMMAND:
      switch (SHORT1FROMMP(parm1)) {

        case SEVEN:
          WinDismissDlg(handle, FIVE);
          return (MRESULT) TRUE;
```

```
      case FIVE:
        WinMessageBox(HWND_DESKTOP, handle,
                       "You Picked Red", "RED", 0, MB_OK);
        return (MRESULT) TRUE;

      case SIX:
        WinMessageBox(HWND_DESKTOP, handle,
                       "You Picked Green","GREEN", 0, MB_OK);
        return (MRESULT) TRUE;


      }
   default:
     return WinDefDlgProc(handle, mess, parm1, parm2);
   }

  return (MRESULT)0;
}
```

Also notice that the accelerator keys are active. Pressing any of the accelerator key sequences will cause the dialog box to pop up immediately. Remember that the accelerator key sequences are CTRL+A, CTRL+B, ALT+A, and ALT+B.

The next chapter covers many of the window controls available through dialog boxes. It may be useful to take a few minutes and look over the dialog editor and the many menus inside it. This will give you a good idea of things to come in the next chapter. Building the dialog box can be fun when using the dialog editor. As you will soon see, setting up the dialog boxes and responding to all the messages generated by the different dialog boxes can be a little complex.

A NOTE ABOUT USING THE DIALOG EDITOR

The dialog editor, a tool provided with the IBM WorkSet/2 Toolkit, is the Presentation Manager-based program IBM supplies to help you easily create dialog resource files. Although the dialog editor is easy to use because it is intuitive, there are a few points about it that you must understand.

First, when saving a resource file from the dialog editor, the default extension is .DLG. This is not the default extension used by the resource compiler. So when using output generated by the default editor, you must either copy the .DLG file to a file with an .RC extension or give the full filename, including the .DLG extension, when invoking the resource compiler. By default, the dialog editor saves a compiled version of your .RC file (which is what you need to link to your Presentation Manager application). To use this file, skip the resource compilation step and, on the command line, simply specify the .RES file to the resource compiler. If your program already exists in a .EXE form, the updated resources can be added to it without recompiling.

Second, in order to create or update the .RES file, you must explicitly save your project before leaving the dialog editor. To do so, select File and then Save. If you don't do this, no changes will be made to the .RES or .DLG files on disk.

Third, once you have saved the compiled .RES and .DLG files, you must return to the command line to recombine your executable and .RES files before the changes will affect your executable program. Use RC.EXE to bind your .RES file created by the dialog editor to your application. If you are using the files straight out of the dialog editor without further modifications, just use the .RES file the dialog editor created for you.

You can use the first example program in this chapter to display just about any of the dialog boxes created with the dialog editor. Of course, the buttons and gadgets will not do anything, but it is interesting to see how easy it is to build and display the various dialog boxes. To try this, simply recombine the .RES file produced by the dialog editor with the program MYDIALOG.EXE; then run it and see what you get.

CONTROL WINDOWS

There are so many different *control windows* available in the OS/2 Presentation Manager that their investigation deserves its own chapter. This chapter examines different control windows and demonstrates the use of a few of them inside dialog boxes. Even though control windows are demonstrated inside dialog boxes, this does not imply that this is the only place window controls are used. Window controls can be used in any window by specifying the control in the frame control flags in the **WinCreateStdWindow()** function. Or you can create control windows separately by calling the **WinCreateWindow()** function. In fact, many standard windows you have seen already in this book have controls, such as the scroll bar window control.

There is one thing about controls that is important to understand: each control is in a window of its own (thus the term control window). But since the control windows themselves appear inside a window (such as the dialog box in this chapter), it appears to the user as if there are groups of controls in a single window. Although this distinction is not very important in practice, it is important to understand this difference when reading documentation on the subject.

In this chapter, the terms control and control window are used interchangeably.

CONTROL TYPES

The Presentation Manager supports many different styles of controls. Some of the more exciting and useful ones are buttons, list boxes, entry fields, combination boxes, spin buttons, notebooks, containers, value sets, and sliders. Each are briefly described here.

Buttons   Pushbuttons, radio buttons, check boxes, and three state buttons all belong to the class of buttons. A button is a control that the user pushes (by clicking the mouse or tabbing to and then pressing ENTER) to activate some response. You have already been using pushbuttons in message boxes. For example, the OK button that we have been using in most message boxes is a pushbutton. There can be one or more pushbuttons in a dialog box. A check box contains one or more buttons that are either checked or not checked. If the item is checked, it means that it is selected. In a check box, more than one item may be selected. A radio button is essentially a check box in which one and only one item may be selected. The three state button is also similar to the check box, but the button can be in one of three states.

List Boxes   A list box displays a list of items from which the user selects one (or more). List boxes are commonly used to display things such as lists of filenames.

Entry Fields   An entry field allows the user to enter a string. Entry fields provide all the necessary text editing features required by the user. Therefore, to input a string, your program simply displays an entry field and waits until the user has finished typing in the string.

Combination Boxes   A combination box is a combination of a list box and an entry field. This type of control is very common. You will see this used in many applications since it allows the user to either select from a list or enter a choice by typing it in.

Spin Buttons   A spin button presents the user with another way to make a choice. The user flips through a list of choices and makes a selection. Only one item is presented at a time, so it is important to group similar data together in this type of window.

Notebooks　A notebook is a control window used to organize groups of controls. The notebook looks just as the name implies, like a notebook. The user can "turn" the pages, or windows, of the notebook to different pages containing different controls.

Containers　A container control is designed to hold objects. This window supports drag and drop operations so the objects in this type of window can be manipulated.

Value Sets　A value set lets you choose among a group of mutually exclusive choices, which makes it similar to the radio buttons. The difference is this control is visually oriented and often contains a mixture of text, numbers, and graphic images.

Sliders　A slider is used to set a value in a variable range. As you can guess, this control acts much like a scroll bar (which is also a window control), but its purpose is completely different. A slider is designed to set values whether or not they are inside the client area. The scroll bar is used to scroll text in a window.

A SAMPLE PROGRAM SHELL

The purpose of this chapter is to examine the different control windows available in the Presentation Manager. To fully implement a control, a custom dialog procedure must be written for each dialog box. Most of the control examples in this chapter will include an example resource file, but not all discussions will develop an example program. In order to try out the different dialog boxes, a generic dialog box driver can be designed to work with all the example dialog resource files presented in this chapter. Developing and reusing a single example driver will allow you to concentrate on the function and design of the dialog boxes.

Please note that the example program shown here is designed to display any dialog, but is not designed to respond to any special messages generated by the different dialog boxes, except to close the dialog box upon any command. The events generated by the different control windows will simply be passed to the default dialog message handler.

This example driver will activate the dialog box of the resource file currently linked in any time the left mouse button is pressed in the sample program window.

```
/* A dialog box display skeleton. */
#define INCL_WIN
#define INCL_GPI

#include <os2.h>
#include "dialog.h"

MRESULT EXPENTRY window_func(HWND, ULONG, MPARAM, MPARAM);
MRESULT EXPENTRY dialog_func(HWND, ULONG, MPARAM, MPARAM);

char class[] = "MyClass";


main()
{
  HAB hand_ab;           /* Anchor Block */
  HMQ hand_mq;           /* message queue */
  HWND hand_frame;       /* Frame */
  QMSG q_mess;           /* message queue */
  ULONG flFlags;         /* Window frame definition */
  unsigned char class[] = "MyClass";  /* class name */

  /* define the frame contents */
  flFlags = FCF_TITLEBAR |      /* have a title bar */
            FCF_SIZEBORDER |    /* be a sizeable window */
            FCF_MINMAX |        /* have min and max buttons */
            FCF_SYSMENU |       /* include a system menu */
            FCF_VERTSCROLL |    /* vertical scroll bar */
            FCF_HORZSCROLL |    /* horizontal scroll bar */
            FCF_SHELLPOSITION;  /* default size and location */


  hand_ab = WinInitialize(0);   /* Get the Anchor Block */

  hand_mq = WinCreateMsgQueue(hand_ab, 0); /* start a queue */

  if(!WinRegisterClass(   /* register this window class */
              hand_ab,                /* anchor block */
              (PSZ) class,            /* class name */
              (PFNWP) window_func,    /* window function */
              CS_SIZEREDRAW,          /* window style */
              0))                     /* no storage */
       exit(1);

  hand_frame = WinCreateStdWindow(
```

```
                 HWND_DESKTOP,/* window type */
                 WS_VISIBLE,  /* frame style */
                 &flFlags,    /* definitions */
                 (PSZ)class,  /* client class */
                 (PSZ)"Dialog Box Test",
                 WS_VISIBLE,   /* client style */
                 0,      /* resource modules */
                 0,      /* resource identifier */
                 NULL);  /* pointer to client handle */

  /* message loop */
  while(WinGetMsg(hand_ab, &q_mess, 0, 0, 0))
    WinDispatchMsg(hand_ab, &q_mess);

  /* Shut down the application window and queue */
  WinDestroyWindow(hand_frame);
  WinDestroyMsgQueue(hand_mq);
  WinTerminate(hand_ab);
}

/* This is the window function. */
MRESULT EXPENTRY window_func(HWND handle, ULONG mess,
                             MPARAM parm1, MPARAM parm2)
{

  switch(mess) {

    case WM_BUTTON1DOWN:    /* left mouse button */
      WinDlgBox(HWND_DESKTOP, handle, dialog_func, 0, DLG1, 0);
      break;

    case WM_ERASEBACKGROUND:
      return (MRESULT)TRUE;

    default:
      return WinDefWindowProc(handle, mess, parm1, parm2);
  }

  return (MRESULT)0;
}

/* This is a skeleton dialog procedure */
MRESULT EXPENTRY dialog_func(HWND handle, ULONG mess,
                             MPARAM parm1, MPARAM parm2)
{
```

```
switch(mess) {

  default:
    return WinDefDlgProc(handle, mess, parm1, parm2);
  }

  return (MRESULT)0;
}
```

The header file DIALOG.H needs to define the resource identifier constants. The following header file will work for all the examples presented in this chapter. Enter it at this time:

```
/* sample header file to define resource
   identifier macro defined constants */

#define DLG1  100
#define ONE   101
#define TWO   102
#define THREE 103
#define FOUR  104
#define FIVE  105
#define SIX   106
#define SEVEN 107
#define EIGHT 108
#define NINE  109
```

Notice the value 100 used in this header file. It is the default value assigned by the dialog editor to the first resource defined. When building dialogs to be used with the simple example shell presented here, either use the default values automatically assigned by the dialog editor or assign the value of 100 to the dialog identifier name. Doing this will allow this example shell to display any dialog box. All the numbers used for resource identifiers are arbitrary, and the actual constant values could be used in their place. It is just good programming practice to define constant values in this manner. It prevents simple mistakes and creates programs that are more easily read and maintained.

ADDING CONTROL WINDOWS

For each example presented in the following sections, a description of the control window is given along with the text of the resource file generated by the dialog editor. Some of the discussions include an example program. For the discussions that do not supply examples, the basic program dialog skeleton can be used to display the sample dialog presented.

BUTTONS

One of the basic buttons, the pushbutton, is used in Chapter 6 to illustrate the use of dialog boxes. All the buttons supplied in the Presentation Manager serve a purpose, and you will no doubt eventually use all of them for one purpose or another.

Pushbuttons, which you have already seen, have but one message to send to an application; that is, the button was pushed. Radio buttons are similar, but these buttons are grouped so that they are mutually exclusive; that is, only one can be selected. Check boxes are either on or off, and three state buttons have a third state indicated by shadowing. An example of how a pushbutton works was given in Chapter 6. Here is a resource file that defines some radio buttons, some check boxes, and some three state buttons. Enter this resource and link it to the example dialog skeleton presented earlier in this chapter:

```
; Sample button box resource file

#include <os2.h>
#include "dialog.h"

DLGTEMPLATE DLG1 LOADONCALL MOVEABLE DISCARDABLE
BEGIN
    DIALOG  "Radio and Three State Buttons", DLG1, 23, 42, 238, 51,
            WS_VISIBLE, FCF_SYSMENU | FCF_TITLEBAR
    BEGIN
        AUTORADIOBUTTON "Radio1", ONE, 7, 34, 47, 10, WS_TABSTOP
        AUTORADIOBUTTON "Radio2", TWO, 7, 24, 49, 10, WS_TABSTOP
        AUTORADIOBUTTON "Radio3", THREE, 7, 14, 44, 10, WS_TABSTOP
        CONTROL         "3-State1", FIVE, 167, 33, 52, 10,
                        WC_BUTTON,
                        BS_AUTO3STATE | WS_TABSTOP | WS_VISIBLE
        CONTROL         "3-State2", SIX, 167, 23, 54, 10,
                        WC_BUTTON,
                        BS_AUTO3STATE | WS_TABSTOP | WS_VISIBLE
```

```
          CONTROL          "3-State3", SEVEN, 167, 12, 48, 10,
                           WC_BUTTON,
                           BS_AUTO3STATE | WS_TABSTOP | WS_VISIBLE
          AUTOCHECKBOX     "Check1", FOUR, 81, 33, 47, 10
          AUTOCHECKBOX     "Check2", EIGHT, 81, 23, 55, 10
          AUTOCHECKBOX     "Check3", NINE, 81, 13, 58, 10
      END
  END
```

Assuming you call this resource file BUTTONS.RC and you named the dialog display skeleton program DIALOG.C, the following resource compiler command will create an executable program called DIALOG.EXE:

RC BUTTONS.RC DIALOG.EXE

When you run the program you will see that all the controls respond when you use the mouse to select or check the box. Of course, as stated earlier, the example dialog function will ignore all the button settings.

LIST BOXES

A list box displays a list of items from which the user selects one (or more). List boxes are commonly used to display things such as filenames. To give the user a list of choices, list boxes must be initialized to the desired list of items.

RESPONDING TO A LIST BOX

To respond to list box events requires some additions to the example skeleton dialog program. When using a list box, you must perform two basic operations. First, you must initialize the list box before the dialog box is first displayed. This consists of sending the list box the list that it will display. (By default, the list box will be empty.) Second, once the list box has been initialized, your program will need to respond to the user selecting an item from the list.

List boxes generate various types of messages. The only one we will use is LN_ENTER. This message is sent when the user has double-clicked on an entry in the list or selected it using the keyboard. This message is contained in SHORT2FROMMP(parm1). Once a selection has been made, you will need to query the list box to find out which item has been selected.

Unlike buttons, a list box is a control that receives messages as well as generates them. You can send a list box any of 26 different messages. However, our example only sends these two:

Macro	Purpose
LM_INSERTITEM	Add a string (selection) to the list box
LM_QUERYSELECTION	Request the index of the item selected

LM_INSERTITEM is a message that tells the list box to add a specified string to the list. That is, the specified string becomes another selection within the box. You will see how to use this message shortly. The LM_QUERYSELEC-TION message causes the list box to return the index of the item within the list box that the user selects. All list box indexes begin with 0.

To send a message to the list box (or any other control) use the **WinSendDlgItemMsg()** API function. Its prototype is shown here:

```
MRESULT APIENTRY WinSendDlgItemMsg(HWND handle,
                                    ULONG ID,
                                    ULONG ID_Msg,
                                    MPARAM parm1,
                                    MPARAM parm2);
```

WinSendDlgItemMsg() sends the message specified by *ID_Msg* to the control (within the dialog box) whose ID is specified by *ID*. The handle of the dialog box is specified in *handle.* Any additional information required by the message is specified in *parm1* and *parm2.* The additional information, if any, varies from message to message. If there is no additional information to pass to a control, the *parm1* and the *parm2* arguments should be 0.

INITIALIZING A LIST BOX

Since a list box is, by default, empty, you will need to initialize it when the dialog box that contains it is first displayed. This proves to be quite simple because each time a dialog box is activated, its window function is sent a WM_INITDLG message. Therefore, you will need to add this case to the outer **switch** statement in the **dialog_func()**.

Chapter 7

```
case WM_INITDLG: /* initialize the list box */
   WinInsertLboxItem(handle, LIT_END, "Apple");
   WinInsertLboxItem(handle, LIT_END, "Orange");
   WinInsertLboxItem(handle, LIT_END, "Pear");
   WinInsertLboxItem(handle, LIT_END, "Grape");

   return (MRESULT)TRUE;
```

WinInsertLboxItem() is a macro that, when expanded, calls the
WinSendDlgItemMsg() with the LM_INSERTITEM message. The position to add the string is put into *parm1*, and the string to add is put into
parm2 by the macro. Using the macro provided makes it easy to add strings
to the list box. In this case, each string is added to the list box at the end of
the list, causing the list to be built in the order it is sent. However,
depending upon how you construct the list box, it is possible to have the
items displayed in any order you desire. If the number of items you send
to a list box exceeds what it can display in its window, vertical scroll bars
will be added automatically so the user can select any item.

PROCESSING A SELECTION

After the list box has been initialized, it is ready for use. Each time
the user selects an item in the list box either by double-clicking or by
positioning the highlight using the arrow keys and then pressing ENTER,
a WM_CONTROL message is passed to the dialog box's window function and the LN_ENTER message is contained in *parm1*. Therefore, you
must add LN_ENTER to the inner **switch** statement of the dialog box's
window function.

Once a selection has been made, you determine which item was chosen
by sending the LM_QUERYSELECTION message to the list box. The list
box then returns the index of the item.

The following example demonstrates how to initialize and process a
list box selection. Each time a selection is made, a message box will display
the string associated with the index of the item selected.

First, enter the resource file that defines the list box:

```
; Sample list box resource file

#include <os2.h>
#include "dialog.h"
```

```
DLGTEMPLATE DLG1 LOADONCALL MOVEABLE DISCARDABLE
BEGIN
     DIALOG   "List box", DLG1, 12, 6, 148, 84, WS_VISIBLE,
             FCF_SYSMENU | FCF_TITLEBAR
     BEGIN
         LISTBOX         ONE, 27, 25, 91, 40
     END
END
```

Name the resource file LISTBOX.RC.

Notice the list box ID is ONE. This is used as the index to the message response function that responds to activity inside the list box as shown in the following program. Enter this program now:

```
/* A list box example. */
#define INCL_WIN
#define INCL_GPI

#include <os2.h>
#include "dialog.h"

MRESULT EXPENTRY window_func(HWND, ULONG, MPARAM, MPARAM);
MRESULT EXPENTRY dialog_func(HWND, ULONG, MPARAM, MPARAM);

char class[] = "MyClass";


main()
{
  HAB hand_ab;              /* Anchor Block */
  HMQ hand_mq;              /* message queue */
  HWND hand_frame;          /* Frame */
  QMSG q_mess;              /* message queue */
  ULONG flFlags;            /* Window frame definition */
  unsigned char class[] = "MyClass";  /* class name */

  /* define the frame contents */
  flFlags = FCF_TITLEBAR |    /* have a title bar */
            FCF_SIZEBORDER |  /* be a sizeable window */
            FCF_MINMAX |      /* have min and max buttons */
            FCF_SYSMENU |     /* include a system menu */
            FCF_VERTSCROLL |  /* vertical scroll bar */
            FCF_HORZSCROLL |  /* horizontal scroll bar */
            FCF_SHELLPOSITION; /* default size and location */
```

```
        hand_ab = WinInitialize(0);  /* Get the Anchor Block */

        hand_mq = WinCreateMsgQueue(hand_ab, 0); /* start a queue */

        if(!WinRegisterClass(    /* register this window class */
                        hand_ab,              /* anchor block */
                        (PSZ) class,          /* class name */
                        (PFNWP) window_func, /* window function */
                        CS_SIZEREDRAW,        /* window style */
                        0))                   /* no storage */
            exit(1);

        hand_frame = WinCreateStdWindow(
                        HWND_DESKTOP,/* window type */
                        WS_VISIBLE,  /* frame style */
                        &flFlags,    /* definitions */
                        (PSZ)class,  /* client class */
                        (PSZ)"A List Box Demo",
                        WS_VISIBLE,  /* client style */
                        0,      /* resource modules */
                        0,      /* resource identifier */
                        NULL);  /* pointer to client handle */

      /* message loop */
    while(WinGetMsg(hand_ab, &q_mess, 0, 0, 0))
      WinDispatchMsg(hand_ab, &q_mess);

    /* Shut down the application window and queue */
    WinDestroyWindow(hand_frame);
    WinDestroyMsgQueue(hand_mq);
    WinTerminate(hand_ab);
}

/* This is the window function. */
MRESULT EXPENTRY window_func(HWND handle, ULONG mess,
                            MPARAM parm1, MPARAM parm2)
{

  switch(mess) {

    case WM_BUTTON1DOWN:    /* left mouse button */
      WinDlgBox(HWND_DESKTOP, handle, dialog_func, 0, DLG1, 0);
      break;
```

```
    case WM_ERASEBACKGROUND:
      return (MRESULT)TRUE;

    default:
      return WinDefWindowProc(handle, mess, parm1, parm2);
  }

  return (MRESULT)0;
}

/* This is the list box dialog procedure */
MRESULT EXPENTRY dialog_func(HWND handle, ULONG mess,
                                MPARAM parm1, MPARAM parm2)
{
APIRET item;
static HWND lbox;
PCHAR fruit[4] = {"Apple", "Orange", "Pear", "Grape"};

  switch(mess)
  {
    case WM_INITDLG: /* initialize the list box */

      /* get the list box handle */
      lbox = HWNDFROMMP(parm1);

      /* insert strings into list box */
      WinInsertLboxItem(lbox, LIT_END, "Apple");
      WinInsertLboxItem(lbox, LIT_END, "Orange");

      /* You can also use a pointer to the string */
      WinInsertLboxItem(lbox, LIT_END, fruit[2]);
      WinInsertLboxItem(lbox, LIT_END, fruit[3]);

      return (MRESULT)TRUE;

    case WM_CONTROL:

      /* get the ID of the control */
      switch (SHORT1FROMMP(parm1))
      {
        case ONE: /* ID of the list box */

          if(SHORT2FROMMP(parm1)==LN_ENTER)
          { /* user double-clicked mouse, or pressed enter */
            /* get the index of the selected item */
```

```
            item = WinQueryLboxSelectedItem(lbox);

            /* display selected item */
            WinMessageBox(HWND_DESKTOP, handle,
                          fruit[item],
                          "", 0, MB_OK);

            return (MRESULT) TRUE;
          }

      default:
        break;
      }

  default:
    return WinDefDlgProc(handle, mess, parm1, parm2);
  }

  return (MRESULT)0;
}
```

Assuming you call the program LISTBOX.C, and you named the resource file LISTBOX.RC, the following commands will build an executable program for you to try:

ICC -B"/PM:PM" LISTBOX.C
RC LISTBOX

When you click the left mouse in the example window, the dialog with the list box will pop up. Selecting one of the items in the list causes a message box to appear. The output of this example program is shown in Figure 7-1.

ENTRY FIELDS

Entry fields are particularly useful because they allow users to enter a string of their own choosing. Before you can use an entry field, you must define one in your resource file. For this example, enter the following resource file:

```
; Sample entry field resource file

#include <os2.h>
#include "dialog.h"

DLGTEMPLATE DLG1 LOADONCALL MOVEABLE DISCARDABLE
BEGIN
    DIALOG   "Entry Field", DLG1, 85, 8, 148, 84, WS_VISIBLE,
             FCF_SYSMENU | FCF_TITLEBAR
    BEGIN
        ENTRYFIELD       "", ONE, 19, 46, FIVE, 8, ES_MARGIN
        LTEXT            "Enter Your Name:", TWO, 17, 65, 85, 8
        PUSHBUTTON       "OK", THREE, 49, 7, 40, 14
    END
END
```

This version adds a pushbutton called OK that will be used to tell the program that you are done editing text in the entry field. It also adds the list box itself. The ID for the list box is TWO. This definition causes a standard entry field to be created that contains the text "Enter Your Name."

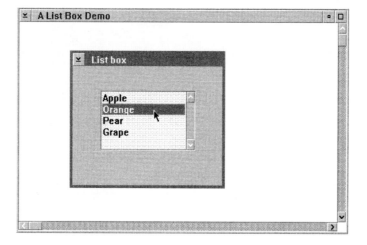

FIGURE 7-1

Sample List Box

Entry fields recognize many messages and generate several of their own. However, for the purposes of this example, there is no need for the program to respond to any messages. As you will see, entry fields perform the editing function on their own. There is no need for program interaction when text is edited. Your program simply decides when it wants to obtain the current contents of the entry field.

Take a moment now and compile the example RC file with the standard dialog box example program. This will allow you to see a standard entry field in action.

COMBINATION BOXES

A combination box is a combination of a list box and an entry field. This type of box is very common. You will see this used in many applications since it allows the user either to select an item from a list or to enter a choice by typing it in.

Using a combination box is just like using the list box and entry field examined in the previous two sections. The following is an example resource file that defines the same functionality presented in the list box and entry field sections:

```
; Sample combo box resource file

#include <os2.h>
#include "dialog.h"

DLGTEMPLATE DLG1 LOADONCALL MOVEABLE DISCARDABLE
BEGIN
    DIALOG  "Combo Box", DLG1, 12, 6, 148, 84, WS_VISIBLE,
            FCF_SYSMENU | FCF_TITLEBAR
    BEGIN
        COMBOBOX        "", ONE, 1, 17, 139, 49, WS_GROUP
        LTEXT           "Enter Your Name:", TWO, 5, 72, 110, 8
        PUSHBUTTON      "OK", THREE, 49, 4, 40, 14
    END
END
```

The advantage of using a combination box over separate list boxes and entry fields is that the **dialog_func()** only needs to query one control to get the user's input. Use the combination box whenever you are looking for one input selection. Use the separate controls when separate inputs are needed.

SPIN BUTTONS

A spin button can add an interesting twist to the presentation of an application's data. The same kind of information can be presented as is found in a list box, but spin buttons are particularly suited for values. The user can flip through a list of this type and very quickly make selections.

A spin button, like a list box, also sends events through the WM_CONTROL message. The following RC file defines a spin button that can hold both characters and numeric information:

```
; Sample spin button resource file

#include <os2.h>
#include "dialog.h"

DLGTEMPLATE DLG1 LOADONCALL MOVEABLE DISCARDABLE
BEGIN
    DIALOG  "Spin Button", DLG1, 12, 6, 148, 84, WS_VISIBLE,
            FCF_SYSMENU | FCF_TITLEBAR
    BEGIN
        CONTROL    "", ONE, 28, 42, 80, 12, WC_SPINBUTTON,
                   SPBS_ALLCHARACTERS | SPBS_MASTER |
                   SPBS_SERVANT | SPBS_JUSTDEFAULT |
                   WS_GROUP | WS_TABSTOP | WS_VISIBLE
    END
END
```

NOTEBOOKS

A notebook is an advanced control that assists the application writer to organize user input into logical sections. Notebooks can be used to classify types of input by creating separate pages for each class. You supply a dialog function for each notebook you define, but each notebook can contain many pages. This makes working with notebook dialogs very easy.

The user can "turn" the pages of the notebook to different windows containing different controls. This complex control is best used in applications that apply many controls to a single task. The notebook control can help the application designer organize a complex set of interdependent controls into one common dialog box.

Don't overlook this control when designing an application, for it can be useful in many ways. To see what a notebook looks like, enter the following resource file and link it into the example dialog skeleton:

```
; Sample notebook resource file

#include <os2.h>
#include "dialog.h"

DLGTEMPLATE DLG1 LOADONCALL MOVEABLE DISCARDABLE
BEGIN
    DIALOG  "NoteBook", DLG1, 74, -37, 148, 132, WS_VISIBLE,
                        FCF_SYSMENU | FCF_TITLEBAR
    BEGIN
        CONTROL    "The Notebook", ONE, 0, 19, 148, 113,
                   WC_NOTEBOOK, BKS_BACKPAGESBR |
                   BKS_MAJORTABRIGHT | BKS_SQUARETABS |
                   BKS_STATUSTEXTLEFT | BKS_TABTEXTLEFT |
                   WS_GROUP | WS_TABSTOP | WS_VISIBLE
        PUSHBUTTON "OK", TWO, 47, 0, 40, 14
    END
END
```

CONTAINERS

A container control is designed to organize objects into like groups. You have seen containers all over the OS/2 Desktop. The folders are containers, and so are the icon views. This control supports drag and drop operations to manipulate objects. Items are dragged in and out of containers.

Containers support the display of bitmaps, icons, and text. The different types of items can be displayed in different ways. Each of these displays is called a *container view*. Different types of container views are available, including an icon view, a name view, a text view, a tree view, and a details view.

The icon view is the view most often seen in the OS/2 Desktop. This is an icon with some text below the icon that names it. The name view displays the text to the right of the icon. Neither the icon view nor the name view limits the number of lines of text displayed or the number of characters per line.

The text view is similar to the icon and name views, but the icon is not present in the text view. Instead, the text acts as the object that can be manipulated. The tree view displays the other views in a treelike organization. The far left object is the root and is known as the parent. Items to the right of the parent are called children and are not displayed unless the parent is selected. Once a child is displayed, it may also be selected, displaying even more children. This type of tree display is often used for graphic representations of disk file structures.

The details view can display multiple fields of information about a single object, including the icon or bitmap, some text, and other values associated with the object. A details view might contain column headings, and the objects can be organized into rows inside the dialog box.

VALUE SETS

A value set lets you choose a visually oriented item. The window of a value set often contains graphic images and bitmaps.

The most common use of the value set control is the graphic image. The user "sees" the choice and selects it. A value set may be used to select the choice of background patterns. In this case, a small sample of each of the images is displayed and the user can simply select the preferred image by clicking on it.

The value set operates much like the radio button. Only one of the displayed images can be selected. Value sets are often combined with other controls in a single dialog box, making user input simpler and more interesting.

SLIDERS

The final control covered in this chapter is the slider. A slider is used to set a value in a variable range. The user sets values by sliding a bar across the page. This can be a very intuitive method of setting many values.

A good use of a slider control is to adjust the frequency setting for sound output, and this is just the type of example developed here for demonstration purposes. In the following example program, every time the slider is moved, the current slider setting will be read and used as the frequency input parameter to the **DosBeep()** API function.

The resource definition file for a slider control is shown here:

```
; Sample slider resource file

#include <os2.h>
#include "dialog.h"

DLGTEMPLATE DLG1 LOADONCALL MOVEABLE DISCARDABLE
BEGIN
    DIALOG  "Speaker Beeper", DLG1, 56, 8, 209, 84, WS_VISIBLE,
            FCF_SYSMENU | FCF_TITLEBAR
    BEGIN
        CONTROL  "", TWO, 3, 22, 206, 9, WC_SLIDER,
                SLS_HORIZONTAL | SLS_CENTER |
                SLS_SNAPTOINCREMENT | SLS_RIBBONSTRIP |
                SLS_HOMELEFT | SLS_PRIMARYSCALE1 |
                WS_GROUP | WS_TABSTOP | WS_VISIBLE
                CTLDATA 12, 0, 200, 0, 20, 0
        CTEXT    "Frequency", FIVE, 65, 43, 60, 8, DT_VCENTER
    END
END
```

A WM_CONTROL message is generated every time the slider value changes. The SLN_SLIDERTRACK notification code, stored in the message parameter *parm1,* is sent even if the mouse button is never released. This will be used to capture the changes as the user slides the control. Sliding the control will cause the speaker to sound for each incremental change in the slider control value. The sample **dialog_func()** is listed here:

```
/* A slider control example. */
#define INCL_WIN
#define INCL_GPI
```

```
#include <os2.h>
#include "dialog.h"

MRESULT EXPENTRY window_func(HWND, ULONG, MPARAM, MPARAM);
MRESULT EXPENTRY dialog_func(HWND, ULONG, MPARAM, MPARAM);

char class[] = "MyClass";


main()
{
  HAB hand_ab;            /* Anchor Block */
  HMQ hand_mq;            /* message queue */
  HWND hand_frame;        /* Frame */
  QMSG q_mess;            /* message queue */
  ULONG flFlags;          /* Window frame definition */
  unsigned char class[] = "MyClass";  /* class name */

  /* define the frame contents */
  flFlags = FCF_TITLEBAR |      /* have a title bar */
            FCF_SIZEBORDER |    /* be a sizeable window */
            FCF_MINMAX |        /* have min and max buttons */
            FCF_SYSMENU |       /* include a system menu */
            FCF_VERTSCROLL |    /* vertical scroll bar */
            FCF_HORZSCROLL |    /* horizontal scroll bar */
            FCF_SHELLPOSITION;  /* default size and location */


  hand_ab = WinInitialize(0);   /* Get the Anchor Block */

  hand_mq = WinCreateMsgQueue(hand_ab, 0); /* start a queue */

  if(!WinRegisterClass(    /* register this window class */
                  hand_ab,                /* anchor block */
                  (PSZ) class,            /* class name */
                  (PFNWP) window_func,    /* window function */
                  CS_SIZEREDRAW,          /* window style */
                  0))                     /* no storage */
      exit(1);

  hand_frame = WinCreateStdWindow(
                  HWND_DESKTOP,/* window type */
                  WS_VISIBLE,  /* frame style */
                  &flFlags,    /* definitions */
```

```
                       (PSZ)class,  /* client class */
                       (PSZ)"Slider Control Demo",
                       WS_VISIBLE,  /* client style */
                       0,      /* resource modules */
                       0,      /* resource identifier */
                       NULL);  /* pointer to client handle */

  /* message loop */
  while(WinGetMsg(hand_ab, &q_mess, 0, 0, 0))
    WinDispatchMsg(hand_ab, &q_mess);

  /* Shut down the application window and queue */
  WinDestroyWindow(hand_frame);
  WinDestroyMsgQueue(hand_mq);
  WinTerminate(hand_ab);
}

/* This is the window function. */
MRESULT EXPENTRY window_func(HWND handle, ULONG mess,
                             MPARAM parm1, MPARAM parm2)

{

  switch(mess) {

    case WM_BUTTON1DOWN:    /* left mouse button */
      WinDlgBox(HWND_DESKTOP, handle, dialog_func, 0, DLG1, 0);
      break;

    case WM_ERASEBACKGROUND:
      return (MRESULT)TRUE;

    default:
      return WinDefWindowProc(handle, mess, parm1, parm2);
  }

  return (MRESULT)0;
}

/* This is the slider dialog procedure */
MRESULT EXPENTRY dialog_func(HWND handle, ULONG mess,
                             MPARAM parm1, MPARAM parm2)
{
ULONG freq;
static HWND lbox;
```

```
switch(mess)
{
  case WM_INITDLG: /* initialize the slider */
    /* get the slider handle */
    lbox = HWNDFROMMP(parm1);

    return (MRESULT)TRUE;

  case WM_CONTROL:

    /* check for the slider drag message. */
    if(SHORT2FROMMP(parm1)==SLN_SLIDERTRACK)
    { /* user is moving the slider, get the new value */
         freq = (ULONG) WinSendMsg(lbox, SLM_QUERYSLIDERINFO,
                         MPFROM2SHORT(SMA_SLIDERARMPOSITION,
                                      SMA_INCREMENTVALUE),
                                                    NULL);

         DosBeep(freq, 75);
         return (MRESULT)TRUE;
    }
  default:
    return WinDefDlgProc(handle, mess, parm1, parm2);
  }

  return (MRESULT)0;
}
```

You will notice as you try this sample program that a trombone effect can be obtained by beeping the speaker while the slider is being moved. To beep the speaker only once when the mouse is released, the SLN_CHANGE notification code should be used in place of the SLN_SLIDERTRACK notification code. Give this a try now to see the effect of changing this one message. The output from the slider control example is shown in Figure 7-2.

CONCLUDING THOUGHTS

While the chapters in this section introduce you to Presentation Manager programming and provide a "quick start" to its essential principles, they only scratch the surface of Presentation Manager programming. If

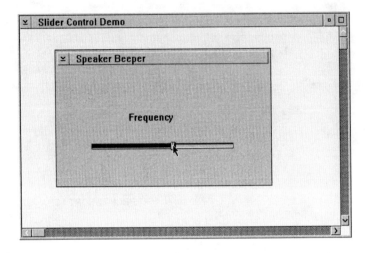

FIGURE 7-2

Sample Slider Control

you want to become an excellent Presentation Manager programmer, you will need to acquire several books on the topic and write a number of programs. Taking a full year to become familiar with all aspects of Presentation Manager programming is not uncommon. However, just be persistent. Your efforts will be rewarded.

ICONS AND GRAPHICS

This chapter explains how to control the appearance of two important items linked with all Presentation Manager applications: the design of the icon that is displayed when an application is minimized and the shape of the mouse pointer. The chapter finishes off with a discussion of the graphics functions available in the Presentation Manager. An example program is developed to demonstrate the drawing capabilities in the Presentation Manager.

USING SYSTEM DEFINED ICONS AND MOUSE POINTERS

The first section of this chapter will explain how to use the set of predefined system icons and mouse pointers. To use your own definition of one of these graphic images you must use the icon editor contained in the IBM WorkSet/2 Toolkit. The user-defined icons and mouse pointers can be loaded into the application through the application's resource definition file. Once loaded, the custom mouse pointer can be used the same way the predefined system icons and mouse pointers are used. The second section in this chapter demonstrates how these custom icons and mouse pointers are developed and used in an application program.

A mouse pointer is nothing more than a special icon, and both the pointer and icon are simply bitmaps. The mouse pointer has a special location defined in its bitmap called a *hot spot*. The hot spot is the exact location the mouse is pointing to, such as the tip of the default mouse pointer. OS/2 keeps track of the screen coordinates of this mouse pointer hot spot, and sends them to the appropriate window as it travels around the screen.

CHANGING THE DEFAULT ICON

Although masked by OS/2, all Presentation Manager applications first create a window class, which defines the attributes of the window, including the shape of the application's icon and mouse pointer. This window class is then registered with the Presentation Manager. Only after these steps have been performed can you actually create a window. In the process, default icon and mouse pointer shapes are defined. Since the shapes of the icon and mouse pointer are defined when a window class is created, you must actively intervene in the window class creation process to alter these items.

Before developing a complete program to demonstrate changing the minimized icon and the mouse pointer, it is necessary to discuss the operation of the various API functions used to manipulate icons and mouse pointers.

To change the default icon to another system defined icon, a message needs to be sent after the window is created. The message to send, WM_SETICON, is sent by the **WinSendMsg()** API function. Its prototype is shown here:

```
WinSendMsg(HWND hand_frame, ULONG msg,
           MPARAM parm1, MPARAM parm2);
```

The *hand_frame* parameter is the frame handle for the window. This is the return value from the call to the API function **WinCreateStdWindow()**. The second parameter is the message to send, and the message being sent determines the final two parameters, *parm1* and *parm2*. In this case, *parm1* will hold the pointer to the new icon, and *parm2* will be 0. To obtain the value for *parm1*, the function **WinQuerySysPointer()** must be called to get the system pointer for the desired icon. The prototype is as follows:

HPOINTER APIENTRY WinQuerySysPointer(HWND *handle*,
LONG *ptr*,
BOOL *load*);

The *handle* parameter is the handle to the parent window. For examples in this book, this parameter will be set to HWND_DESKTOP. The desired system pointer value (the icon pointer) is placed into *ptr*. The parameter *load*, if set to TRUE, tells the system to make a copy of the current pointer before returning the handle. This is used if the application is going to modify the bitmap of the current pointer.

Table 8-1 lists the system defined icons normally used for minimized applications. Actually, you can also use any of the system pointers listed in Table 8-2 since the Presentation Manager does not distinguish between mouse system pointers and icon system pointers.

The best location to change the icon is directly following the **WinCreateStdWin()** call. The following code fragment shows how the icon can be changed to the SPTR_ICONQUESTION system defined icon.

```
hand_frame = WinCreateStdWindow(
                HWND_DESKTOP,/* window type */
                WS_VISIBLE,   /* frame style */
                &flFlags,     /* definitions */
                (PSZ)class,   /* client class */
                (PSZ)"Icon and Mouse Pointer Test",
                WS_VISIBLE,   /* client style */
                0,            /* resource modules */
                0,            /* resource identifier */
                NULL);        /* pointer to client handle */

/* get the system pointer to the desired icon */
icon = WinQuerySysPointer(HWND_DESKTOP,
                    SPTR_ICONQUESTION,
                    FALSE);

/* set the icon to the desired system pointer */
WinSendMsg(hand_frame, WM_SETICON, (MPARAM)icon, (MPARAM)0);
```

This fragment will be used in the next sample program following the next section.

Macro	Icon Description
SPTR_APPICON	Default application icon
SPTR_FILE	Single file icon
SPTR_ICONERROR	Exclamation point
SPTR_ILLEGAL	Used to indicate something illegal
SPTR_ICONWARNING	Warning icon
SPTR_MULTFILE	Multiple file icon
SPTR_FOLDER	Icon to represent a folder
SPTR_PROGRAM	Executable program icon
SPTR_ICONINFORMATION	Information icon
SPTR_ICONQUESTION	Question mark

TABLE 8-1

System Defined Icons

Macro	Pointer Description
SPTR_ARROW	Default arrow pointer
SPTR_TEXT	I-beam pointer
SPTR_WAIT	Clock
SPTR_SIZEWE	Horizontal double-headed arrow
SPTR_SIZENS	Vertical double-headed arrow
SPTR_SIZENWSE	Double-headed arrow pointing northwest and southeast
SPTR_SIZENESW	Double-headed arrow pointing northeast and southwest
SPTR_SIZE	Pointer used during sizing
SPTR_MOVE	Pointer used while dragging

TABLE 8-2

System Defined Pointers

CHANGING THE DEFAULT MOUSE POINTER

Changing the default mouse pointer is very similar to changing the default icon. To change the mouse pointer from the default shape, you will first need to get the handle of the desired pointer shape using the API function **WinQuerySysPointer()**. The prototype for this function was shown in the previous section, but is repeated here for completeness:

HPOINTER APIENTRY WinQuerySysPointer(HWND *handle*,
                                                                    LONG *ptr*,
                                                                    BOOL *load*);

The *handle* parameter is the handle to the parent window which will be set to HWND_DESKTOP for all examples used here. The system pointer value (mouse pointer) is placed into *ptr*. The parameter *load*, if set to TRUE, tells the system to make a copy of the current pointer before returning the handle. A list of most of the common system pointers used for mouse pointers is given in Table 8-2. You can also use any of the system icons listed in Table 8-1 since the Presentation Manager does not distinguish between icon system pointers and mouse system pointers.

Once you have a handle to the desired mouse pointer, you set the current mouse pointer with a call to **WinSetPointer()**. The prototype for this function looks like this:

BOOL APIENTRY WinSetPointer(HWND *handle*,
                                                HPOINTER *new_ptr*);

Here, *handle* is the parent window handle, HWND_DESKTOP, and *new_ptr* is the handle for the new mouse pointer. This value is the return value from the API function **WinQuerySysPointer()** that you used to get the handle to the mouse pointer.

It is often necessary for the application program to save the current mouse pointer before installing a new pointer. This is so the original mouse pointer can be restored. The API function **WinQueryPointer()** is used to retrieve the handle to the current mouse pointer. The prototype for this function is shown here:

HPOINTER APIENTRY WinQueryPointer(HWND *handle*);

The interesting part of this function call is the return value. This is where you will find the handle to the current mouse pointer.

DISPLAYING THE ICON AND MOUSE POINTER

The following program uses the functions described in the previous two sections of this chapter to change the default icon to a question mark. The program also changes the mouse pointer into a clock shape whenever the right mouse button is pressed. When the left mouse button is pressed, the mouse pointer is restored to its original shape.

```c
/* An example of switching icons and mouse pointers */

#define INCL_WIN

#include <os2.h>

MRESULT EXPENTRY window_func(HWND, ULONG, MPARAM, MPARAM);

char class[] = "MyClass";

main()
{
  HAB hand_ab;            /* anchor block */
  HMQ hand_mq;            /* message queue */
  HWND hand_frame;        /* frame */
  QMSG q_mess;            /* message queue */
  ULONG flFlags;          /* window frame definition */
  unsigned char class[] = "MyClass";  /* class name */
  HPOINTER icon;          /* new icon being used */

  /* define the frame contents */
  flFlags = FCF_TITLEBAR |     /* have a title bar */
            FCF_SIZEBORDER |   /* be a sizeable window */
            FCF_MINMAX |       /* have min and max buttons */
            FCF_SYSMENU |      /* include a system menu */
            FCF_VERTSCROLL |   /* vertical scroll bar */
            FCF_HORZSCROLL |   /* horizontal scroll bar */
            FCF_SHELLPOSITION; /* default size and location */

  hand_ab = WinInitialize(0);  /* get the anchor block */

  hand_mq = WinCreateMsgQueue(hand_ab, 0); /* start a queue */

  if(!WinRegisterClass(   /* register this window class */
                 hand_ab,              /* anchor block */
                 (PSZ) class,          /* class name */
                 (PFNWP) window_func,  /* window function */
```

```
                        CS_SIZEREDRAW,        /* window style */
                        0))                   /* no storage */
        exit(1);

    hand_frame = WinCreateStdWindow(
                    HWND_DESKTOP,/* window type */
                    WS_VISIBLE,  /* frame style */
                    &flFlags,    /* definitions */
                    (PSZ)class,  /* client class */
                    (PSZ)"Icon and Mouse Pointer Test",
                    WS_VISIBLE,  /* client style */
                    0,           /* resource modules */
                    0,           /* resource identifier */
                    NULL);       /* pointer to client handle */

    /* get the system pointer to the desired icon */
    icon = WinQuerySysPointer(HWND_DESKTOP,
                              SPTR_ICONQUESTION,
                              FALSE);

    /* set the icon to the desired system pointer */
    WinSendMsg(hand_frame, WM_SETICON, (MPARAM)icon, NULL);

     /* message loop */
    while(WinGetMsg(hand_ab, &q_mess, 0, 0, 0))
      WinDispatchMsg(hand_ab, &q_mess);

    /* shut down the application window and queue */
    WinDestroyWindow(hand_frame);
    WinDestroyMsgQueue(hand_mq);
    WinTerminate(hand_ab);
}

/* this is the window function */
MRESULT EXPENTRY window_func(HWND handle, ULONG mess,
                            MPARAM parm1, MPARAM parm2)
{
   HPOINTER new_pointer;
   static HPOINTER old_pointer;
   static HPOINTER curr_pointer;

   switch(mess) {

     case WM_CREATE:
```

```
        /* save the original mouse pointer on creation */
        /* if no original pointer, use the default */
        old_pointer = WinQueryPointer(HWND_DESKTOP);
        if(old_pointer == NULLHANDLE)
           old_pointer = WinQuerySysPointer(HWND_DESKTOP,
                                            SPTR_ARROW,
                                            FALSE);


        /* set the current pointer to the original */
        curr_pointer = old_pointer;

        break;

   case WM_BUTTON2DOWN: /* process right button */

        /* get the handle of the new pointer */
        new_pointer = WinQuerySysPointer(HWND_DESKTOP,
                                         SPTR_WAIT,
                                         FALSE);

        /* set the mouse pointer to the new shape */
        WinSetPointer(HWND_DESKTOP, new_pointer);
        curr_pointer = new_pointer;
        break;

   case WM_BUTTON1DOWN: /* process left button */
        /* set the mouse pointer back to the original shape */
        WinSetPointer(HWND_DESKTOP, old_pointer);
        curr_pointer = old_pointer;
        break;

   case WM_MOUSEMOVE:

        /* when the mouse moves, the system will restore the
           original mouse pointer. Set the mouse pointer
           and return TRUE to prevent the system from
           reacting to the mouse move */

        WinSetPointer(HWND_DESKTOP, curr_pointer);
        return (MRESULT)TRUE;

   case WM_ERASEBACKGROUND:
        return (MRESULT)TRUE;

   default:
```

```
      return WinDefWindowProc(handle, mess, parm1, parm2);
  }
  return (MRESULT)0;
}
```

Notice that the program processes the WM_MOUSEMOVE message. This is done to preserve the current mouse pointer during movement. If the mouse leaves the focus of the example window, the example program no longer provides the mouse pointer shape. As soon as the mouse returns to the focus of the example program, the current mouse pointer of the example program is again displayed. If the WM_MOUSEMOVE message were passed on to the default window message handler, the system would restore the default mouse pointer every time the mouse was moved.

The output of the example program is shown in Figure 8-1. Notice the icon in the upper left-hand corner. It's a question mark. Also notice the mouse pointer is now a picture of a clock.

Take a few minutes and try some of the different icons and mouse pointers. To try other icons, replace the macro in the call to **WinQuerySysPointer()** in the **main()** function with other system icons

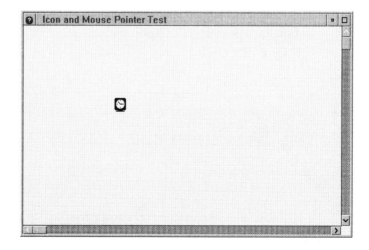

FIGURE 8-1

Sample Output Using a Standard System Icon and Pointer

listed in Table 8-1. To try other mouse pointers, replace the macro in the call to **WinQuerySysPointer()** inside the **window_func()** procedure with other system pointers listed in Table 8-2.

USING CUSTOM ICONS AND MOUSE POINTERS

Before continuing with the following examples, you must create a pointer resource. As with other graphical resources, the best way to create your own pointer is to use the IBM WorkSet/2 icon editor.

CREATING THE ICON AND MOUSE POINTER

Take a minute now and create your own icon and a mouse pointer. The icon editor is quite intuitive to use. If you encounter problems, refer to the extensive online documentation or the manuals supplied with the Toolkit. When you save the files, name them MYICON.ICO and MYMOUSE.PTR respectively, so they can be used by the sample program without any changes to the code presented in this section. Figure 8-2 shows the icon editor with the sample icon used in the sample program in this section.

Once you have created the icon and mouse pointer, you will need to include them in your application's resource file. The following lines will define the icon and mouse pointer, making them available to the application program:

```
#include "icon.h"
POINTER MYMOUSE MYMOUSE.PTR
ICON MYICON MYICON.ICO
```

The header file ICON.H should contain the following lines:

```
#define MYMOUSE 111
#define MYICON 222
```

To use the icon defined in a resource file, simply add the FCF_ICON macro to the **flFlags** variable in the example program. This variable holds the window creation flags in the **main()** function. Next, include the ID number in the call to **WinCreateStdWindow()** in the resource identifier field. The Presentation Manager takes care of the rest of the work.

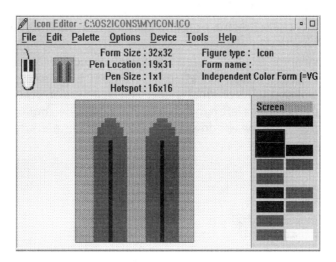

FIGURE 8-2
Icon Editor Screen

To use the mouse pointer you have defined in the resource file takes a bit more work, but once you have done the work, you may display the pointer whenever you want. Using a custom mouse pointer is similar to using a system default mouse pointer, except the custom mouse pointer must first be loaded through a call to WinLoadPointer(). This function will retrieve the system handle for the custom mouse pointer much the same way the function **WinQuerySysPointer()** retrieved the handles for the system defined pointers and icons. The prototype for this function is given here:

> HPOINTER APIENTRY WinLoadPointer(HWND *handle*,
> > > HMODULE *mod*,
> > > ULONG *id*);

Again, the *handle* parameter is set to HWND_DESKTOP, the parent window. The parameter *mod* is the module name of the bit image. Usually this is set to 0 because the bit images are linked into the executable file by the resource compiler. Here, *id* is the unique ID number assigned to the pointer in the resource file.

DISPLAYING THE CUSTOM ICON AND MOUSE POINTER

The following program uses the icon and mouse pointer you created. Like the previous example program, the mouse pointer changes into your custom designed mouse pointer whenever the right mouse button is pressed. When the left mouse button is pressed, the mouse pointer is restored to its original shape. The custom icon you designed is displayed in the upper left-hand corner of the window, but to get a good look at it, minimize the window. Figure 8-3 shows sample output from this program.

```
/* An example of a custom icon mouse pointer */

#define INCL_WIN

#include <os2.h>
#include "icon.h"

MRESULT EXPENTRY window_func(HWND, ULONG, MPARAM, MPARAM);

char class[] = "MyClass";


main()
{
  HAB hand_ab;           /* anchor block */
  HMQ hand_mq;           /* message queue */
  HWND hand_frame;       /* frame */
  QMSG q_mess;           /* message queue */
  ULONG flFlags;         /* window frame definition */
  unsigned char class[] = "MyClass";  /* class name */
  HPOINTER icon;         /* the new icon system pointer */

  /* define the frame contents */
  flFlags = FCF_ICON |           /* use the indicated icon */
            FCF_TITLEBAR |       /* have a title bar */
            FCF_SIZEBORDER |     /* be a sizeable window */
            FCF_MINMAX |         /* have min and max buttons*/

            FCF_SYSMENU |        /* include a system menu */
            FCF_VERTSCROLL |     /* vertical scroll bar */
            FCF_HORZSCROLL |     /* horizontal scroll bar */
            FCF_SHELLPOSITION;   /* default size and location*/


    hand_ab = WinInitialize(0);  /* get the anchor block */
```

```
   hand_mq = WinCreateMsgQueue(hand_ab, 0); /* start a queue*/


   if(!WinRegisterClass(   /* register this window class */
                  hand_ab,             /* anchor block */
                  (PSZ) class,         /* class name */
                  (PFNWP) window_func, /* window function*/

                  CS_SIZEREDRAW,       /* window style */
                  0))                  /* no storage */
     exit(1);

   hand_frame = WinCreateStdWindow(
                  HWND_DESKTOP,/* window type */
                  WS_VISIBLE,  /* frame style */
                  &flFlags,    /* definitions */
                  (PSZ)class,  /* client class */
                  (PSZ)"Custom Icon and Mouse Pointer",
                  WS_VISIBLE,  /* client style */
                  0,           /* resource modules */
                  MYICON,      /* resource identifier */
                  NULL);       /* pointer to client handle */

    /* message loop */
   while(WinGetMsg(hand_ab, &q_mess, 0, 0, 0))
     WinDispatchMsg(hand_ab, &q_mess);

   /* shut down the application window and queue */
   WinDestroyWindow(hand_frame);
   WinDestroyMsgQueue(hand_mq);
   WinTerminate(hand_ab);
}

/* This is the window function */
MRESULT EXPENTRY window_func(HWND handle, ULONG mess,
                            MPARAM parm1, MPARAM parm2)
{
   HPOINTER new_pointer;
   static HPOINTER old_pointer;
   static HPOINTER curr_pointer;

   switch(mess) {

     case WM_CREATE:
```

```
     /* save the original mouse pointer on creation */
     /* if no original pointer, use the default */
     old_pointer = WinQueryPointer(HWND_DESKTOP);
     if(old_pointer == NULLHANDLE)
        old_pointer = WinQuerySysPointer(HWND_DESKTOP,
                                         SPTR_ARROW,
                                         FALSE);

     /* set the current pointer to the original */
     curr_pointer = old_pointer;

     break;

case WM_BUTTON2DOWN: /* process right button */

     /* get the handle of the new pointer */
     new_pointer = WinLoadPointer(HWND_DESKTOP,
                                  0,
                                  MYMOUSE);

     /* set the mouse pointer to the new shape */
     WinSetPointer(HWND_DESKTOP, new_pointer);
     curr_pointer = new_pointer;
     break;

case WM_BUTTON1DOWN: /* process left button */
     /* set the mouse pointer back to the original shape */
     WinSetPointer(HWND_DESKTOP, old_pointer);
     curr_pointer = old_pointer;
     break;

case WM_MOUSEMOVE:

     /* when the mouse moves, the system will restore the
        original mouse pointer. Set the mouse pointer
        and return TRUE to prevent the system from
        reacting to the mouse move */

     WinSetPointer(HWND_DESKTOP, curr_pointer);
     return (MRESULT)TRUE;

case WM_ERASEBACKGROUND:
     return (MRESULT)TRUE;
```

```
    default:
      return WinDefWindowProc(handle, mess, parm1, parm2);
  }
  return (MRESULT)0;
}
```

USING GRAPHICS

The creators of OS/2 left the task of graphics display to the Presentation Manager. It is very difficult to implement graphics outside the Presentation Manager. This section contains an explanation of how to use Presentation Manager graphics and an example graphics program.

THE CURRENT POSITION APPROACH TO GRAPHICS

The Presentation Manager maintains a pointer to the currently active screen location. The Presentation Manager graphics system makes use of

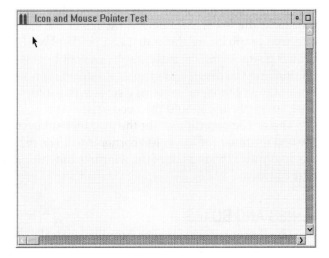

FIGURE 8-3

Sample Output From the Custom Icon and Mouse Pointer Test

this current location to streamline many of its graphics services, such as those that draw lines and boxes. To understand how, consider first the more traditional approach to the basic graphics functions.

In a traditional graphics system, the function that draws a line will be defined something like this:

drawline(startX, startY, endX, endY)

Here, both the starting and ending points of the line are specified explicitly in the function parameters. In general, in the traditional method all graphics functions specify both the beginning and ending points of the object to be drawn (where applicable, of course). However, the Presentation Manager uses a fundamentally different approach based upon the current position. In this method, the call to the line drawing function specifies only the endpoints of the line. The start of the line is the current position. That is, the line drawing service found in the Presentation Manager draws a line from the current position to the specified endpoint. The same principle applies to the service that draws a box. You simply call the box drawing function with the coordinates of the corner opposite the current position and the box is drawn using the current position and the specified opposite corner.

The reason that the Presentation Manager uses the current position approach is speed. Because each parameter in a call takes time to push onto the stack, the fewer parameters, the faster the call is executed. The most effective graphics are those that can be displayed very quickly. In many drawing situations, the next graphics event begins where the last one left off, making the display of graphical information very fast. Of course, the Presentation Manager contains a service that allows you to set the current position explicitly, should the need arise.

The screen coordinates for the graphics subsystem are the same as for the text routines: the lower left corner is 0,0. The maximum X and Y values are determined by the size of the window and, ultimately, by the resolution of the screen.

DRAWING LINES AND BOXES

The Presentation Manager supplies several graphics functions. However, we will explore only three of the most common: **GpiSetPel()**, **GpiLine()**, and **GpiBox()**. These services draw a point, line, and box, respectively. Their prototypes are shown here:

LONG APIENTRY GpiSetPel(HPS *p_space*, POINTL *loc*);

LONG APIENTRY GpiLine(HPS *p_space*, POINTL *loc*);

LONG APIENTRY GpiBox(HPS *p_space*, LONG *style*, PPOINTL *loc*,
                              LONG *horiz_round*, LONG *vert_round*);

Here, *p_space* is the handle of the presentation space being written to. All functions use the current foreground color to draw the object. For **GpiSetPel()**, the structure pointed to by *loc* contains the coordinates to the pel that will be written. The current position is unchanged by this service.

For **GpiLine()**, the structure pointed to by *loc* contains the endpoint of the desired line. The start of the line is the current position. After the call to **GpiLine()**, the current position is set to the end of the line specified by *loc*.

For **GpiBox()**, the structure pointed to by *loc* is the corner opposite the current position. Through these two corners a rectangle is drawn. The value of *style* determines whether the box is outlined, filled, or both. The valid values, along with their macro names, are shown here. The current position is unchanged by this service.

Macro Name	Value	Meaning
DRO_FILL	1L	Fill the box
DRO_OUTLINE	2L	Outline the box
DRO_OUTLINEFILL	3L	Fill and outline the box

Outlining and filling are done in the current drawing color. If any of these drawing functions are called using invalid coordinates, an error is returned.

SETTING THE CURRENT POSITION

To explicitly set the current position, use **GpiSetCurrentPosition()**, whose prototype is shown here:

BOOL APIENTRY GpiSetCurrentPosition(HPS *p_space*, PPOINTL *loc*);

Here, *p_space* is the handle of the presentation space, and the structure pointed to by *loc* contains the coordinates of the pel to make the current

position. If you specify an invalid coordinate, the service returns
FALSE/TRUE; it returns TRUE on success.

A SHORT GRAPHICS DEMO PROGRAM

The following program demonstrates the graphics services just discussed. The program provides services to draw blue lines and red boxes.
Of course, if you have a black and white monitor, you will only see black
lines and black boxes.

When the left mouse is pressed in the graphics example window, the
current position is recorded. When the button is released, a line is drawn
from the point the button was pressed to the point where the button was
released. The right button will draw the boxes. When the right button is
pressed, the location is recorded. When the button is released, a box is
drawn using the mouse press and mouse release as the positions of the
opposite corners of the box.

```
/* This program demonstrates some graphics services */

#define INCL_WIN
#define INCL_GPI

#include <os2.h>

MRESULT EXPENTRY window_func(HWND, ULONG, MPARAM, MPARAM);

char class[] = "MyClass";


main()
{
  HAB hand_ab;              /* anchor block */
  HMQ hand_mq;              /* message queue */
  HWND hand_frame;          /* frame */
  QMSG q_mess;              /* message queue */
  ULONG flFlags;            /* window frame definition */
  unsigned char class[] = "MyClass";  /* class name */

  /* define the frame contents */
  flFlags = FCF_TITLEBAR |    /* have a title bar */
            FCF_SIZEBORDER |  /* be a sizeable window */
            FCF_MINMAX |      /* have min and max buttons */
            FCF_SYSMENU |     /* include a system menu */
            FCF_VERTSCROLL |  /* vertical scroll bar */
```

```
                FCF_HORZSCROLL |    /* horizontal scroll bar */
                FCF_SHELLPOSITION; /* default size and location */

    hand_ab = WinInitialize(0);   /* get the anchor block */

    hand_mq = WinCreateMsgQueue(hand_ab, 0); /* start a queue */

    if(!WinRegisterClass(    /* register this window class */
                hand_ab,                /* anchor block */
                (PSZ) class,            /* class name */
                (PFNWP) window_func,    /* window function */
                CS_SIZEREDRAW,          /* window style */
                0))                     /* no storage */
        exit(1);

    hand_frame = WinCreateStdWindow(
                HWND_DESKTOP,/* window type */
                WS_VISIBLE,  /* frame style */
                &flFlags,    /* definitions */
                (PSZ)class,  /* client class */
                (PSZ)"Graphics Example",
                WS_VISIBLE,  /* client style */
                0,           /* resource modules */
                0,           /* resource identifier */
                NULL);       /* pointer to client handle */
    /* message loop */
    while(WinGetMsg(hand_ab, &q_mess, 0, 0, 0))
        WinDispatchMsg(hand_ab, &q_mess);

    /* Shut down the application window and queue */
    WinDestroyWindow(hand_frame);
    WinDestroyMsgQueue(hand_mq);
    WinTerminate(hand_ab);
}


/* This is the window function */
MRESULT EXPENTRY window_func(HWND handle, ULONG mess,
                            MPARAM parm1, MPARAM parm2)
{
static  HPS p_space;
        POINTL coords;

    switch(mess) {

        case WM_PAINT:
```

```
      /* initialize */
      p_space = WinBeginPaint(handle, 0, 0);
      GpiSetBackMix(p_space, BM_OVERPAINT);
      break;

   case WM_BUTTON1DOWN:
   case WM_BUTTON2DOWN:

      /* set the current location when either button is
pressed */
      coords.x = SHORT1FROMMP(parm1);
      coords.y = SHORT2FROMMP(parm1);
      GpiSetCurrentPosition(p_space, &coords);
      break;

   case WM_BUTTON1UP:

      /* when button is released, draw the line */
      coords.x = SHORT1FROMMP(parm1);
      coords.y = SHORT2FROMMP(parm1);
      GpiSetColor(p_space, CLR_BLUE);
      GpiLine(p_space, &coords);
      break;

   case WM_BUTTON2UP:

      /* when button is released, draw a filled box */
      coords.x = SHORT1FROMMP(parm1);
      coords.y = SHORT2FROMMP(parm1);
      GpiSetColor(p_space, CLR_RED);
      GpiBox(p_space, DRO_FILL, &coords, 0, 0);
      break;

   case WM_ERASEBACKGROUND:
      return (MRESULT)TRUE;

   case WM_CLOSE:

      /* end the paint session */
      WinEndPaint(handle);

   default:
      return WinDefWindowProc(handle, mess, parm1, parm2);
   }
```

```
    return (MRESULT)0;
}
```

You might find it interesting to change the drawing color or play with the various graphics functions available in the Presentation Manager. Figure 8-4 shows sample output from this program.

CONCLUDING THOUGHTS

While the chapters in this section introduce you to OS/2 Presentation Manager programming and provide a "quick start" to understanding the essential principles, they only scratch the surface of Presentation Manager programming. To become a truly effective Presentation Manager programmer, you will need to acquire several books on the topic and write a number of programs. Although the amount of time and effort required to learn Presentation Manager programming may be great, be persistent. Programming in the Presentation Manager can be a rewarding experience.

FIGURE 8-4

Sample Output From the Graphics Example

PART

THREE

Exploring the API

In this section, many of the core API services are discussed. Several of these services exist to help the programmer take full advantage of the power of OS/2. There are many processes that occur in the background, out of view from the user. These processes can exploit the power of OS/2. A solid understanding of the core services is important for several reasons, not the least of which is to provide support for such things as interprocess communication and dynamic link libraries.

Several example programs are included in the following chapters. Many of these examples are written without using the Presentation Manager, so as not to cloud the issue with overhead code. But all the concepts discussed in this section apply to Presentation Manager programs.

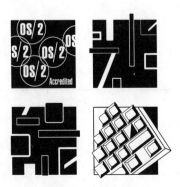

AN INTRODUCTION TO MULTITASKING

The preceding chapters in this book have introduced you to some very important OS/2 API services. This chapter introduces you to OS/2's multitasking capabilities, in which much of OS/2's power lies. So, if you are new to a multitasking environment, this is where the real fun begins!

Multitasking can dramatically increase the efficiency of most applications. For example, in a software development situation, multitasking allows you to edit, compile, and test simultaneously. In a word processor, part of the program can input text, while another part formats it for printing, and yet another part actually prints the document. The entire point of a multitasking, single-user system such as OS/2 is to allow the user to achieve greater throughput by reducing needless idle time to a minimum.

This chapter covers some of the basic OS/2 multitasking services. Chapter 10 builds upon the material presented here and discusses inter-process and inter-thread communication and synchronization issues. The time you invest in understanding the concepts presented here will really pay off later.

OS/2 implements multitasking on both a process and a thread level. Hence, OS/2 provides two sets of multitasking services: one to create and support processes, and one to create and support threads. This chapter looks at both, beginning with processes.

 Note: As you know from the preceding chapters, when you write OS/2 compatible programs, you generally do so using the Presentation Manager user interface. However, for the sake of simplicity, the examples shown in this section will not. The reason for this is to keep the examples as short and to the point as possible. As you know, even a minimal Presentation Manager program includes many lines of code that simply display a window on the screen. Instead, the examples in this chapter use normal C-like output, thus reducing their length. This prevents the point of the example from being "buried" inside dozens of lines of extraneous code. However, in real applications that you write for OS/2, you will want to use the Presentation Manager user interface, and there is nothing that prevents the API services discussed here from being used in a Presentation Manager program.

A WORD OF CAUTION

Before we begin, it is important to emphasize one important point from the start: you must never make any assumptions about the way multitasking routines will be executed by OS/2. You must never assume that one routine will execute before another, or that it will execute for a given number of milliseconds. For example, if you need one multitasked routine to execute before another, perhaps to initialize something, you must explicitly design this into your program. It is not acceptable to find, through experimentation, that one multitasked routine always executes before another and then use this "fact" in your program, for three important reasons:

▶ First, future versions of OS/2 may schedule tasks differently. (Actually, nothing in the OS/2 documentation says that you can assume anything about the way OS/2 schedules tasks even within the same version.)

▶ Second, at a future point, OS/2 may be designed to run on a multiple-CPU computer, thus allowing true concurrent execution of multiple tasks, in which two tasks that might have been sequenced in a single CPU system will be run simultaneously.

▶ Third, future versions of OS/2 may change the way time slices are allocated, causing the "first" routine to begin execution but not finish before the "second" begins.

 Remember: When you are dealing with multitasked routines, there is no valid way to experimentally determine which routine will be executed "first," unless you have explicitly provided for this in your program.

To write solid multitasked code, you must assume that all multitasked routines are actually executed simultaneously, whether in your current environment they are or not. Most of the troubles you will experience when you use multitasking in your programs will be caused by your forgetting this important point.

PROCESSES VERSUS THREADS

The distinction between a process and a thread was covered in Part One of this book, and is summarized here. A thread is a dispatchable piece of code. That is, the OS/2 scheduler executes threads. A thread does not own resources. A process consists of at least one thread and may have several. A process does own resources. Very loosely, a process is a program and a thread is somewhat like a subroutine in that program.

MULTIPLE PROCESSES

OS/2 has nine services, shown in Table 9-1, that are used to oversee the creation and operation of multiple processes. The process functions are

Service	Function
DosWaitChild()	Waits for a child process to terminate
DosExecPgm()	Loads and executes another process
DosExit()	Terminates the current process
DosExitList()	Registers functions to be called when the process terminates
DosGetInfoBlocks()	Returns a process's information block
DosSelectSession()	Makes specified session foreground
DosSetSession()	Sets a sessions status
DosStartSession()	Starts a new session
DosStopSession()	Stops a session

TABLE 9-1

OS/2 Session-based Services

available when you define INCL_DOSPROCESS before including the OS2.H header file. You can include all DOS function definitions by defining INCL_DOS before including the OS2.H header file, but this will include all DOS functions, structures, and variables, which carry a lot of overhead. As you can probably tell by looking at the table, OS/2 lets your program begin the concurrent execution of another program. The program that executes the second process is called the *parent*, and the program that the parent executes is called the *child*.

Most of the time when you want one program to cause the execution of another, related program, you will use **DosExecPgm()**. The main use for **DosStartSession()** is at system initialization, when you might want to begin several sessions automatically.

We will begin with a look at **DosExecPgm()** and its support functions.

STARTING A PROCESS

To execute a second process from a currently executing program, use **DosExecPgm()**, which has this prototype:

APIRET APIENTRY DosExecPgm(PCHAR *pObjname,*
LONG *cbObjname,*

ULONG *execFlag*,
PSZ *pArg*,
PSZ *pEnv*,
PRESULTCODES *pRes*,
PSZ *pName*);

The buffer pointed to by *pObjname* receives a message that helps to explain the cause of a failure to successfully execute the specified program, should one occur. The *cbObjname* parameter specifies the size of the fail buffer. The *execFlag* parameter specifies how the child program will be executed. It's most common values are listed in the following table.

Macro	Value	Meaning
EXEC_SYNC	0	Execute synchronously
EXEC_ASYNC	1	Execute asynchronously, discard termination code
EXEC_ASYNCRESULT	2	Execute asynchronously, save termination code
EXEC_TRACE	3	Execute in debug mode
EXEC_BACKGROUND	4	Detach child

When the child program is synchronously executed, the parent suspends execution until the child has terminated, at which time the parent resumes. In a DOS environment, this is the only way that one program can run another. However, in OS/2's multitasking environment, synchronous execution will seldom be used and is not of much interest. When the child is run asynchronously, both the parent and child execute concurrently. If the parent needs extensive information about how the child terminated, then you will want to call **DosExecPgm()** with the *execFlag* set to 2; if not, use the value 1. The debug mode is used for tracing. If you want to detach the child, use the value 4.

The parameters *pArg* and *pEnv* point, respectively, to arrays that hold any command line arguments and environment variables required by the child process. Either or both may be null. The array pointed to by *pArg* begins with the null terminated name of the program, followed by a double-null terminated list of the arguments. For example, if the child program's name is "TEST" and you want to pass it the argument "HELLO THERE", you would call **DosExecPgm()** with *args* pointing to this string:

Chapter 9

```
"TEST\0HELLO THERE\0\0"
```

The environment variables are passed to the child as null terminated strings with the last string being double-null terminated.

The structure pointed to by *pRes* receives information concerning the termination of the child process. The structure is defined like this:

```
typedef struct _RESULTCODES {
                            ULONG codeTerminate;
                            ULONG codeResult;
                            } RESULTCODES;
```

If the child is executed asynchronously, then *codeTerminate* holds the process identifier (PID) associated with the child process. For asynchronous execution, the *codeResult* field is not used. If the child is executed synchronously, *codeTerminate* will be 0 for normal termination, 1 for a hardware error, 2 for system trap, and 3 if the process was killed. For synchronous execution, *codeResult* holds the child's exit code.

Finally, the array pointed to by *pName* contains the drive, path, and name of the program to be executed.

As with all the API services, **DosExecPgm()** returns zero if successful and non-zero otherwise.

As a first example, this program first asynchronously executes a program called TEST.EXE and then begins printing to the screen from both the parent and child processes.

```
/* This program asynchronously executes a second process. */

#define INCL_DOSPROCESS
#include <os2.h>

main()
{
    CHAR pObjname[128];
    RESULTCODES result;

    if(DosExecPgm(pObjname, sizeof(pObjname), EXEC_ASYNC,
                NULL, NULL, &result, "TEST.EXE"))
            printf("\nERROR from DosExecPgm\n");

    printf("Hello from main!\n");
    DosSleep(25);
```

```
   printf("Hi, main again!!\n");

   DosExit(EXIT_PROCESS, 0);
}
```

Use this for the TEST.EXE program.

```
/* This is called from the parent process */

#define INCL_DOSPROCESS
#include <os2.h>

main()
{
   printf("Hello from test.\n");
   DosSleep(50);
   printf("Hi, test, again.\n");
}
```

When both programs are executing, you will see the series greetings displayed on the screen. Because of the difference in the **DosSleep()** parameter, the parent and child alternate printing to the screen. (You might want to try varying the sleep parameters to see the effect. This will give you insight into how the OS/2 scheduler works.) The ways to insure this are discussed in Chapter 10.

When the child begins executing, it inherits the parent's environment, including all open file handles (except those with the inheritance flag set to 0). The child can access these files without opening them. Of course, the parent's environment can be overridden or augmented by the contents of the environment array passed at the time of the **DosExecPgm()** call.

With a slight modification to the **DosExecPgm()** call in the parent program, the command line argument "Hi Child" can be passed to the TEST.EXE program, as shown here:

```
/* This program starts a process and passes an argument
   to the process it creates.
*/

#define INCL_DOSPROCESS
#include <os2.h>

main()
{
```

```
         CHAR pObjname[128];
         RESULTCODES Res;

         if(DosExecPgm(pObjname, sizeof(pObjname), EXEC_ASYNC,
                     "TEST\0Hi child\0\0",NULL,&Res,"TEST.EXE"))
                 printf("\nERROR from DosExecPgm\n");

         printf("Hello from main!\n");
         DosSleep(25);
         printf("Hi, main again!!\n");

         DosExit(EXIT_PROCESS, 0);
}
```

This version of TEST.EXE prints the argument before proceeding:

```
/* This is called from the parent process. */

#define INCL_DOSPROCESS
#include <os2.h>

main(int argc, char *argv[])
{
    printf("My parent passed me: %s %s\n",argv[1], argv[2]);
    printf("Hello from test.\n");
    DosSleep(50);
    printf("Hi, test, again.\n");
}
```

 Remember: (1) A parent can execute more than one child process, and (2) a child process can execute its own child processes.

WAITING FOR A PROCESS TO TERMINATE

It is not uncommon in multitasking environments for the parent process to wait, at some point, until an asynchronous child process has finished. For example, a database program may initiate a sort process and then continue processing user input. However, the parent will have to wait until the sort is complete before processing a print database request. Put another way, it is very common for a parent and an asynchronously executing child process to concurrently execute until some special event causes the parent to wait for the child to finish. This differs from simple synchronous execution, in which the parent and child never execute concurrently. To allow the parent to wait for a child, OS/2 includes the **DosWaitChild()** service, whose prototype is shown here:

```
APIRET APIENTRY DosWaitChild(ULONG action,
                             ULONG option,
                             PRESULTCODES pres,
                             PPID ppid,
                             PID pid);
```

The parameter specifies whether **DosWaitChild()** should wait for the termination of just the specified process, or of the specified process and all (if any) of its child processes. If *action* is 0 (DCWA_PROCESS), **DosWaitChild()** waits for the specified process only. If *action* is 1 (DCWA_PROCESSTREE), then **DosWaitChild()** waits for the specified process and any of its children.

The *option* parameter specifies whether **DosWaitChild()** will actually wait for the specified process to terminate or simply return immediately. If its value is 0 (DCWW_WAIT), it waits for the process to terminate. If it is 1 (DCWW_NOWAIT), it returns immediately with the result codes of a process that has already terminated. However, if the specified process is still executing when **DosWaitChild()** is called with the no-wait option, it returns an error.

The structure pointed to by *pres* is of type RESULTCODES and is the same as described earlier in the discussion of **DosExecPgm()**.

The variable pointed to by *ppid* will hold the process identifier PID of the terminating process as set by **DosWaitChild()**.

The *pid* parameter specifies the process identifier of the process to wait for. If it is 0, then the first child process to terminate causes a return, and the PID of this child is loaded into the *ppid* parameter. Otherwise, **DosWaitChild()** waits only for the specified process.

If the specified process does not exist, **DosWaitChild()** returns an error.

The following program executes the TEST.EXE program shown earlier and waits for it to end.

```
/* This program starts a process, then waits for it to exit.
*/

#define INCL_DOSPROCESS
#include <os2.h>
```

```
main()
{
    CHAR pObjname[128];
    RESULTCODES Res, waitRes;
    PID proc;

    if(DosExecPgm(pObjname, sizeof(pObjname), EXEC_ASYNC,
                "TEST\0Hi child\0\0",NULL,&Res,"TEST.EXE"))
            printf("\nERROR from DosExecPgm\n");

    DosWaitChild(DCWA_PROCESS, DCWW_WAIT, &waitRes,
                &proc, Res.codeTerminate);

    printf("Hello from main!\n");
    DosSleep(25);
    printf("Hi, main again!!\n");

    DosExit(EXIT_PROCESS, 0);
}
```

In this program, notice how the process identifier of TEST.EXE is first returned in the *Res.codeTerminate* field by **DosExecPgm()** and then used by **DosWaitChild()** to specify the specific process to be waited for.

It is important to understand that when **DosWaitChild()** is called using its wait mode, the calling process is suspended, thus freeing the CPU.

KILLING A PROCESS

The parent can terminate a child process. To understand the need for this, imagine that you have created a large relational database system. The main (parent) process includes all the user input and query functionality. However, to achieve uninterrupted use, you allocate such time-consuming tasks as printouts, sorting, mail-merges, and backups to separate child processes, which are executed only when needed. In such a system, it is very likely that, from time to time, you will need to terminate one or more child processes because they are no longer needed. To accomplish this task, OS/2 provides **DosKillProcess()**, which has this prototype:

APIRET APIENTRY DosKillProcess(ULONG *action*, PID *pid*);

Here, if the *action* parameter is 0 (DKP_PROCESSTREE), then the specified process plus all of its descendants (if any) are killed. If it is 1 (DKP_PRO-

CESS), then only the specified process is terminated. The *pid* parameter is the process ID for the process to be stopped.

DosKillProcess() returns zero if successful and returns non-zero if a failure occurs. One way it can fail is if the specified child process does not exist.

To see **DosKillProcess()** in action, try this program, which first executes the TEST.EXE program, waits 25 milliseconds, and then kills the child process before it can print any messages. When all works correctly, the message "child process terminated" is printed. If the child process has already terminated, when the parent tries to kill it with the **DosKillProcess()**, it fails, and the message "child process already terminated" appears. To see this message, increase the amount of time the parent process sleeps. Increasing the **DosSleep()** parameter to 225 will allow enough time for the child process to terminate before the parent process can issue the **DosKillProcess()** command.

```
/* This program starts a process, waits a bit,
   then terminates it with a kill command.
*/

#define INCL_DOSPROCESS
#include <os2.h>

main()
{
    CHAR pObjname[128];
    RESULTCODES Res;
    PID proc;

    if(DosExecPgm(pObjname, sizeof(pObjname), EXEC_ASYNC,
               "TEST\0Hi child\0\0",NULL,&Res,"TEST.EXE"))
           printf("\nERROR from DosExecPgm\n");

    printf("Hello from main!\n");
    DosSleep(25);

    if(DosKillProcess(DKP_PROCESSTREE, Res.codeTerminate))
           printf("child process already terminated\n");
    else
           printf("child process terminated\n");

    DosExit(EXIT_PROCESS, 0);
}
```

CREATING AN EXIT FUNCTION LIST

Since it is possible for a parent function to unexpectedly terminate a child process, it may be necessary to insure that the child has some means of dying a clean death. For example, you will want the child to flush any disk buffers and close all files. There may be special hardware devices that need to be reset, and it may even be appropriate to notify the user that the process is being killed. To allow the child to perform these tasks, a special list of functions is called whenever a process (child or parent) terminates. The functions that comprise this list are called *exit functions*. Collectively, they are referred to as the *exit function list*. OS/2 provides the **DosExitList()** service to support the exit function list. Its prototype is shown here:

APIRET APIENTRY DosExitList(ULONG *ordercode*,
PFNEXITLIST *pfn*);

The value of *ordercode* determines what **DosExitList()** does. The valid values are shown here:

Macro	Value	Meaning
EXLST_ADD	1	Add function to the exit list
EXLST_REMOVE	2	Remove function from the exit list
EXLST_EXIT	3	Exit current function, move to next

To add or remove a function from the list, you must pass a pointer to the function in the *pfn* parameter. The function must be declared as follows:

VOID APIENTRY func(ULONG *uiTermCode*);

The function will be passed a termination code, in the *uiTermCode* parameter, which will be one of the following values:

Macro	Value	Meaning
TC_EXIT	0	Normal termination
TC_HARDERROR	1	Unrecoverable error
TC_TRAP	2	System trap error (16-bit child)
TC_KILLPROCESS	3	Process was killed
TC_EXCEPTION	4	Exception error (32-bit child)

Your exit function can take different actions based upon the termination code, if so desired.

The basic approach to establishing an exit function is to first call **DosExitList()** to add the function to the list. At termination, the last thing your function must do is call **DosExitList()** with the *ordercode* parameter set to 3 (EXLST_EXIT), to cause OS/2 to move on to the next function in the list. If for some reason you want to remove a function that you previously added to the list, call **DosExitList()** with *ordercode* set to 2 (EXLST_REMOVE).

There is one very important thing to remember about an exit function: it cannot be terminated by OS/2. This means that your exit functions should be very short and never under any circumstances delay the termination of the process for more than a few milliseconds. Keep in mind that the environment surrounding the exit function is dying; it is imperative that your function do what it needs to do as quickly as possible. An incorrectly constructed exit function cannot crash OS/2, but it can make it impossible for OS/2 to complete its termination of the process, and thereby degrade system performance.

As a simple example, the following program puts the function **exfunc()** into the exit list and then prints 100 numbers. Upon termination, the **exfunc()** function is called, and it displays a message indicating that the process is terminating normally.

```
/* This program creates an exit function which is called
   when the program terminates.
*/

#define INCL_DOSPROCESS
#include <os2.h>

VOID APIENTRY exfunc(ULONG);

main()
{
  int i;

  DosExitList(EXLST_ADD, exfunc);
  for(i=0; i<100; i++)
    printf("%d ",i);

  DosExit(EXIT_PROCESS, 0);
}
```

```
VOID APIENTRY exfunc(ULONG ulTermCode)
{
    printf("\nProgram terminating with code: %d\n",
        ulTermCode);
    DosExitList(EXLST_EXIT, 0);
}
```

ERROR CHECKING

A wide variety of errors can occur when you create or manipulate processes. For example, in a given situation OS/2 may not be able to create a new process, because all process identifiers are already allocated. In your applications, it is important to watch for errors and take appropriate action should one occur.

CREATING NEW SESSIONS

When you used **DosExecPgm()** to start new processes, these new processes ran in the same session (sometimes called a *screen group*) as the parent. While this is very useful for related processes that interact with each other to form a unit, it is not very desirable when the processes are not related. For this reason, OS/2 allows you to start a process in its own session by using the **DosStartSession()** service, whose prototype is shown here:

APIRET APIENTRY DosStartSession(PSTARTDATA *psd*,
                                        PULONG *pidSession*,
                                        PPID *ppid*);

The structure pointed to by *psd* is defined like this:

```
typedef struct _STARTDATA
    {
        USHORT  Length;      /* size of this struct */
        USHORT  Related;     /* session relation */
        USHORT  FgBg;        /* foreground / background */
        USHORT  TraceOpt;    /* trace active flag */
        PSZ     PgmTitle;    /* session title */
        PSZ     PgmName;     /* program to execute */
```

```
PBYTE    PgmInputs;     /* command line arguments */
PBYTE    TermQ;         /* termination queue */
PBYTE    Environment;   /* environment to use */
USHORT   InheritOpt;    /* inherit the environment */
USHORT   SessionType;   /* one of five session types */
PSZ      IconFile;      /* named icon or null */
ULONG    PgmHandle;     /* used for window calls */
USHORT   PgmControl;    /* how to start program */
USHORT   InitXPos;      /* X pos, lower left corner */
USHORT   InitYPos;      /* Y pos, lower left corner */
USHORT   InitXSize;     /* length of X coordinate */
USHORT   InitYSize;     /* length of Y coordinate */
PSZ      ObjectBuffer;  /* fail buffer */
ULONG    ObjectBuffLen; /* buffer length*/
} STARTDATA;
```

The *Length* field must hold the length of the STARTDATA structure. If *Related* is 0, the new session is completely independent of the parent. If it is 1, the new session is a child of the parent. If *FgBg* is 0, the new session will become the foreground task; if it is 1, the new session becomes a background task. The new session can only become a foreground task if the parent is in the foreground when it creates the new session.

If *TraceOpt* is 0, the new session is not set up for tracing; if it is 1, the new session may be traced. The string pointed to by *PgmTile* is the name of the session and may be null. The string pointed to by *PgmName* is the name of the program that will begin running in the new session. The string pointed to by *PgmInputs* contains any command line arguments needed by the program and may be null. The string pointed to by *TermQ* is the name of the termination queue and may be null. (OS/2 queues will be discussed later in this book.)

Environment holds the current environment information. If the next field, *InheritOpt*, is set to 1, it causes the new session to inherit the current session's environment, including any open file handles.

The new session can be one of five types: full screen, windowed, Presentation Manager, DOS, or windowed DOS. The *SessionType* holds one of the five session types. The only restriction is that a DOS session cannot start another session. A custom icon can be specified in the *IconFile* field, and can be null, causing the default icon to be used. The *PgmHandle* is used to specify how the window is started: a setting of 2 will cause the window to be maximized on startup; setting this field to 1 will create a minimized window session.

The next four fields, *InitXPos, InitYPos, InitXSize,* and *InitYSize,* specify the starting location and the size of the new window being created. The last two fields hold additional message information passed back when the **DosStartSession()** call fails.

The *pidSession* parameter points to a variable that receives the session identifier when the call returns. The *ppid* parameter points to a variable that receives the process identifier of the process run in the newly created session.

The definitions required for using the session manager functions, structures, and variables are included when you define INCL_DOSSESMGR before including OS2.H in your program. You can see this define being used in the following sample program.

This program begins a new session called "beep session" and starts running the BEEP.EXE program. When you try this program, remember that you will need to have BEEP.EXE in the current working directory.

```
/* This program starts a new session called "beep session",
   and runs the program BEEP.EXE.
*/

#define INCL_DOSPROCESS
#define INCL_DOSSESMGR
#include <os2.h>

main()
{
    STARTDATA sdata;
    ULONG idSession;
    PID   pid;
    CHAR  buff[CCHMAXPATH];
    APIRET retCode;

    sdata.Length = sizeof(sdata);
    sdata.Related = 0;         /* no relation */
    sdata.FgBg = 0;            /* foreground session */
    sdata.TraceOpt = 0;        /* trace off */
    sdata.PgmTitle = "beep session";
    sdata.PgmName = "beep.exe";
    sdata.PgmInputs = NULL;  /* no arguments */
    sdata.TermQ = NULL;
    sdata.Environment = NULL;
    sdata.InheritOpt = 1;    /* inherit environment */
    sdata.SessionType = 0;   /* default session */
```

```
    sdata.IconFile = NULL;   /* no icon */
    sdata.PgmHandle = 0;
    sdata.PgmControl = 2;    /* window controls */
    sdata.InitXPos = 0;
    sdata.InitYPos = 0;
    sdata.InitXSize = 0;
    sdata.InitYSize = 0;
    sdata.ObjectBuffer = buff;
    sdata.ObjectBuffLen = sizeof(buff);

    retCode = DosStartSession(&sdata, &idSession, &pid);
    if(retCode != 0)
       printf("Error in DosStartSession\n");

    DosExit(EXIT_PROCESS, retCode);
}
```

Compile the following example program, name it BEEP.EXE, and place it in the current directory.

```
/* This program simply beeps. Name this program BEEP.EXE. */

#define INCL_DOSPROCESS
#include <os2.h>

main()
{
    DosExit(EXIT_PROCESS, DosBeep(600, 400));
}
```

In this program the new session is not a child of the parent, and it becomes the foreground task. It is advised to always check for errors, because in actual practice the call to **DosStartSession()** is susceptible to a wide variety of errors. For example, OS/2 may not be able to start another session, because all its session identifiers may be allocated.

If the program BEEP.EXE specified in the *PgmName* field of the STARTDATA structure is not found, the parent session will print the message "Error in DosStartSession".

SELECTING AND STOPPING A SESSION

If your program starts a child session, then your program can switch to that session using **DosSelectSession()**, whose prototype is shown here:

APIRET APIENTRY DosSelectSession(ULONG *idSession*);

Here, *idSession* is the session identification number of the session to switch to. The *idsession* value is obtained during the call to **DosStartSession()**. The second parameter to **DosstartSession()** is a pointer to a type ULONG, which is assigned the session identification number during the call.

You can only use **DosSelectSession()** to switch to a child session or back to the parent. You cannot select an independent session. To switch to the parent, call **DosSelectSession()** with *idSession* assigned a value of 0.

The parent session can stop a child session using the **DosStopSession()** service, which has this prototype:

APIRET APIENTRY DosStopSession(ULONG *scope*,
                               ULONG *idSession*);

If the *scope* parameter is 0 (STOP_SESSION_SPECIFIED), only the specified session is terminated. If it is 1 (STOP_SESSION_ALL), the specified session plus any children of that session are terminated. The *idSession* parameter holds the session identification code of the session to be terminated, and is only used when *scope* is set to STOP_SESSION_SPECIFIED; otherwise, it is ignored. **DosStopSession()** returns zero if no error occurs.

THREADS

The single most important thing to understand about OS/2's multitasking model is that it is thread (rather than process) based. A thread is the unit of code dispatched by the scheduler. All the programs you have seen up to this point have consisted of a single thread. That is, the entire program was one thread of execution. However, this need not always be the case, because OS/2 lets you, the programmer, define threads of execution within a program. This allows a single program to create concurrently executing routines which can, if used correctly, greatly enhance the efficiency of your program. In fact, OS/2 also allows you to set the priority of the threads within a program, so that you can choose what routines get the greatest access to the CPU. The thread-based services are listed in Table 9-2.

Service	Function
DosCreateThread()	Creates a thread of execution
DosResumeThread()	Restarts a suspended thread
DosSetPriority()	Sets a thread's priority
DosSuspendThread()	Suspends a thread's execution

TABLE 9-2

OS/2 Thread-based Services

In the first half of this chapter you saw how to create concurrently executing processes. While the multitasking of processes is a wonderful improvement over single-tasking and allows a number of divergent applications to share CPU time, it is not, generally speaking, the approach you should take when you want to multitask pieces of a single application. Instead, you should use multiple threads within the application.

Another important point about threads and processes is that each process can have up to 4095 separate threads, and there can be up to 4095 separate processes. You can use as many threads as you need (up to the maximum amount) in a single process.

Each thread inherits the environment of the process it is part of. This includes open files, virtual address space, and environmental strings. If one thread in a process opens a file, for example, other threads can use that file handle. All threads in a program share the same code and data segments, so access to global data and routines is unrestricted.

The thread that begins a process's execution is called either the *main thread* or *thread 1.* It is somewhat special, as you will soon see. There is always at least one thread running for each process. When the last thread dies, the process itself ends. A thread can either be running, not running, or blocked from running. Only one thread will be running on the system at any given moment.

Frankly, OS/2's thread-based multitasking system is one of its most exciting, and powerful, features.

CREATING THREADS

To create a thread of execution your program uses the **DosCreateThread()** service, whose prototype is shown here:

APIRET APIENTRY DosCreateThread(PTID *ptid*,
PFNTHREAD *pfn*,
ULONG *param*,
ULONG *flag*,
ULONG *cbStack*);

Here, *pfn* is a pointer to a function that is the entry point into the thread. The function must be declared as VOID with one ULONG parameter. The single ULONG parameter may be passed to the thread by *param*. You can control the execution of the thread with *flag*: if bit one is set to 0, execution begins immediately; but if the first bit is set to 1, execution of the thread is suspended until the application calls **DosResumeThread()**.

The size of the stack is specified by the *cbStack* parameter. Each thread uses its own stack. This region must be at least 512 bytes long, but you really should allow at least 2048, if you will be using any of the API services inside the thread.

Upon return from the call, *ptid* will point to the thread's ID number.

The following short program uses **DosCreateThread()** to create and execute two threads.

```
/* This program uses DosCreateThread to activate two
   concurrently executing threads.
*/

#define INCL_DOSPROCESS
#include <os2.h>

VOID APIENTRY thread1(ULONG);
VOID APIENTRY thread2(ULONG);

main()
{
   TID ptid;

   printf("This is the main thread.\n");
   printf("thread 1 beeps low, thread 2 beeps high.\n");

   DosCreateThread(&ptid, thread1, 0, 0, 4096);
   DosCreateThread(&ptid, thread2, 0, 0, 4096);

   DosSleep(1000);  /* wait for the children to finish */
   DosExit(EXIT_PROCESS, 0);
}
```

```
VOID APIENTRY thread1(ULONG unused)
{
   DosBeep(400, 400);
}

VOID APIENTRY thread2(ULONG unused)
{
   DosBeep(700, 700);
}
```

Each thread, including the main program thread, terminates when the end of the function is encountered. However, you can terminate a thread conditionally by calling **DosExit()**, whose prototype is shown here:

VOID APIENTRY DosExit(ULONG *action*, ULONG *result*);

If *action* is 0 (EXIT_THREAD), only the current thread is terminated. If it is 1 (EXIT_PROCESS), the entire process is killed. The value of *result* is passed to the calling process.

If the main thread terminates, it terminates the process, even if other threads in the process are still active. Keep this in mind when designing your multithread applications.

Frankly, there is a problem using **DosCreateThread()** directly with high-level languages. First, it is possible that not all high-level language library functions will be reentrant. If a library function is not reentrant, it cannot be called by two different threads at the same time without causing trouble. Although all the API services are reentrant, it is possible that language runtime libraries will not be. This is the reason that **DosBeep()** was used in the sample program rather than **printf()**. Most standard C libraries will not work with multiple threads. Second, because each thread has its own stack, a high-level language that performs runtime stack overflow checking will report false stack overflow errors. Generally, you can work around this problem by using a compiler option to turn off runtime stack checking. However, you will lose the advantage of runtime stack overflow checking.

WAITING FOR THREADS TO FINISH

Because the entire process dies when the main thread dies, it is important to keep the main thread alive until all desired program activity has finished. More generally, it is important for your program to know when the various threads of execution have either completed or are at least in a safe state, so that the program can terminate. Although Chapter 9 covers OS/2 inter-process and inter-thread communication and synchronization services, which provide a solution to this problem, we will still need a solution (if only temporarily) for our examples. The one shown here can safely be used in many applications, but should not be construed as a general solution. (The reasons for this will be made clear in Chapter 10.)

The approach and the examples developed here are designed to serve two purposes. First, they introduce the basic notion of thread synchronization and communication and will make the concept of the *semaphore*, OS/2's standard synchronization method, easier to understand and appreciate. Second, they serve as illustrations of some key multitasking concepts.

In general, when you need to wait until a thread finishes, you establish a flag which the thread sets when it is done executing. Another thread simply examines this flag to see if the other thread is executing or not. For example, you can rewrite the previous example so that it automatically terminates when both threads have terminated, as shown here:

```
/* This program uses DosCreateThread to activate two
   concurrently executing threads, and then waits until
   each thread has set a global flag.
*/

#define INCL_DOSPROCESS
#include <os2.h>

VOID APIENTRY thread1(ULONG);
VOID APIENTRY thread2(ULONG);

UCHAR flag1=0;
UCHAR flag2=0;

main()
{
    TID ptid;
    printf("This is the main thread.\n");
    printf("thread 1 beeps low, thread 2 beeps high.\n");

    DosCreateThread(&ptid, thread1, 0, 0, 4096);
    DosCreateThread(&ptid, thread2, 0, 0, 4096);

    while(flag1==0 || flag2==0) DosSleep(25);  /* wait */
```

```
    DosExit(EXIT_PROCESS, 0);
}

VOID APIENTRY thread1(ULONG unused)
{
    DosBeep(400, 400);
    flag1=1;
}

VOID APIENTRY thread2(ULONG unused)
{
    DosBeep(700, 700);
    flag2=1;
}
```

As you can see, the program waits for the other threads to terminate with this wait loop:

```
while(flag1 == 0 || flag2 == 0); /* wait */
```

However, this leaves much to be desired, for two reasons:

▶ First, it keeps the main thread active (and soaking up CPU time) while it is doing no productive work.

▶ Second, and perhaps more important, is that the **while** loop is compute-bound.

   Unlike waiting for a keypress, which causes the thread to suspend, the **while** loop keeps the thread in a constant state of being ready-to-run. Remember, a suspended thread demands no CPU cycles. However, a thread that is compute-bound is always able to run and is therefore given CPU cycles. This fact causes the program to run quite slowly, much slower than you might have thought ahead of time. In the next section, you will see a solution to this problem.

WAITING EFFICIENTLY

Throughout this book the **DosSleep()** service has been used without much explanation. Now is the time for you to learn how important **DosSleep()** can be. The **DosSleep()** function causes the thread that calls it to suspend for a specified number of milliseconds. Keep in mind that **DosSleep()** is not simply a time-delay loop, which would eat up CPU time.

Instead, it actually instructs the OS/2 scheduler to suspend the calling thread for the specified time.

The central issue here is that **DosSleep()** is not simply a delay function. Instead, its careful use allows you to increase the efficiency of your applications. Any time that your program enters a polling loop that is not extremely time-critical, you should insert a call to **DosSleep()** so that other threads can have more CPU cycles.

THREAD PRIORITIES

As stated in Part One, OS/2 has four categories of execution priorities: idle, regular, foreground, and time-critical. Within each category, there are 32 priority levels, 0 through 31. By default all threads within a process have the same priority: regular, level 0. However, you can alter a thread's priority using the **DosSetPriority()** service, which has this prototype:

```
APIRET APIENTRY DosSetPriority(ULONG scope,
                               ULONG class,
                               LONG delta,
                               ULONG PorTid);
```

If the *scope* parameter is equal to 0 (PRTYS_PROCESS), then all the threads within the calling process will have their priority altered. If *scope* is 1 (PRTYS_PROCESSTREE), then all the threads in the calling process plus any child processes are affected. If *scope* is 2 (PRTY_THREAD), then only the specified thread's priority is changed.

The *class* parameter determines which priority class the specified thread or threads will become. It can take the following values:

Macro	Value	Priority Class
PRTYC_NCHANGE	0	No change
PRTYC_IDLETIME	1	Idle
PRTYC_REGULAR	2	Regular
PRTYC_TIMECRITICAL	3	Time-critical
PRTYC_FOREGROUNDSERVER	4	Foreground task

The *delta* parameter is a signed integer in the range -31 to 31, which will be added to the current priority setting. For example, if *delta* is 5 and the current priority setting is 7, then the new priority, after the call, will be 12.

The *PorTid* parameter specifies the process or thread that will have its priority changed.

You can find out a thread's priority using the **DosGetPriority()** service, which has this prototype:

APIRET APIENTRY DosGetInfoBlocks(PTIB *pptib,
                                            PPIB *pppib);

A call to **DosGetInfoBlocks()** will fill the *pptib* parameter with the information pertaining to the current thread, and fill the *pppib* parameter with the information pertaining to the current process. This information is used in calls to **DosSetPriority()** to identify and change the priority of threads and/or processes.

SUSPENDING THREADS

A thread's execution can be suspended using **DosSuspendThread()**, which has this prototype:

APIRET APIENTRY DosSuspendThread(TID *tid*);

Here, *tid* is the thread identifier of the thread to be suspended. When a thread is suspended, the scheduler does not grant it access to the CPU. You can only suspend threads that are within the same process as the **DosSuspendThread()** call.

A thread suspended by **DosSuspendThread()** stays suspended until it is restarted by a call to **DosResumeThread()**, which has this prototype:

APIRET APIENTRY DosResumeThread(TID *tid*);

Here, *tid* is the thread's identifier. **DosResumeThread()** can only restart a thread that was previously stopped by a call to **DosSuspendThread()**.

To see how these services work, try this program, in which the first thread alternately stops and restarts the second thread each time through its main loop. The second thread simply counts numbers until the first thread terminates.

```
/* This program uses DosCreateThread() to activate two
   concurrently executing threads, and then illustrates
```

```
        the use of DosSuspendThread() and DosResumeThread().
*/

#define INCL_DOSPROCESS
#include <os2.h>

VOID APIENTRY thread1(ULONG);
VOID APIENTRY thread2(ULONG);

CHAR flag1=0;
CHAR flag2=0;

TID tid1, tid2;

main()
{
   printf("This is the main thread.\n");

   DosCreateThread(&tid1, thread1, 0, 0, 4096);
   DosCreateThread(&tid2, thread2, 0, 0, 4096);

   while(flag1==0 || flag2==0) DosSleep(25);  /* wait */

   DosExit(EXIT_PROCESS, 0);
}

VOID APIENTRY thread1(ULONG unused)
{
   int i;
   char flag;

   flag = 0;
   DosSleep(1000);  /* allow time for thread 2 to start */
   for(i=0; i<100; i++)
   { /* loop, each time either suspend or restart thread 2 */
     printf("Thread 1 (%d) - ", i);
     flag = !flag;
     if(flag != 0)
     {
        if(DosSuspendThread(tid2) != 0)
           printf("Error in suspending thread\n");
        else
           printf("suspending thread 2 \n");
     }
     else
```

```
      {
         if(DosResumeThread(tid2) != 0)
            printf("Error in restarting thread\n");
         else
            printf("restarting thread 2 \n");
      }
   }
   flag1 = 1; /* set flag to allow parent to terminate. */
}

VOID APIENTRY thread2(ULONG unused)
{
   int i;
   /* loop and wait, see how far it gets */
   for(i=0; i<30000 && flag1==0; i++)
      DosSleep(10);
   printf("thread 2 completed %d loops. \n", i);

   flag2 = 1;  /* set flag to allow parent to terminate. */
}
```

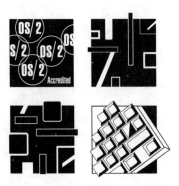

C H A P T E R

10

SERIALIZATION AND INTER-PROCESS COMMUNICATION

Now that you know the basics of OS/2's multitasking capabilities, it is time to learn about some important concepts and API services that allow you to bring multiply-executing processes and threads under control. As you will see in this chapter, there are two major issues that arise in a multitasking environment which must be addressed. First, there must be some way to serialize access to certain resources, so that only one task has access to the resource at any one time. Second, there must be some way for one process to communicate with another. The purpose of this chapter is to explore OS/2's solutions to these problems.

THE SERIALIZATION PROBLEM

OS/2 must provide special services that allow access to a shared resource to be serialized, because without help from the operating system, there is no way for one program (or thread) to know that it has sole access to a resource. To understand this, imagine that you are writing programs for a multitasking operating system that does not provide any serialization support. Further, imagine that you have two multiply-executing processes, A and B, both of which, from time to time, require access to some resource R (such as a disk drive) that must only be accessed by one task at a time. As a means of preventing one program from accessing R while the other is using it, you try the following solution. First, you establish a variable called **flag**, that can be accessed by both programs. Your programs initialize **flag** to 0. Next, before each piece of code that accesses R, you wait for the flag to be cleared (0), then you set the flag, access R, and finally clear the flag. That is, before either program accesses R, it executes this piece of code:

```
while(flag) ; /* wait for flag to be zero */
flag = 1;     /* set flag so another process knows
                 that you are using resource R */

/* code which accesses resource R */

flag = 0;     /* clear the flag. */
```

The idea behind this code is that neither process will access R if **flag** is set. Conceptually, this approach is in the spirit of the correct solution. However, in actual fact it leaves much to be desired for one simple reason: it won't always work! Let's see why.

Using the code just given, it is possible for both processes to access R at the same time. The **while** loop is, in essence, performing repeated load and compare instructions on **flag** or, in other words, it is testing the flag's value. The next line of code sets the flag's value. The trouble is that it is possible for these two operations to be performed in two separate time slices. Between the two time slices, the value of **flag** might have been changed by a different process, thus allowing R to be accessed by both processes at the same time. To understand this, imagine that process A enters the **while** loop and finds that **flag** is 0, which is the green light to access R. However, before it can set **flag** to 1, its time slice expires and process B resumes execution. If B executes its **while**, it too will find that **flag** is not set and assume that it is safe to access R. However, when A resumes it will also begin accessing R. The crucial point of the problem is that the testing of **flag** and the setting of **flag** do not comprise one uninterrupted operation. Rather, as just illustrated, they can be separated by a time slice of the other process. No matter how you try, there is no way, using only application-level code, that you can absolutely guarantee that one and only one process will access R at one time.

The solution to the serialization problem is as elegant as it is simple. The operating system, in this case OS/2, provides a routine that in one uninterrupted operation, tests and, if possible, sets a flag. In the language of operating systems engineers, this is called a *test and set* operation. For historical reasons, the flags used to control serialization are called *semaphores*. The OS/2 services that allow you to use them are discussed in the next section.

OS/2 SEMAPHORES

OS/2 provides twenty services that are used to create and access semaphores. These functions are shown in Table 10-1. The semaphore services are broken down into three major categories: event semaphores, mutex (mutual exclusion) semaphores, and muxwait (multiple wait) semaphores. The most important use of these services is to allow separate processes or threads to synchronize their activity. As described in the previous section, one important use of semaphores is to control access to a shared resource. However, they have other uses, such as allowing one task to signal another that an event has occurred.

CHOOSING THE RIGHT SEMAPHORE

OS/2 lets you use semaphores to synchronize the actions of threads within a process or the actions of separate processes. To this end, OS/2 supports three different types of semaphores: *event*, *mutex*, and *muxwait*.

The event semaphore is used by threads in a process to signal other threads within this and other processes that a particular event has occurred, such as the allocation of a block of memory. One thread may want to write to a block of memory, but must first wait for another thread to allocate the memory.

A mutex semaphore is used when you must limit activity between two or more threads or processes. Using a mutex semaphore, only one thread is allowed to execute at any given time. This type of semaphore is used when threads or processes are sharing a resource that demands exclusive access. A good example of this is when two threads are writing to the same file.

The muxwait semaphore is the compound semaphore. This type of semaphore allows a process or thread to wait for one or all of a group of semaphores to be either cleared or posted. A group of semaphores may contain up to 64 event or mutex semaphores, but event and mutex semaphores cannot be mixed within the same muxwait semaphore.

Service	Function
DosCreateEventSem()	Create an event semaphore
DosCreateMutexSem()	Create a mutex semaphore
DosCreateMuxSem()	Create a muxwait semaphore
DosOpenEventSem()	Open an event semaphore
DosOpenMutexSem()	Open a mutex semaphore
DosOpenMuxSem()	Open a muxwait semaphore
DosCloseEventSem()	Close an event semaphore
DosCloseMutexSem()	Close a mutex semaphore
DosCloseMuxSem()	Close a muxwait semaphore
DosQueryEventSem()	Request semaphore posting count
DosQueryMutexSem()	Request owner information
DosQueryMuxWaitSem()	Request semaphore records
DosWaitEventSem()	Wait for an event semaphore
DosRequestMutexSem()	Request a mutex semaphore
DosWaitMuxWaitSem()	Wait for a muxwait semaphore
DosResetEventSem()	Reset an event semaphore
DosReleaseMutexSem()	Release a mutex semaphore
DosAddMuxWaitSem()	Add a semaphore to the list
DosDeleteMuxWaitSem()	Remove a semaphore from the list
DosPostEventSem()	Post an event semaphore

TABLE 10-1

The OS/2 Semaphore Services

EVENT SEMAPHORES

One of the first things you learn about the OS/2 semaphore API functions is that you can't use just one! The semaphore routines work in conjunction with each other, so you need to learn about a few before any examples can be developed.

To use an event semaphore, first create a semaphore using the **DosCreateEventSem()** service, which has this prototype:

```
APIRET APIENTRY DosCreateEventSem(PSZ name,
                                  PHEV handle,
                                  ULONG flags,
                                  BOOL32 init);
```

Here, *name* is a pointer to a string that is the name of the semaphore. This string must have the prefix "\SEM32\". The parameter *handle* is a pointer to the handle of the semaphore. A list of attributes describing the semaphore is kept in *flags*, and the initial state of the semaphore (set or cleared) is put into *init*.

To cause a thread to suspend execution until a specified semaphore is posted, use **DosWaitEventSem()**, whose prototype is shown here:

```
APIRET APIENTRY DosWaitEventSem (HEV handle,
                                 ULONG timeout);
```

The *handle* parameter contains the handle of the event semaphore to wait for. The *timeout* parameter determines how long, in milliseconds, the calling thread will suspend if the semaphore is not cleared first. If the value of *timeout* is -1 (SEM_INDEFINITE_WAIT), the service will wait indefinitely.

To post a semaphore, use **DosPostEventSem()**, whose prototype is shown here:

```
APIRET APIENTRY DosPostEventSem(HEV handle);
```

The semaphore to be posted is identified by the semaphore handle stored in the parameter *handle*. The posting of a semaphore signals other threads that they may continue execution.

The next few sections show how to use these services to synchronize program activity.

AN EVENT SEMAPHORE EXAMPLE

As you may recall from the previous chapter, one trouble with multi-thread programs is that the main thread must stay alive and wait for the other threads in the process to terminate. In that chapter a temporary solution was offered which involved the main thread looping while it waited for flags to be set by the other threads. It was pointed out that although this solution worked in the specific situation, it should not be generalized. As you should know by now, a major problem with this solution is that it wastes CPU cycles. A better solution is to use event semaphores, because when a thread waits for a semaphore, it suspends until that semaphore is cleared. When the thread is suspended, it does not consume any CPU cycles.

The following program uses event semaphores to signal the termination of two threads.

```
/* The main program thread waits for two event semaphores
   to be posted from two different threads before terminating.
*/

#define INCL_DOSPROCESS
#define INCL_DOSSEMAPHORES

#include <os2.h>
#include <stdio.h>
#include <string.h>

VOID EXPENTRY thread1(ULONG);
VOID EXPENTRY thread2(ULONG);

HEV handle1;
HEV handle2;
UCHAR sem1[16];
UCHAR sem2[16];
TID tid1;
TID tid2;

main()
{
    printf("This is the main thread.\n");
    printf("thread 1 beeps low, thread 2 beeps high.\n");

    /* Create two event semaphores, initially set */
    strcpy(sem1, "\\SEM32\\SEM1");
```

```
   strcpy(sem2, "\\SEM32\\SEM2");
   DosCreateEventSem(sem1, &handle1, 0, 0);
   DosCreateEventSem(sem2, &handle2, 0, 0);

   /* Start two threads */
   DosCreateThread(&tid1, thread1, 0, 0, 4096);
   DosCreateThread(&tid2, thread2, 0, 0, 4096);

   /* Wait for the second semaphores to be posted. */
   DosWaitEventSem(handle2, SEM_INDEFINITE_WAIT);

   DosExit(EXIT_PROCESS, 0);
}


VOID EXPENTRY thread1(ULONG unused)
{
   DosBeep(400, 400);

   /* Post an event for sem1 */
   DosPostEventSem(handle1);
}


VOID EXPENTRY thread2(ULONG unused)
{
   /* Wait for the first thread to finish. */
   DosWaitEventSem(handle1, SEM_INDEFINITE_WAIT);
   DosBeep(700, 700);

   /* Post an event for sem2 */
   DosPostEventSem(handle2);
}
```

The program establishes two event semaphores, **sem1** and **sem2**. The main thread creates the semaphores before creating the child threads. Next, the program creates the child threads and waits for the semaphores to be posted by the child threads.

You might find it interesting to try a time-out value in place of SEM_INDEFINITE_WAIT, such as 200, to see the effect. The program will run for a short while and then terminate when the time-out limit is reached. Given a short enough value in *timeout*, the child threads may not have time to beep before the process exits.

Remember: any thread within the same process can directly access an event semaphore. If the thread is in a different process, the desired semaphore must first be opened using the **DosOpenEventSem()** function, the prototype of which is shown here:

APIRET APIENTRY DosOpenEventSem(PSZ *name*, PHEV *handle*);

All that is needed to open a semaphore that was created in another process is the *name* of the semaphore. When opening a semaphore by name, set the *handle* parameter to 0. For example, you can access **sem1** of the previous program by opening the event semaphore from a different process, as shown in the following code fragment:

```
{
  HEV handle;
  DosOpenEventSem("\\SEM32\\sem1", &handle);

  /* wait for thread1 of the other process to finish */
  DosWaitEventSem(handle, SEM_INDEFINITE_WAIT);
    .
    .
    .
}
```

MUTEX SEMAPHORES

As was discussed at the beginning of this chapter, one of the key aspects of semaphore usage is that some means of testing and setting a semaphore in one uninterrupted operation must be provided. In the examples given so far, this operation was not needed, because the semaphores simply signaled the conclusion of some event. However, to use a semaphore to serialize access to a shared resource, there must be a way for your program to wait until a semaphore is cleared and then set the semaphore in one operation. A mutex semaphore is considered cleared if it is unowned, and set if it is owned. Owned means that nobody else can use the resource until it is released; unowned means that the resource is free to be accessed by another thread or process.

When you need to synchronize access to a shared resource between two or more mutually exclusive threads or processes, an application can use a mutex semaphore. To create a mutex semaphore, call **DosCreate-MutexSem()**, which has this prototype:

> APIRET APIENTRY DosCreateMutexSem(PSZ *name*,
> PHMTX *handle*,
> ULONG *flags*,
> BOOL32 *init*);

All of the parameters are similar to those in the **DosCreateEventSem()** API function described in the previous section. The *name* parameter is a null terminated string naming the semaphore, and must be prefixed by "\SEM32\". The handle of the semaphore will be returned in *handle*. The *flags* parameter sets the attributes, and the *init* parameter sets the initial state of the semaphore, in this case, *owned* or *unowned.*

After creating a mutex semaphore, ownership can be requested and released by different threads and processes. To request ownership of a mutex semaphore, use the **DosRequestMutexSem()** function. The prototype is shown here:

> APIRET APIENTRY DosRequestMutexSem(HMTX *handle*,
> ULONG *timeout*);

Here, *handle* is the semaphore handle, and *timeout* is the amount of time in milliseconds to wait for the semaphore. Requesting a mutex semaphore is much like waiting for an event semaphore, but the difference is that a mutex semaphore is owned by only one thread or process at a time, even if more than one thread or process is waiting for the semaphore.

After finishing with the mutually exclusive access, the semaphore should be released, so that other threads or processes waiting for the semaphore can have access to the resource being controlled by the semaphore. To release a mutex semaphore, the **DosReleaseMutexSem()** function is called. The prototype is shown here:

> APIRET APIENTRY DosReleaseMutexSem(HMTX *handle*);

The parameter *handle* is the handle of the semaphore to be released.

A MUTEX SEMAPHORE EXAMPLE

The following program creates a mutex semaphore called **sem1** and executes two child threads that will treat the **DosBeep()** function as a

shared resource, using the mutex semaphore to call the function synchronously. The main thread waits for both child processes to end by also
requesting access to the mutex semaphore. The child processes request use
of the shared resource by requesting ownership of the mutex semaphore.

It is **DosRequestMutexSem()** that enables a program to sequence
access to a shared resource. The basic method of operation is to put a call
to **DosRequestMutexSem()** at the beginning of any code that accesses a
shared resource. This way, the code will only execute when it has
control of the resource. At the end of this code, put a call to
DosReleaseMutexSem() to release the semaphore. The code that lies
between the call to **DosRequestMutexSem()** and **DosReleaseMutex-
Sem()** is often referred to as a *critical section*. This general approach
is shown here:

```
/* This program creates two threads which will treat the
   DosBeep() function as a shared resource by using a mutex
   semaphore. The main thread will use the same mutex
   semaphore to wait for the child threads to end.
*/

#define INCL_DOSPROCESS
#define INCL_DOSSEMAPHORES

#include <os2.h>
#include <stdio.h>
#include <string.h>

VOID EXPENTRY thread1(ULONG);
VOID EXPENTRY thread2(ULONG);

HMTX handle1;
UCHAR sem1[16];
TID tid;

main()
{

    /* Create a mutex semaphores, initially set */
    strcpy(sem1, "\\SEM32\\SEM1");
    DosCreateMutexSem(sem1, &handle1, 0, 0);

    /* Start two threads */
    DosCreateThread(&tid, thread1, 0, 0, 4096);
```

```
   DosCreateThread(&tid, thread2, 0, 0, 4096);

   printf("This is the main thread.\n");
   printf("thread 1 beeps low, thread 2 beeps high.\n");
   printf("The child threads are running, wait.\n");

   /* Wait for the mutex semaphore. */
   DosRequestMutexSem(handle1, SEM_INDEFINITE_WAIT);

   /* Release the mutex semaphore. */
   DosReleaseMutexSem(handle1);

   DosExit(EXIT_PROCESS, 0);
}

VOID EXPENTRY thread1(ULONG unused)
{
   /* Wait for the mutex semaphore. */
   DosRequestMutexSem(handle1, SEM_INDEFINITE_WAIT);

   DosBeep(400, 400);

   /* Release the mutex semaphore. */
   DosReleaseMutexSem(handle1);
}

VOID EXPENTRY thread2(ULONG unused)
{
   /* Wait for the mutex semaphore. */
   DosRequestMutexSem(handle1, SEM_INDEFINITE_WAIT);
   DosBeep(700, 700);

   /* Release the mutex semaphore. */
   DosReleaseMutexSem(handle1);
}
```

A process that creates a semaphore is said to own it. When the process that owns a semaphore terminates, the semaphore is automatically closed. However, your program can explicitly close a semaphore. To close a mutex semaphore, use the API function **DosCloseMutexSem()**. Its prototype is shown here:

APIRET APIENTRY DosCloseMutexSem(HMTX *handle*);

Here, *handle* is the handle of the semaphore that is to be closed. There are also similar functions to close event semaphores and muxwait semaphores. All of the close functions take one parameter: the handle to the semaphore.

As with event semaphores, for a second process to access a mutex semaphore it must first open it using **DosOpenMutexSem()**, which has this prototype:

APIRET APIENTRY DosOpenMutexSem(PSZ *name*,
                                                    PHMTX *handle*);

The parameters are the same as in the event semaphore: *name* is the name of the semaphore, and *handle* will contain the handle of the opened semaphore.

MUXWAIT SEMAPHORES

Now that you know how the two basic types of semaphores are maintained, it is time to see how to use combinations of semaphores to serialize access to a shared resource. The example that we will develop illustrates a very common situation found in multitasking programs: one task produces something that a second task consumes. This is often called a *producer-consumer* relationship. The key problem in tasks that have this relationship is that the consumer must wait until the producer has finished producing whatever it is that it produces before the consumer takes it. You do not want the consumer taking a half-created object. Serialization of producer and consumer tasks is achieved through the use of semaphores.

To accomplish complex synchronization, OS/2 provides the muxwait semaphores. These semaphores allow you to combine one or more event or mutex semaphores into one semaphore. This one semaphore can be used to wait for one member of a list of semaphores, or to wait for all of the semaphores on the list. This makes the muxwait semaphores very powerful and flexible.

To create a muxwait semaphore, the **DosCreateMuxWaitSem()** function is used. The prototype is shown here:

```
APIRET APIENTRY DosCreateMuxWaitSem(PSZ name,
                                    PHMUX handle,
                                    ULONG count,
                                    PSEMRECORD rec,
                                    ULONG flags);
```

Here, the *name* and *handle* parameters are similar to those in the other semaphore create calls. That is, *name* is a string that holds the name of the semaphore, and *handle* holds the handle of the semaphore. The third parameter, *count*, holds the number of entries in *rec*, which is a pointer to an array of semaphore records. The *flags* parameter specifies the attributes of the semaphore. If *flags* is initialized to DCMW_WAIT_ANY, then the muxwait semaphore is cleared whenever any one of the event semaphores in the list are posted or any one of the mutex semaphores in the list are released. If *flags* is initialized to DCMW_WAIT_ALL, then all of the event semaphores in the list need to be posted, or all of the mutex semaphores in the list need to be cleared, for the muxwait semaphore to clear.

    After the creation of a muxwait semaphore, a program calls **DosWaitMuxWaitSem()** to wait (if necessary) for the specified semaphores to be cleared or posted. The prototype for this function is shown here:

```
APIRET APIENTRY DosWaitMuxWaitSem(HMUX handle,
                                  ULONG timeout,
                                  PULONG user);
```

Here, *handle* is the handle of the muxwait semaphore to wait for, and *timeout* is the number of milliseconds to wait. The last parameter, *user*, will contain the handle of a semaphore. The semaphore handle that *user* contains is dependent on the type of muxwait semaphore that was created. If the muxwait semaphore was waiting for any one of the listed semaphores, then the handle of the first semaphore to be released or posted will be returned in *user*. If the semaphore was designated to wait for all of the semaphores, then the handle of the last semaphore to get posted or released is returned in *user*.

A MUXWAIT SEMAPHORE EXAMPLE

    To illustrate the use of a muxwait semaphore, a producer-consumer situation will be developed in a short program that creates two threads called, appropriately, **producer** and **consumer**. The producer will create a string in two steps. The central issue here is that the memory storing the string is a shared resource, and we want to insure that only one task at a time is accessing it.

The program shown here uses two event semaphores called **sem1** and **sem2** to control access to an array. The two semaphores will be combined into a muxwait semaphore to control access to the string until it is complete.

```c
/* This program creates two event semaphores which will
   control the building and printing of a string. The
   semaphores are used separately and together in a muxwait
   semaphore. The main thread will use the muxwait semaphore
   to wait for the child threads to build a string.
*/

#define INCL_DOSPROCESS
#define INCL_DOSSEMAPHORES

#include <os2.h>
#include <stdio.h>
#include <string.h>

VOID EXPENTRY thread1(ULONG);
VOID EXPENTRY thread2(ULONG);

HEV handle1;
HEV handle2;
HMUX handle3;
UCHAR sem1[16];
UCHAR sem2[16];
UCHAR sem3[16];
SEMRECORD rec[2];
ULONG user;
UCHAR string[32];
TID tid;

main()
{
    /* Create a two event semaphores, initially set */
    strcpy(sem1, "\\SEM32\\SEM1");
    strcpy(sem2, "\\SEM32\\SEM2");
    DosCreateEventSem(sem1, &handle1, 0, 0);
    DosCreateEventSem(sem2, &handle2, 0, 0);
```

```
   /* Create a muxwait semaphore. */
   strcpy(sem3, "\\SEM32\\SEM3");
   rec[0].hsemCur = (PULONG) handle1;
   rec[1].hsemCur = (PULONG) handle2;
   DosCreateMuxWaitSem(sem3, &handle3, 2,
                       rec, DCMW_WAIT_ALL);

   /* Start two threads */
   DosCreateThread(&tid, thread1, 0, 0, 4096);
   DosCreateThread(&tid, thread2, 0, 0, 4096);

   /* Wait for the mutex semaphore. */
   DosWaitMuxWaitSem(handle3, SEM_INDEFINITE_WAIT, &user);

   printf("%s\n", string);

   DosExit(EXIT_PROCESS, 0);
}


VOID EXPENTRY thread1(ULONG unused)
{
   /* build first part of the string */
   strcpy(string, "Hello, ");

   /* Post the first event semaphore. */
   DosPostEventSem(handle1);
}

VOID EXPENTRY thread2(ULONG unused)
{
   /* Wait for the first event semaphore. */
   DosWaitEventSem(handle1, SEM_INDEFINITE_WAIT);

   /* Build the second part of the string */
   strcat(string, "Semaphores");
   /* Post the second event semaphore. */
   DosPostEventSem(handle2);
}
```

In this simple example, no serious harm will result if access to the shared resource is not serialized. However, in almost all real-world applications, lack of serialization will spell disaster. For example, failure to correctly serialize access to the printer will cause the output of several tasks to be intermixed.

SYNCHRONIZING CRITICAL SECTIONS OF CODE

OS/2 provides a second method of synchronizing multiple threads within a single process that differs from semaphores. In this second approach, your program temporarily halts the execution of all but one thread within the process, thus preventing a shared resource from being accessed by two different threads at the same time. The OS/2 services **DosEnterCritSec()** and **DosExitCritSec()** are used to stop and restart, respectively, all threads in a process except the one that calls these services. Their prototypes are shown here.

APIRET APIENTRY DosEnterCritSec(VOID);

APIRET APIENTRY DosExitCritSec(VOID);

Neither service takes a parameter.

The theory behind these services is that there is a (typically) short critical section of code that accesses some shared resource. To insure that the critical section is safe from interruption, **DosEnterCritSec()** is called at the beginning of the code, suspending all other threads. When the critical section has ended, **DosExitCritSec()** is called, restarting all other threads. This general approach is shown here:

```
DosEnterCritSec();

/* critical section code is put here */

DosExitCritSec();
```

Keep in mind that there can be several places in your program where **DosEnterCritSec()** is called. Because it suspends the execution of all threads, except the caller, there is no chance that a second thread will call **DosEnterCritSec()** when the first is in a critical section.

This program shows how **DosEnterCritSec()** and **DosExitCritSec()** work. Here, **thread1** suspends the execution of **thread2** until it has completed. This has the effect, in this situation, of serializing the execution of **thread1** and **thread2**, and the advantages of multitasking are lost.

```
/* This program demonstrates the DosEnterCritSec() and
   DosExitCritSec() services. Thread1 will complete before
```

```
   Thread2, because Thread1 halts the execution of the other
   threads in the program.
*/

#define INCL_DOSPROCESS
#define INCL_DOSSEMAPHORES

#include <os2.h>
#include <stdio.h>
#include <string.h>

VOID EXPENTRY thread1(ULONG);
VOID EXPENTRY thread2(ULONG);

HEV handle1;
HEV handle2;
HMUX handle3;
UCHAR sem1[16];
UCHAR sem2[16];
UCHAR sem3[16];
SEMRECORD rec[2];
ULONG user;
TID tid;

main()
{
   /* Create a two event semaphores, initially set */
   strcpy(sem1, "\\SEM32\\SEM1");
   strcpy(sem2, "\\SEM32\\SEM2");
   DosCreateEventSem(sem1, &handle1, 0, 0);
   DosCreateEventSem(sem2, &handle2, 0, 0);

   /* Create a muxwait semaphore. */
   strcpy(sem3, "\\SEM32\\SEM3");
   rec[0].hsemCur = (PULONG) handle1;
   rec[1].hsemCur = (PULONG) handle2;
   DosCreateMuxWaitSem(sem3, &handle3, 2,
                       rec, DCMW_WAIT_ALL);

   /* Start the two threads */
   DosCreateThread(&tid, thread1, 0, 0, 4096);
   DosCreateThread(&tid, thread2, 0, 0, 4096);

   /* Wait for the semaphore to quit. */
   DosWaitMuxWaitSem(handle3, SEM_INDEFINITE_WAIT, &user);
```

```
    DosExit(EXIT_PROCESS, 0);
}

VOID EXPENTRY thread1(ULONG unused)
{
  int i;

  DosEnterCritSec();
    for(i=0; i<100; i++)
      printf("thread 1(%d)\n", i);
  DosExitCritSec();

    /* Post the first event semaphore. */
    DosPostEventSem(handle1);
}

VOID EXPENTRY thread2(ULONG unused)
{
  int i;

  for(i=0; i<100; i++)
    printf("thread 2(%d)\n", i);

    /* Post the second event semaphore. */
    DosPostEventSem(handle2);
}
```

Generally speaking you will want the critical section code to be as short as possible, so that the rest of the threads do not remain idle for extended periods of time.

 Caution: For the vast majority of situations, you should use semaphores to synchronize multiple tasks, not **DosEnterCritSec()**. The reason for this is quite simple: **DosEnterCritSec()** stops all threads in the process, whether they need to be stopped or not. This degrades the total performance of your program. The critical section services are in OS/2 for those special situations in which you want to stop the execution of all other threads for a reason, such as a catastrophic error. They should not become your main method of serializing tasks.

INTER-PROCESS COMMUNICATION

As you saw earlier in this chapter, semaphores allow one process to communicate with another process, mostly to achieve some form of synchronized activity. However, OS/2 supports three other forms of inter-process communication (IPC). These are shared memory, pipes, and queues. This section takes a look at two of these: shared memory and pipes.

SHARED MEMORY

By default, the memory used by one process is logically separate from that used by another. (OS/2 might actually use the same piece of memory for two or more processes because of swapping, but from a logical point of view, neither program can actually touch another's memory.) However, you can create a shared block of memory which two or more processes can access and use to exchange information. Of all the OS/2 IPC methods, shared memory is the most flexible, because it gives you total control of both form and content of the information being shared. However, this freedom comes at a price: it is up to your programs to manually handle the data interchanges.

To allocate a segment of shared memory, use the **DosAllocShared-Mem()** function. Its prototype is shown here:

APIRET APIENTRY DosAllocSharedMem(PPVOID *address*,
                                PSZ *name*,
                                ULONG *size*,
                                ULONG *flags*);

The pointer to the allocated memory is placed into *address*. The optional name of the shared memory is specified by *name*, which must be preceded by the string "\SHAREMEM\". The value of *size* specifies the size of the block in bytes. The size allocated is rounded up to the next page size boundary. The *flags* parameter specifies the attributes for the shared memory. The attributes for *flags* include the values listed in Table 10-2.

Macro	Value	Description
PAG_READ	0x0001	Memory has read access
PAG_WRITE	0x0002	Memory has write access
PAG_EXECUTE	0x0004	Memory has execute access
PAG_GUARD	0x0008	Access to memory is guarded
PAG_COMMIT	0x0010	Memory is initially committed
OBJ_TILE	0x0040	Allocate in first 512MB of memory
OBJ_GETTABLE	0x0100	Allow access from other processes
OBJ_GIVEABLE	0x0200	Memory can be given to processes

TABLE 10-2

Attribute Flags for Shared Memory Accesses

For another process to obtain access to shared memory allocated by another process, it must call **DosGetNamedSharedMem()**, which has this prototype:

APIRET APIENTRY DosGetNamedSharedMem(PVOID *address*,
PSZ *name*,
ULONG *flags*);

Here, *address* will hold the base address of the shared memory object. The *name* parameter is the name of the desired shared memory, and it must match the name used when the memory was allocated. The parameter *flags* must be at least one of the following: PAG_READ, PAG_WRITE, PAG_EX-ECUTE, or PAG_GUARD, as described in Table 10-2.

The following program allocates a shared memory object called MEM1, writes a string to it, and then executes a child process, called SHRTEST, which reads the string from the shared memory and displays it on the screen.

```
/* This program writes a string into shared memory and
   then executes a child process. The child
   process reads the string from the shared memory
   and displays it on the screen.
*/
```

```
#define INCL_DOSMEMMGR
#define INCL_DOSPROCESS

#include <os2.h>
#include <stdio.h>
#include <bsememf.h>

main()
{
  UCHAR fail[128];
  RESULTCODES result;
  PBYTE address;

   /* allocate some unnamed shared memory */
   if(DosAllocSharedMem((PPVOID)&address, "\\SHAREMEM\\MEM1",
                         1000, PAG_WRITE | PAG_COMMIT))
   {
     printf("allocation of shared memory failed\n");
     DosExit(EXIT_PROCESS, 1);
   }

   /* put a string into shared memory */
   strcpy(address, "This is a test of shared memory.");

   /* Execute the child process, wait for termination. */
   if(DosExecPgm(fail, 128, EXEC_SYNC, NULL, NULL,
                  &result,"SHRTEST.EXE"))
   {
     printf("DosExec failed");
     DosExit(EXIT_PROCESS, 1);
   }

  DosExit(EXIT_PROCESS, 0);
}
```

The SHRTEST program is shown here:

```
/* Read a string from shared memory and print it
   to the screen.
*/

#define INCL_DOSMEMMGR

#include <os2.h>
#include <stdio.h>
```

```
#include <bsememf.h>
main()
{
  HEV handle;
  PBYTE address;

  if(DosGetNamedSharedMem((PPVOID)&address,
                          "\\SHAREMEM\\MEM1", PAG_READ))
  {
    printf("error obtaining shared memory.\n");
    DosExit(EXIT_PROCESS, 1);
  }

  printf("%s \n", address);

  DosExit(EXIT_PROCESS, 0);
}
```

Even though these sample programs use shared memory for character string data, you can use shared memory to hold any types of objects you desire.

There is one very important thing to remember about using shared memory: you must be sure to allocate enough to hold the largest object you wish to put into it. If your program tries to write past the end of the allocated memory, a memory protection fault will be generated, causing the process to terminate.

PIPES

OS/2 lets two processes communicate with each other via a *pipe*, which is a special type of file maintained by the operating system. Once the pipe has been created, routines read and write to and from the pipe using the standard **DosRead()** and **DosWrite()** file I/O services. These and other I/O functions are covered thoroughly in Chapter 11.

To create a pipe, use **DosCreateNPipe()**, which has the prototype shown here:

APIRET APIENTRY DosCreateNPipe(PSZ *name*,
                                        PHPIPE *handle*,

           ULONG *omode,*
           ULONG *pmode,*
           ULONG *outsize,*
           ULONG *insize,*
           ULONG *timeout*);

Here, *name* is the name of the pipe, and must be preceded by the string "\PIPE\". The variable pointed to by *handle* receives the handle for the pipe. The *omode* parameter holds the attributes for the open mode. Table 10-3 is a list of the flags that can be combined to create the desired mode.

The *pmode* parameter is related to the *omode* parameter, but controls the mode of the pipe. It too holds a set of flags, but is complicated by the fact that the first 8 bits hold the number of instances to allow. This can be simply set to NP_UNLIMITED_INSTANCES, unless you need to control the number of accesses to the pipe. The important flag settings are listed in Table 10-4.

The parameters *outsize* and *insize* tell the system how large to make the inbound and outbound buffers of the pipe. The *timeout* parameter is used only when the first instance of this named pipe is being created. If this parameter is set to 0, the system wide default is used.

Macro	Value	Description
NP_ACCESS_INBOUND	0x0000	Inbound access (default)
NP_ACCESS_OUTBOUND	0x0001	Outbound access
NP_ACCESS_DUPLEX	0x0002	In/Outbound access
NP_INHERIT	0x0000	Child inherits (default)
NP_NOINHERIT	0x0080	Cannot be inherited
NP_WRITEBEHIND	0x0000	Writes to remote pipes may be buffered by system (default)
NP_NOWRITEBEHIND	0x4000	Remote pipes are written to immediately

TABLE 10-3

Macros Used for Open Mode

Macro	Value	Description
NP_UNLIMITED_INSTANCES	0x00FF	Unlimited instances
NP_READMODE_BYTE	0x0000	Byte read mode (default)
NP_READMODE_MESSAGE	0x0100	Message read mode
NP_TYPE_BYTE	0x0000	Byte pipe type (default)
NP_TYPE_MESSAGE	0x0400	Message pipe type
NP_WAIT	0x0000	Wait on I/O (default)
NP_NOWAIT	0x8000	No wait on I/O

TABLE 10-4

Macros Used for Pipe Mode

Pipes are very easy to use for communication, but there is one more step to the process before pipes can be used. The process that creates the pipe must call **DosConnectNPipe()** to allow access to the pipe. The prototype is shown here:

APIRET APIENTRY DosConnectNPipe(HPIPE *handle*);

The parameter *handle* is the handle of the pipe to connect. This is the handle that was returned by the call to **DosCreateNPipe()**. Without this call, the pipe cannot be accessed either by the creator of the pipe, or by other processes. A call to **DosConnectNPipe()** puts the pipe into a listening mode. After this call, the process that created the call can begin communicating, using the **DosRead()** and **DosWrite()** services. Other processes can also communicate through the pipe with these same services, but must first gain access to the pipe through a call to **DosOpen()**. For more information on these file I/O API services, see Chapter 11 of this book.

After finishing with the current communication, the pipe can be disconnected with a call to **DosDisConnectNPipe()**. The prototype for this function is shown here:

APIRET APIENTRY DosDisConnectNPipe(HPIPE *handle*);

Again, *handle* is the handle of the pipe, the handle which was returned by the call to **DosCreateNPipe()**, and used in the call to connect the pipe. After disconnecting a pipe, it can again be used to communicate, if it is put back into listing mode with another call to **DosConnectNPipe()**.

A Pipe Example Program

The following program creates a pipe and prepares it for access. While this is happening, a child process is opening the pipe and waiting to read from it. When the parent process writes a string to the pipe, the child process reads it and displays it on the screen.

```
/* This program opens a pipe and writes a string
   into the pipe. A child process opens the pipe and
   reads in the string, then displays it on the screen.
*/

#define INCL_DOSNMPIPES
#define INCL_DOSFILEMGR
#define INCL_DOSPROCESS

#include <os2.h>
#include <stdio.h>

main()
{
  UCHAR fail[128];
  RESULTCODES result;
  HPIPE handle;
  ULONG written;

    /* create a named pipe */
    if(DosCreateNPipe("\\PIPE\\PIPE1", &handle,
                      NP_ACCESS_OUTBOUND,
                      NP_UNLIMITED_INSTANCES,
                      255, 255, 0))

    {
      printf("Pipe creation failed.\n");
      DosExit(EXIT_PROCESS, 1);
    }

    /* Start up a child process */
    if(DosExecPgm(fail, 128, EXEC_ASYNC, NULL, NULL,
                  &result,"PIPETEST.EXE"))
    {
      printf("DosExec failed");
```

```
    DosExit(EXIT_PROCESS, 1);
  }

  /* Put the pipe into listing mode. */
  if(DosConnectNPipe(handle))
  {
    printf("Conection failed");
    DosExit(EXIT_PROCESS, 1);
  }

  /* Write a string into the pipe. */
  if(DosWrite(handle, "Hello from the parent",
                      21, &written))
  {
    printf("DosWrite failed");
    DosExit(EXIT_PROCESS, 1);
  }

  DosExit(EXIT_PROCESS, 0);
}
```

Enter this second program and name it PIPETEST.C. This will allow
the parent process to call the program through the **DosExecPgm()** function, which expects the child program to be named PIPETEST.EXE.

```
/* Read a string from a pipe and print it to the screen. */

#define INCL_DOSNMPIPES
#define INCL_DOSFILEMGR

#include <os2.h>
#include <stdio.h>

main()
{
  HPIPE handle;
  ULONG action;
  UCHAR buff[32];
  ULONG read;

  /* Open the pipe */
  if(DosOpen("\\PIPE\\PIPE1", &handle, &action, 0,
             FILE_READONLY, OPEN_ACTION_OPEN_IF_EXISTS,
             OPEN_ACCESS_READONLY | OPEN_SHARE_DENYNONE, 0))
  {
```

```
      printf("error opening pipe.\n");
      DosExit(EXIT_PROCESS, 1);
    }

    /* Read from the pipe. */
    if(DosRead(handle, buff, 32, &read))
    {
      printf("error reading pipe\n");
      DosExit(EXIT_PROCESS, 1);
    }

    /* Now null terminate the string and print it out. */
    buff[read] = '\0';
    printf("String received through the pipe: %s \n", buff);

}
```

JUST A SCRATCH ON THE SURFACE

This and the previous chapter have introduced you to the most important and fundamental aspects of OS/2's multitasking capabilities. But we have only scratched the surface of the multitasking environment provided by OS/2. It is not enough just to know how to use the appropriate OS/2 services to create a multithread or multiprocess application. You must learn to use multitasking effectively. The two reasons you will want to use multitasking are to increase the performance of your program, and to prevent the user from being idle while your program performs some lengthy task. While it is beyond the scope of this book to discuss the various theories and approaches to writing multitasking applications, you should give much thought to how both data and execution flow through your program, looking for discrete tasks that can be concurrently executed. With a little practice, this process will become second nature.

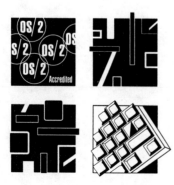

11

FILE I/O

The OS/2 file I/O subsystem is amazingly straightforward and provides a very efficient means of accessing disk files as well as other devices. At its core are four services: **DosOpen()**, **DosRead()**, **DosWrite()**, and **DosClose()**. If you are familiar with C's unbuffered I/O system, you will be pleased to learn that these services parallel **open()**, **read()**, **write()**, and **close()**. In fact, many of the file services are similar to C I/O functions. Even if you are unfamiliar with these C functions, the OS/2 file system is very easy to learn and use.

The OS/2 file I/O services are shown in Table 11-1 along with a short description of each. Notice that all of the functions begin with the prefix *Dos*.

As has been the case with many of the OS/2 services, the OS/2 file system closely parallels the C file system. For most low-performance applications you will probably want to use the C file I/O functions, because they are more portable and, in a few cases, slightly easier to use. However, for high-performance or, depending upon the actual implementation of your C compiler, for multithread applications, you should rely on the OS/2 file services.

One final point: OS/2 provides the capability to directly access the disk, bypassing the disk's logical structure. However, this direct control of the disk hardware is a topic beyond the scope of this book.

In general, you would only want to access the disk directly when creating special disk utility programs, such as a file recovery program, not for general programming tasks.

Service	Function
DosResetBuffer()	Flushes the buffers associated with a file
DosSetCurrentDir()	Changes the current directory
DosSetFilePtr()	Changes the location of the file pointer
DosClose()	Closes a file
DosDelete()	Deletes a file
DosDupHandle()	Duplicates a file handle
DosSetFileLocks()	Locks a file
DosFindClose()	Closes a directory search file handle
DosFindFirst()	Finds the first file in the directory that matches the specified filename
DosFindNext()	Finds the next file in the directory that matches the specified filename
DosCreateDir()	Makes a subdirectory
DosMove()	Rename a file
DosSetFileSize()	Resizes a file
DosOpen()	Opens a file
DosQueryFSInfo()	Returns information about the disk system
DosQueryCurrentDir()	Returns information about the current directory
DosQueryCurrentDisk()	Returns information about the current disk
DosQueryFHState()	Returns information about a handle
DosQueryFileInfo()	Returns information about a file
DosQuerySysInfo()	Returns information about a file's mode
DosQueryFSInfo()	Returns information about the file system

TABLE 11-1

File I/O Subsystem Services

Service	Function
DosQueryHType()	Returns a handle's type
DosQueryVerify()	Returns the state of the verify flag
DosRead()	Reads data from a file
DosDeleteDir()	Removes a subdirectory
DosScanEnv()	Looks for a specified environmental variable
DosSearchPath()	Searches for a filename, given a path
DosSetDefaultDisk()	Changes the default drive
DosSetFHState()	Sets a file handle's state
DosSetFileInfo()	Changes information associated with a file
DosCopy()	Copies a file or directory
DosSetFSInfo()	Changes the file system information
DosSetMaxFH()	Sets the maximum number of file handles
DosSetVerify()	Changes the state of the verify flag
DosWrite()	Writes data to a file

TABLE 11-1

File I/O Subsystem Services (continued)

FILE HANDLES

The OS/2 file subsystem operates on files via a file's handle, which is obtained when the file is first opened. A file handle, like all other OS/2 handles, is a 32-bit value. You must obtain a valid file handle before attempting to use any of the file I/O services. The handle is obtained either through a successful call to **DosOpen()** or by using one of the built-in handles discussed later.

FILE POINTERS

All open disk files have associated with them a *file pointer*, which is used to keep track of the location in the file that is currently being accessed. The file pointer is automatically maintained by OS/2 when read or write operations occur. For example, if a file is 100 bytes long and your program has just read the first 50 bytes, then the value of the file pointer is 50. It is also possible for your program to set the value of the file pointer in order to reach a specific point in the file.

OPENING AND CLOSING FILES

Before you can access a file, you must obtain a handle to it. To do this, use the **DosOpen()** service, the prototype of which is shown here:

```
APIRET APIENTRY  DosOpen(PSZ filename,
                         PHFILE fhandle,
                         PULONG action,
                         ULONG  size,
                         ULONG attr,
                         ULONG openflags,
                         ULONG mode,
                         PEAOP2 op2);
```

Here, *filename* must be a null terminated string that contains a valid path and filename for the file to be opened. The *fhandle* parameter points to the integer that will contain the file's handle upon return from a successful call.

The *action* parameter points to a value which holds the action taken by a successful **DosOpen()**. If the call failed, the value pointed to by *action* has no meaning. The value that *action* points to will be one of these:

Macro	Value	Meaning
FILE_EXISTED	0x0001	File was existent
FILE_CREATED	0x0002	File was created
FILE_TRUNCATED	0x0003	File length was truncated

The *size* parameter specifies an initial length, in bytes, for a new or truncated file. This value may be 0. This parameter has no effect on a file that is opened for read operations.

The value of the *attr* parameter determines a file's attributes. It only applies to newly created files. The value of *attr* can be any valid combination of the following:

Macro	Value	Type of File
FILE_NORMAL	0x0000	normal
FILE_READONLY	0x0001	read-only
FILE_HIDDEN	0x0002	hidden
FILE_SYSTEM	0x0004	system
FILE_DIRECTORY	0x0010	directory
FILE_ARCHIVED	0x0020	archived

The value of the *openflags* parameter determines what action **DosOpen()** takes, depending upon whether the specified file exists or not. Its value can be a combination of the values shown here:

Macro	Value	Action
OPEN_ACTION_FAIL_IF_EXISTS	0x0000	Open file, fail if the file already exists
OPEN_ACTION_OPEN_IF_EXISTS	0x0001	Open file if it exists, fail if it does not
OPEN_ACTION_REPLACE_IF_EXISTS	0x0002	Open file, replace it if it exists
OPEN_ACTION_CREATE_IF_NEW	0x0010	Open file, create if it does not exist

The value of the *mode* parameter must specify the access mode as well as the share mode of a file that is being created. As you probably know, all files may be accessed one of three different ways: read-only, write-only, or read/write. For a single-tasking operating system, these access codes fully describe how the files may be accessed. However, in OS/2, a multitasking system, the access mode of a file is not sufficient to fully describe the file, because it does not take into account the possibility of two or more processes attempting to access the file at the same time. To handle this situation, all OS/2 files also have associated with them a *share* attribute, which is one of the following:

Share Attribute	Meaning
Deny write-share	Only the process that opened the file may write to it, but other processes may read from it.
Deny read-share	Only the process that opened the file may read from it, but other processes may write to it.
Deny read/write-share	Only the process that opened the file may read or write to the file; all other processes are barred access.
Deny-none	Any process may access the file at any time, in any way.

In addition to the access and file sharing specifics, OS/2 lets you control a few things about the way the file system operates. You can control the setting of the inheritance flag, which determines whether a child process inherits a file handle from the parent. You can tell the file system to return all I/O errors to the calling routine instead of to the system critical error routine. You can tell OS/2 that you do not want write operations to return until the information being written is actually put on the physical device instead of simply written to a buffer. Finally, you can tell OS/2 that the drive is being accessed directly on a sector by sector basis, bypassing the disk's logical structure.

The values for the access, file sharing, and miscellaneous flag settings are shown in Table 11-2. You combine the attributes to create the value desired for the *mode* parameter. To combine the values, simply OR them together.

The last parameter is used to pass the address of the extended attribute buffer. For most file operations, including the examples in this book, this value will be 0, meaning that no extended attributes will be defined.

When the file is first opened, the file pointer is set to the beginning of the file and has the value of 0.

Unless the write-to-device flag has been set, the OS/2 file system writes output to a buffer, not to the actual physical file, until that buffer is

Macro	Value	Meaning
OPEN_ACCESS_READONLY	0x0000	Read-only file
OPEN_ACCESS_WRITEONLY	0x0001	Write-only file
OPEN_ACCESS_READWRITE	0x0002	Read/write file
OPEN_SHARE_DENYREADWRITE	0x0010	Deny read/write sharing
OPEN_SHARE_DENYWRITE	0x0020	Deny write sharing
OPEN_SHARE_DENYREAD	0x0030	Deny read sharing
OPEN_SHARE_DENYNONE	0x0040	No access denied
OPEN_FLAGS_NOINHERIT	0x0080	File handles not passed on to child process
OPEN_FLAGS_SEQUENTIAL	0x0100	Sequential access
OPEN_FLAGS_RANDOM	0x0200	Random access
OPEN_FLAGS_NO_CACHE	0x1000	Output not put in cache
OPEN_FLAGS_FAIL_ON_ERROR	0x2000	Report errors to caller
OPEN_FLAGS_WRITE_THROUGH	0x4000	Do not return until the information is written to device
OPEN_FLAGS_DASD	0x8000	Signals the system that direct device access will take place

TABLE 11-2

File Mode Values

full. As you may know, virtually all operating systems buffer disk input and output by even multiples of a sector. For example, when your program requests information, the file system automatically reads a full sector, even if only a partial sector is needed. Subsequent sequential read requests can then obtain information from the buffer without waiting for disk access. The same happens on output: data is buffered until a full sector can be written to disk, thus bypassing a number of time-consuming disk write operations, each of which would write just a few bytes. The buffered method is used to improve performance and is not unique to OS/2. However, you must insure that the contents of the buffer have been written to the file before your program terminates, or before the handle associated with that file is destroyed. Also, there are a finite number of file handles available in the file system (20 by default), so there needs to be some way to release a file handle for reuse when you are done with a file. To accomplish these goals OS/2 provides the **DosClose()** service, whose prototype is shown here:

APIRET APIENTRY DosClose(HFILE *fhandle*);

where *fhandle* must be a previously acquired file handle.

Before any meaningful examples can be developed using **DosOpen()** and **DosClose()**, you need to learn about **DosWrite()**, the subject of the next section.

WRITING TO A FILE

To write information to a file, use the **DosWrite()** service, whose prototype is shown here:

APIRET APIENTRY DosWrite(HFILE *fhandle*,
                  PVOID *buf*,
                  ULONG *count*,
                  PULONG *num_bytes_written*);

The *fhandle* parameter must be a valid, previously obtained file handle. The region pointed to by *buf* holds the information that will be written to the file. The *count* parameter specifies the length of the buffer, or more properly, the number of bytes in the buffer that should be written to the file. Finally, the *num_bytes_written* parameter points to a value that holds the number of bytes actually written upon return from the call. If an error occurs and it is not possible to write all the bytes requested, then the value returned in *num_bytes_written* will be different from the number requested.

OS/2 file operations are binary in nature and no character translations take place. (What you write is what you get!) Also, the file system performs no formatting and is byte-oriented. That is, if you wish to write data other than characters, you must treat the data as a group of bytes. For example, there is no OS/2 service that writes **floats** directly. (You will see how to write other types of data later in this chapter.)

Each time you write to the file, the file's file pointer is automatically advanced by the number of bytes written.

A SIMPLE FIRST EXAMPLE

To see how **DosOpen()**, **DosWrite()**, and **DosClose()** work together, examine the following program, which creates a new disk file called TEST.TST and writes the line "Hello OS/2 World!" to it. (Make sure a file named TEST.TST does not already exist.)

```
/* This program writes output to a disk file.
   If the file exists, the open will fail.*/

#define INCL_DOS

#include <os2.h>
#include <stdio.h>

main()
{
  ULONG fh;
  ULONG action;
  ULONG count;
  CHAR buf[80];

  strcpy(buf, "Hello, OS/2 World!");
```

```
/* create the file, no file sharing */
if(DosOpen("test.tst", /* filename */
          &fh,          /* pointer to handle */
          &action,      /* pointer to result */
          0,            /* initial length */
          FILE_NORMAL,/* normal file */
          OPEN_ACTION_CREATE_IF_NEW | /* create file, */
          OPEN_ACTION_FAIL_IF_EXISTS, /* fail if exists */
          OPEN_ACCESS_WRITEONLY | /* write only with */
          OPEN_SHARE_DENYREADWRITE,/* no sharing allowed */
          0))    /* no extended attributes */
{
  printf("error in opening file");
  exit(1);
}

/* write a short message to it */
if(DosWrite(fh, buf, strlen(buf), &count))
  printf("error in write operation");

/* close the file */
if(DosClose(fh))
  printf("error closing file");
}
```

The first time this program is run, it creates the file called TEST.TST and writes output to it. However, if you try to run the program a second time, you will see the error message "error in opening file". The reason this happens is that the value of the *openflags* parameter specifies that the file will be created only if it does not already exist.

Notice that this program checks for error returns from **DosOpen()**, **DosWrite()**, and **DosClose()**. As you probably know, errors are very common when dealing with files. A frequently encountered error is forgetting to put a diskette into the drive. Another one is running out of space on a disk. For these reasons, it is imperative to check for errors whenever you open a file or write to it. (Remember that closing a file may involve a write operation if a buffer must be written to disk. Hence, **DosClose()** must be checked.) Unlike the screen or keyboard services in which most of the functions are (more or less) guaranteed success, and error checking is generally unnecessary, many of the file system services have a significant likelihood of failure due to uncontrollable circumstances. You simply must check for errors and take appropriate action if one occurs.

A VARIATION

As mentioned, the program just shown will only work if the file does not already exist. It is possible to change the value of the *openflags* parameter so that the file will be opened if it already exists or created if it doesn't. This can be accomplished by using the value 0x11. This version of the program is shown here:

```
/* This program writes output to a disk file.
   If the file exists, it is replaced.
*/

#define INCL_DOS

#include <os2.h>
#include <stdio.h>

main()
{
  ULONG fh;
  ULONG action;
  ULONG count;
  CHAR buf[80];

  strcpy(buf, "Hello again, OS/2 World!");

  /* create the file, no file sharing */
  if(DosOpen("test.tst", /* filename */
            &fh,         /* pointer to handle */
            &action,     /* pointer to result */
            0,           /* initial length */
            FILE_NORMAL,/* normal file */
            OPEN_ACTION_CREATE_IF_NEW | /* create file, */
            OPEN_ACTION_REPLACE_IF_EXISTS, /* replace */
            OPEN_ACCESS_WRITEONLY |  /* write only with */
            OPEN_SHARE_DENYREADWRITE,/* no sharing allowed */
            0))   /* no extended attributes */
  {
    printf("error in opening file");
    exit(1);
  }

  /* write a short message to it */
  if(DosWrite(fh, buf, strlen(buf), &count))
    printf("error in write operation");
```

```
/* close the file */
if(DosClose(fh))
  printf("error closing file");
}
```

When you run this program it will open an existing TEST.TST file and write the new message to it—overwriting any existing contents. (Later you will see how to append information to a file.) If TEST.TST does not exist, it will be created.

READING FROM A FILE

To read information from a file, use the **DosRead()** service, which has this prototype:

APIRET APIENTRY DosRead(HFILE *fhandle*,
                        PVOID *buf*,
                        ULONG *count*,
                        PULONG *num_read*);

The *fhandle* parameter is a valid, previously obtained file handle associated with the file you wish to read from. The region pointed to by *buf* receives the information read. The value of *count* determines how many bytes are read from the file. The length of the buffer receiving them must be at least *count* bytes in length. The value pointed to by *num_read* will contain the number of bytes actually read after the call returns. The number of bytes requested and the number of bytes actually read may differ, either because the end of the file has been reached, or because an error has occurred.

OS/2 automatically updates the file pointer after each read operation.

As an example, the following program will read and display the contents of a text file. You must specify the name of the file on the command line.

```
/* This program displays an entire file. */

#define INCL_DOS
```

```
#include <os2.h>
#include <stdio.h>

main(int argc, char *argv[])
{
  HFILE fh;
  ULONG action;
  ULONG num_bytes;
  CHAR buf[513];

  if(argc!=2)
  {
    printf("Usage: %s <filename>\n", argv[0]);
    exit(1);
  }

  /* open the file, no file sharing */
  if(DosOpen(argv[1],    /* the file to open */
             &fh,        /* pointer to handle */
             &action,    /* pointer to result */
             0,          /* initial length */
             FILE_NORMAL,/* normal file */
             OPEN_ACTION_FAIL_IF_NEW | /* do not create */
             OPEN_ACTION_OPEN_IF_EXISTS, /* open if exists */
             OPEN_ACCESS_READONLY |   /* read only with */
             OPEN_SHARE_DENYREADWRITE,/* no sharing allowed */
             0))   /* no extended attributes */
  {
    printf("error in opening file");
    exit(1);
  }

  do
  {
    if(DosRead(fh, buf, 512, &num_bytes))
    {
      printf("error reading file");
      exit(1);
    }
    buf[num_bytes] = '\0'; /* null terminate the buffer */
    printf(buf);
  } while(num_bytes);

  if(DosClose(fh))
```

```
    printf("error closing file");
}
```

As this program illustrates, the easiest way to know when you have reached the end of the file is when the value of the *num_bytes* parameter is zero. The **DosRead()** function does not return an EOF character.

One thing to notice about this program is that the buffer used to hold the data is one byte longer than the number of bytes requested to be read. This is because the buffer must be transformed into a null terminated string so that it can be used as a parameter to **printf()**. Not every application will require this step, of course.

RANDOM ACCESS

The OS/2 file system supports byte-addressable random access through the **DosSetFilePtr()** service, which has this prototype:

APIRET APIENTRY DosSetFilePtr(HFILE *fhandle*,
$\qquad$ LONG *distance*,
$\qquad$ ULONG *origin*,
$\qquad$ PULONG *loc*);

The *fhandle* parameter must contain a valid, previously obtained file handle. The **DosSetFilePtr()** service works only upon actual disk files and cannot be used with other devices. The value of *distance* determines how far, in bytes, the file pointer is to be moved relative to the origin. This is a signed value and may be either positive or negative. The value of *origin* determines how the value of *distance* is interpreted, as shown here.

Macro	Value	Effect
FILE_BEGIN	0	Move specified number of bytes from the start of the file
FILE_CURRENT	1	Move specified number of bytes from the current location
FILE_END	2	Move specified number of bytes from the end of the file

The value pointed to by *loc* will hold the current value of the file pointer upon return.

The following program makes use of the **DosSetFilePtr()** service to let you scan a text file in both the forward and backward directions. You must specify the name of the file on the command line. The program supports these commands:

Command	Meaning
S	Go to beginning of the file
E	Go to the end of the file
B	Go back 512 bytes
F	Go forward 512 bytes
Q	Quit

When it begins execution the first 512 bytes of the file are shown.

```
/* A file browse program */

#define INCL_DOS

#include <os2.h>
#include <stdio.h>

main(int argc, char *argv[])
{
  ULONG fh;
  ULONG action;
  ULONG num_bytes;
  CHAR buf[513], ch;
  ULONG pos;
  LONG p;

  if(argc!=2)
  {
    printf("Usage: %s <filename>\n", argv[0]);
    exit(1);
  }

  /* open the file, no file sharing */
  if(DosOpen(argv[1],    /* the file to open */
            &fh,         /* pointer to handle */
            &action,     /* pointer to result */
```

```
              0,            /* initial length */
              FILE_NORMAL,/* normal file */
              OPEN_ACTION_FAIL_IF_NEW | /* do not create */
              OPEN_ACTION_OPEN_IF_EXISTS, /* open if exists */
              OPEN_ACCESS_READONLY |   /* read only with */
              OPEN_SHARE_DENYREADWRITE,/* no sharing allowed */
              0))   /* no extended attributes */
{
  printf("error in opening file");
  exit(1);
}

/* main loop */
pos = 0;
do
{
  if(DosRead(fh, buf, 512, &num_bytes))
  {
    printf("error reading file");
    exit(1);
  }
  buf[num_bytes] = '\0'; /* null terminate the buffer */
  printf(buf); /* display the buffer */

  /* see what to do next */
  ch = tolower(getc(stdin));
  switch(ch)
  {
    case 'e': /* move to end, the last 512 bytes */
      DosSetFilePtr(fh, -512, FILE_END, &pos);
      break;
    case 's': /* move to start, the first 512 bytes */
      DosSetFilePtr(fh, 0, FILE_BEGIN, &pos);
      break;
    case 'f': /* move forward */
      /* forward is automatic, so no change is required */
      pos += num_bytes;
      break;
    case 'b': /* move backward */
      p = pos - 512;
      if(p < 0)
        p = 0;
      DosSetFilePtr(fh, p, FILE_BEGIN, &pos);
  }
```

```
  } while(ch != 'q');

  if(DosClose(fh))
    printf("error closing file");
}
```

APPENDING TO A FILE

The way to add information to the end of a file is to first advance the file pointer to the end and then begin writing the new data. To accomplish this, you could open the file for read/write operations and read the file until the end was reached. But this method is very inefficient. The best way to get to the end of the file is to use **DosSetFilePtr()** in a statement similar to this:

```
DosSetFilePtr(fh, 0, FILE_END, &pos);
```

This tells OS/2 to move the file pointer to the end of the file. The 2 in the *origin* parameter and the 0 in the *distance* parameter insure that the file pointer will be at the physical end of the file.

The following program uses this method to add lines of text, entered at the keyboard, to the file TEST.TST. To stop inputting lines, enter the word "quit" on a separate line.

```
/* This program opens a file, reads lines from the keyboard,
   and appends each line to the end of the file.
*/

#define INCL_DOS

#include <os2.h>
#include <stdio.h>
#include <string.h>

main()
{
  ULONG fh;
  ULONG action;
  ULONG pos;
  ULONG count;
```

```
CHAR buf[513];

/* open the file, no file sharing */
if(DosOpen("test.tst", /* the file to open */
           &fh,         /* pointer to handle */
           &action,     /* pointer to result */
           0,           /* initial length */
           FILE_NORMAL,/* normal file */
           OPEN_ACTION_CREATE_IF_NEW | /* create or */
           OPEN_ACTION_OPEN_IF_EXISTS, /* open if exists */
           OPEN_ACCESS_READWRITE |   /* read/write with */
           OPEN_SHARE_DENYREADWRITE,/* no sharing allowed */
           0))   /* no extended attributes */
{
  printf("error in opening file");
  exit(1);
}

/* go to the end of the file */
DosSetFilePtr(fh, 0, FILE_END, &pos);

/* continue adding to the file until the word "quit" is
   entered
*/
do
{
  gets(buf);

  if(DosWrite(fh, buf, strlen(buf), &count))
    printf("error in write operation");
} while(stricmp("quit", buf));

/* close the file */
if(DosClose(fh))
  printf("error closing file");
}
```

READING AND WRITING OTHER DATA TYPES

You can use the OS/2 file system services to read and write data types other than characters (bytes) by treating a variable of a different type as a

buffer and using its address and length in the calls to **DosRead()** and
DosWrite(). (Remember, you can obtain the size of any data type using the
sizeof compile time operator.) For example, the following program first
writes a **double** to the file TEST.TST and then reads it back, displaying the
value to the screen for verification.

```
/* This program illustrates how to write a double value to
   a file and read it back
*/
#define INCL_DOS

#include <os2.h>
#include <stdio.h>

main()
{
  ULONG fh;
  ULONG action;
  ULONG pos;
  ULONG count;
  double dbl;

  /* create or overwrite a file, no file sharing */
  if(DosOpen("test.tst", /* the file to open */
             &fh,        /* pointer to handle */
             &action,    /* pointer to result */
             0,          /* initial length */
             FILE_NORMAL,/* normal file */
             OPEN_ACTION_CREATE_IF_NEW | /* create or */
             OPEN_ACTION_REPLACE_IF_EXISTS, /* overwrite */
             OPEN_ACCESS_READWRITE |   /* read/write with */
             OPEN_SHARE_DENYREADWRITE, /* no sharing allowed
*/
             0))   /* no extended attributes */
  {
    printf("error in opening file");
    exit(1);
  }

  dbl = 101.125;
  /* write a double value to the file */
  if(DosWrite(fh, &dbl, sizeof(dbl), &count))
    printf("error in write operation");

  /* clear the dbl variable */
```

```
dbl = 0.0;

/* reset the file pointer to start of file */
DosSetFilePtr(fh, 0, FILE_BEGIN, &pos);

if(DosRead(fh, &dbl, sizeof(dbl), &count))
{
  printf("error reading file");
  exit(1);
}

printf("%lf \n", dbl); /* print the value read in */

/* close the file */
if(DosClose(fh))
  printf("error closing file");
}
```

You can use this same basic approach on more complex data types such as arrays, unions, and structures. Just be sure that you are passing the address of the variable to **DosRead()** or **DosWrite()**, not its actual value.

READING AND WRITING TO A DEVICE

The OS/2 file system lets you access certain devices as if they were files. For example it is possible to open the console (screen and keyboard), and then read and write to it. To open a device, you must use that device's name in the **DosOpen()** call in place of a filename. The devices supported by OS/2 are,

clock$	con	mouse$
com1	kbd$	nul
com2	lpt1	pointer$
com3	lpt2	prn
com4	lpt3	screen$

Of the most interest are **com1** through **com4**, because these are the serial communication ports, and **lpt1** through **lpt3** and **prn**, because these are the printer ports.

One thing to keep in mind is that not all devices support all modes of operation. For example, if you open **screen$**, you may write to the screen but not read from it. Also, as you will see, disk files support random access operations, but devices do not.

This program opens the keyboard, reads a line of text, and displays the contents of the buffer.

```
/* This program reads input from the keyboard */

#define INCL_DOS

#include <os2.h>
#include <stdio.h>

main()
{
  ULONG fh;
  ULONG action;
  ULONG pos;
  ULONG count;
  CHAR buf[80];

  /* open the keyboard, no sharing */
  if(DosOpen("kbd$",          /* the keyboard */
            &fh,              /* pointer to handle */
            &action,          /* pointer to result */
            0,                /* initial length */
            FILE_NORMAL,      /* normal file */
            OPEN_ACTION_CREATE_IF_NEW | /* create or */
            OPEN_ACTION_OPEN_IF_EXISTS, /* open */
            OPEN_ACCESS_READONLY |      /* read only with */
            OPEN_SHARE_DENYREADWRITE,   /* no sharing */
            0))   /* no extended attributes */
  {
    printf("error accessing the keyboard.");
    exit(1);
  }

  if(DosRead(fh, buf, 80, &count))
    printf("error in read operation");
```

```
  buf[count] = '\0'; /* null terminate */
  printf(buf);

  if(DosClose(fh))
    printf("error closing the keyboard");

}
```

The following program opens **lpt1** and writes a message to it.

```
/* This program writes output to the printer */

#define INCL_DOS

#include <os2.h>
#include <stdio.h>
#include <string.h>

main()
{
  ULONG fh;
  ULONG action;
  ULONG pos;
  ULONG count;
  CHAR buf[80];

  strcpy(buf, "Hello, OS/2 Printer");

  /* open the printer, no sharing */
  if(DosOpen("lpt1",        /* the keyboard */
          &fh,               /* pointer to handle */
          &action,           /* pointer to result */
          0,                 /* initial length */
          FILE_NORMAL,    /* normal file */
          OPEN_ACTION_CREATE_IF_NEW | /* create or */
          OPEN_ACTION_OPEN_IF_EXISTS, /* open */
          OPEN_ACCESS_WRITEONLY |     /* write only with */
          OPEN_SHARE_DENYREADWRITE,/* no sharing */
          0))    /* no extended attributes */
  {
    printf("error accessing the printer.");
    exit(1);
  }

  if(DosWrite(fh, buf, strlen(buf), &count))
```

```
      printf("error in write operation");

   if(DosClose(fh))
      printf("error closing the printer");

}
```

It is quite easy to read from and write to devices using the file system. OS/2 can automatically route input and output to and from the various devices without your program needing intimate knowledge of the system's configuration or the device drivers.

OS/2 STANDARD DEVICES

OS/2 has three built-in file handles, which are associated with three standard devices. These handles are created when your program begins executing. The handles and their meaning are shown here:

Device	Handle	Meaning
stdin	0	Standard input
stdout	1	Standard output
stderr	2	Standard error (output)

By default, standard input is associated with the keyboard, standard output with the screen, and standard error with the screen. However, because OS/2 supports I/O redirection of its standard devices, input and/or output can be routed to disk files or to other devices.

The following program writes a message to standard output.

```
/* This program writes output to standard output */
#define INCL_DOS

#include <os2.h>
#include <stdio.h>
#include <string.h>

main()
{
```

```
ULONG count;
CHAR buf[24];

strcpy(buf, "Hello OS/2 World!");

/* write a short message to it */
if(DosWrite(1, buf, strlen(buf), &count))
  printf("error in write operation");
}
```

Notice that the program does not have to open standard output, because this is automatically done by OS/2 when the program begins. Further, the program does not close standard output, because this too is performed automatically. If this program is called STDOUT, then executing it using this command line causes the message to be written to the screen:

```
STDOUT
```

However, using this command line cause the message to be written to a file called MESS:

```
STDOUT > MESS
```

DISPLAYING THE DIRECTORY

It is very common for an application program to need to display the contents of a directory, so that the user can make a file selection. Fortunately, OS/2 makes this very easy to do through its **DosFindFirst()** and **DosFindNext()** services. Their prototypes are shown here:

APIRET APIENTRY DosFindFirst(PSZ *mask,*
                        PHDIR *handle,*
                        ULONG *attr,*
                        PVOID *info,*
                        ULONG *buflength,*
                        PULONG *count,*
                        ULONG *level);*

APIRET APIENTRY DosFindNext(HDIR *handle*,
                             PVOID *info*,
                             ULONG *buflength*,
                             PULONG *count*);

In **DosFindFirst()**, the *mask* parameter is a null terminated string that holds the file name you are looking for. This string can include the * and **?** wildcard characters. A directory handle is returned in the variable pointed to by *handle*. This handle is used in subsequent calls to **DosFileNext()**. Prior to the call to **DosFindFirst()**, *handle* must contain the value 1 (HDIR_SYSTEM), or 0xFFFFFFFF (HDIR_CREATE). If its value is 1, OS/2 supplies a default handle. However, if you will be searching for more than one specific file, then use 0xFFFFFFFF, which causes OS/2 to return a handle that can be used in subsequent calls to **DosFindNext()**. The *attr* parameter specifies the type of file you are looking for. It can be any valid (non-mutually exclusive) combination of the following values:

Macro	Value	File Type
FILE_READONLY	0x0001	Include read-only files
FILE_HIDDEN	0x0002	Include hidden files
FILE_SYSTEM	0x0004	Include system files
FILE_DIRECTORY	0x0010	Include subdirectories
FILE_ARCHIVE	0x0020	Include archive files
MUST_HAVE_READONLY	0x0100	Just read-only files
MUST_HAVE_HIDDEN	0x0200	Just hidden files
MUST_HAVE_SYSTEM	0x0400	Just system files
MUST_HAVE_DIRECTORY	0x1000	Directories only
MUST_HAVE_ARCHIVE	0x2000	Just archive files

The structure type pointed to by *info* depends on the value specified in *level*. The structure is filled with information about the file if a match is found.

The *buflength* parameter specifies the length of the structure in *info*. The value pointed to by *count* specifies the number of matches to find and holds the number of matches found upon return. It is generally best to give *count* a value of 1. If no match is found, 0 is returned. The *level* parameter is used to specify the level of information requested. The default level is 1, and is the level of return even if *level* is set to 0.

For **DosFindNext()**, the parameters have the same meaning as those for **DosFindFirst()**.

If you are looking for only one specific file and fully specify that file's name (no wildcards) in the call to **DosFindFirst()**, you will not need to use **DosFindNext()**. However, if you are searching for (potentially) several matches, the basic method is to first call **DosFindFirst()** to obtain the first match (if any), as well as a directory handle. This directory handle is then used in subsequent calls to **DosFindNext()**.

There are two ways to determine when the last match has been found. First, both **DosFindFirst()** and **DosFindNext()** fail and return an error code if no match is found. Second, the *count* parameter will be zero when no (more) matches are found.

The following program lists the current working directory. It displays the file's name and length.

```
/* This program lists the directory */

#define INCL_DOS

#include <os2.h>
#include <stdio.h>

void show_dir(void);

main()
{
  show_dir();
}

/* Display the directory */
void show_dir()
{
  FILEFINDBUF3 f;
  HDIR hdir;
  ULONG count;

  hdir = HDIR_CREATE; /* cause a new handle to be returned */
  count = 1;  /* find the first match */
  DosFindFirst("*.*", &hdir, 0, &f, sizeof(f), &count, 1);
  do
  {
    printf("%-13s %d\n", f.achName, f.cbFile);
    DosFindNext(hdir, &f, sizeof(f), &count);
```

```
  } while(count);
  DosFindClose(hdir);
}
```

ACCESSING INFORMATION ABOUT THE DISK SYSTEM

It is not uncommon for an application to need various pieces of information about the disk system, including such things as the total free storage, the number of bytes per sector, or the number of sectors per cluster. To obtain this information, OS/2 supplies the **DosQueryFSInfo()** service, which has this prototype:

APIRET APIENTRY DosQueryFSInfo(ULONG *drive*,
ULONG *info-type*,
PVOID *info*,
ULONG *buflength*);

The *drive* parameter specifies the number of the drive you want to receive information about. If it is 0, the default drive is used. Otherwise, use 1 for drive A, 2 for drive B, and so on. The *info-type* parameter specifies what type of information will be returned. If it is 1, then upon return *info* points to a structure of type FSALLOCATE, which is defined like this:

```
typedef struct _FSALLOCATE {
        ULONG idFileSystem; /* system identifier */
        ULONG cSectorUnit;  /* sectors per cluster */
        ULONG cUnit;        /* total number of sectors */
        ULONG cUnitAvail;   /* available sectors */
        ULONG cbSector;     /* bytes per sector */
} FSALLOCATE;
```

In some OS/2 literature a cluster is referred to as a *unit*, but this book will continue to use cluster, because it is the more common name.

This program displays the number of bytes per sector, the number of sectors per cluster, the total disk space, and the total free disk space for the default drive. The total disk space is computed by multiplying the number of bytes per sector by the number of sectors per cluster by the number of clusters on the disk. The free space is computed by multiplying the number of bytes per sector by the number of sectors per cluster by the number of clusters available.

```
/* Demonstrate the DosQueryFSInfo service and display the number
    of bytes per sector, sectors per cluster, total disk
    space,and available disk space
*/

#define INCL_DOS

#include <os2.h>
#include <stdio.h>

main()
{
  FSALLOCATE f;

  DosQueryFSInfo(0, 1, &f, sizeof(f));

  printf("Bytes per sector: %ld\n", f.cbSector);
  printf("Sectors per cluster: %ld\n", f.cSectorUnit);
  printf("Total disk space: %ld\n",
        f.cbSector * f.cSectorUnit * f.cUnit);
  printf("Total available disk space: %ld\n",
        f.cbSector * f.cSectorUnit * f.cUnitAvail);
}
```

EXAMINING AND CHANGING THE DIRECTORY

OS/2 provides two important directory services called **DosQueryCurrentDir()** and **DosSetCurrentDir()**, which are used to return the pathname of the current directory and to change the current directory. Their prototypes are shown here:

APIRET APIENTRY DosQueryCurrentDir(ULONG *drive*,
                                   PBYTE *path*,
                                   PULONG *size*);

APIRET APIENTRY DosSetCurrentDir(PSZ *path*);

In **DosQueryCurrentDir()**, the *drive* parameter specifies the drive to be operated on. To specify the default drive, use 0 for *drive*. For drive A use 1, for drive B use 2, and so on. Upon return, the character array pointed to by *path* will hold the pathname of the directory. The integer pointed to by *size* must hold the length of the array pointed to by *path* prior to the call. It returns the length of the pathname.

In **DosSetCurrentDir()**, *path* points to the character array that holds the new directory pathname.

This program first displays the current directory name, switches to the root directory, and then switches back to the original directory.

```
/* Displaying and changing the directory    */

#define INCL_DOS

#include <os2.h>
#include <stdio.h>

main()
{
  CHAR olddirname[64], newdirname[64];
  ULONG size;

  size = 63;

  DosQueryCurrentDir(0, olddirname, &size);
  printf("current directory: %s\n", olddirname);
  DosSetCurrentDir("\\");
  DosQueryCurrentDir(0, newdirname, &size);
  printf("current directory: %s\n", newdirname);
  DosSetCurrentDir(olddirname);
  DosQueryCurrentDir(0, newdirname, &size);
  printf("current directory: %s\n", newdirname);

}
```

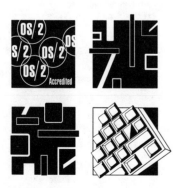

CREATING AND USING DYNAMIC LINK LIBRARIES

Before concluding this book we will examine one of OS/2's most important features: dynamic link libraries. Through the use of dynamic link libraries, your programs can be made more efficient and more maintainable. This chapter begins with an overview of dynamic linking, both at loadtime and runtime, and concludes with several examples. It is possible to create dynamic link libraries that have a single thread of execution or that have multiple threads. However, in this chapter we will be concerned only with single-thread dynamic link libraries.

Throughout the remainder of this chapter, the term *dynlink* will be used interchangeably with *dynamic link. Dynlink* was coined by the developers of OS/2 and its use seems appropriate.

WHAT IS DYNAMIC LINKING?

Put simply, dynamic linking is the process whereby references to external subroutines and/or data are resolved when the program is loaded. A linker, whether static or dynamic, has two main functions. First, it combines separately compiled modules and libraries into an executable program. Second, it resolves references to external functions or data. For example, if you have a main program file that uses library functions, when the program is compiled, only place-holding information is generated when a library function is called because the compiler has no way of knowing that function's location in memory. It is the linker's job to resolve these addresses.

Dynamic linking differs from static linking in one important way: when the linking takes place. When a program is statically linked, all functions that it requires are physically bound together in its .EXE file when it is compiled. However, in a dynamic linking situation, parts of a program reside in one or more dynlink libraries that are linked to the main program at loadtime. Here is a key point: the main program and its dynlink libraries are individually linked statically. However, the main program and its dynlinks are not statically linked to each other. Instead the final linking is performed by the OS/2 loader.

Although final linking is done by the loader, your program still needs to be linked by the linker. When your program calls a dynlink routine, an external reference is generated. When the linker encounters this reference, it generates code that will cause the appropriate dynamic linked library to be loaded when the program is executed. The entire loadtime linking process is invisible to the user. To understand just how transparent dynamic linking is, remember that the OS/2 API services are implemented as dynlinks.

DYNLINK ADVANTAGES

Dynamic linking has several advantages over the more traditional static linking. First, there is a great savings in disk space because each program does not contain the code found in the libraries. That is, when several programs that use the same library functions are statically linked, each program file contains copies of the library functions. However, when the same programs are dynamically linked, this duplication of code is avoided.

Another important advantage of dynamic linking is that it simplifies the chore of program maintenance. Because the routines in a dynlink library are separate from the main program, it is possible to upgrade or repair a dynlink routine without recompiling the entire program. For example, an accounting package could be upgraded when tax laws change by simply changing a dynlink library. When the program is executed, the new routine is automatically used.

IMPORTANT DYNLINK FILES

Each dynlink library is supported by a minimum of four separate files. First, there is the file that contains the source code to the dynlink routines. Most likely, this will be a C source file. The compiler transforms this file into a standard .OBJ file, which is the second file.

The third file is the definition file that is associated with the source file. This definition file could have the same name as the source file, but use the .DEF extension. The definition file contains several pieces of information that describe the dynlink library. (You will learn more about definition files a little later.)

Finally, there is the dynlink library itself. All dynlink library files must use the .DLL extension and must reside in the dynamic link directory. The .DLL file is created by the same linker used to provide static linking. It takes the .OBJ files created by the compiler and converts it into a dynlink file.

CREATING A SIMPLE DYNLINK LIBRARY

In this section a simple dynamic link library will be developed. Along the way you will learn several important requirements that must be met.

DYNLINK FUNCTIONS

All dynlink functions reside separately from the calling program's code. Dynlink functions, like the window and dialog functions presented in Part 2, must be declared with linkage type EXPENTRY. The return type also needs to be declared for all functions residing in a library even if there is no return value. (In this case the return type is VOID.)

Data within a dynlink function can be of two different types: *shared* data and *instance* data. Shared data, also known as global data, is shared among all processes that call the dynlink function. Instance data is just the opposite. Each process that calls the dynlink function has its own unique copy of the data. How the data is handled is defined in the .DEF file. Exact use of the .DEF file definitions is discussed in the sections that follow.

A SIMPLE DYNLINK LIBRARY

The following code will be used to create a very small dynlink library that contains only one function: **my_write()**. Assume that this file is called LIBTEST.C

```
/* A small library example. */

#include <os2.h>
#include <string.h>

VOID EXPENTRY my_write(PSZ s)
{
  ULONG written;

  DosWrite(1, s, strlen(s), &written);
  return;
}
```

Before this file can be transformed into a dynlink library, its definition file must be created. Although we will examine definition files in detail in the next section, the one shown here contains the minimal elements necessary to successfully convert LIBTEST.C into a dynlink library. Call this file LIBTEST.DEF.

```
LIBRARY libtest
EXPORTS my_write
```

The LIBRARY statement specifies the name of the dynlink library. The .DLL extension is assumed. The EXPORTS statement lists those functions in the dynlink library that are accessible by other programs. (A dynlink library can contain internal functions that are not usable by other programs.) The definition file is case sensitive and it must be entered as shown. Call this file LIBTEST.DEF.

To create the dynlink library, use this command:

```
ICC /Ge- LIBTEST.C LIBTEST.DEF
```

The /Ge- option tells the compiler to create a dynlink library instead of an executable file. In order for OS/2 to find the dynlink library, you must copy the resulting LIBTEST.DLL into the directory specified by the

LIBPATH environment variable found in the CONFIG.SYS file. OS/2 will also find the library if it is in the current directory.

ACCESSING DYNLINK FUNCTIONS

Creating the dynlink library and its support files is only one-half the story. You must follow a few special steps in order for your application program to access the dynlink functions. For example, this short program uses the **my_write()** function to output a string to the screen. Assume the name of this program is TEST.

```
/* Sample function to test library. */

#include <os2.h>

VOID EXPENTRY my_write(PSZ);

main()
{
  my_write("dynlink libraries work");
  return 0;
}
```

In order to access the dynlink library LIBTEST.DLL, it is necessary to create a definition file for the application program that names the functions in the library. (In the next section you will see that this is not always true.) In the application definition file, the dynlink functions accessed by the program are listed in an IMPORT command. A valid application definition file for this program is shown here:

```
NAME test WINDOWCOMPAT
IMPORTS libtest.my_write
```

The first line states the name of the program. The second line specifies which files will be imported from the LIBTEST.DLL dynlink library.

When you link the program, you must specify the application definition file on the linker command line. For example, assuming that the main program and definition files are called TEST, use this command to compile the program:

```
ICC TEST.C TEST.DEF
```

IMPORT LIBRARIES

Creating an *import library*, while unnecessary for accessing dynlink libraries, makes accessing the functions in a dynlink library a bit simpler. An import library allows your application and the dynlink libraries to be linked without requiring explicit naming of each of the library functions inside your application definition file. The OS/2 API libraries are import libraries. This is how you can access the API functions without explicitly naming the functions in a definition file. Import libraries are generated by the IMPLIB utility program using the dynlink's definition file. The general form of an IMPLIB command is shown here:

```
IMPLIB OUTPUT.LIB FILENAME.DEF
```

where OUTPUT.LIB is the name of the created import library and FILENAME.DEF is the definition file for the dynlink library. To create the import library for LIBTEST.DLL, use this command:

```
IMPLIB LIBTEST.LIB LIBTEST.DEF
```

Once created, the dynlink library can be accessed simply by linking directly to the import library. No definition file specifying each function in the dynlink library is needed.

The previous example program, TEST, can be compiled and linked to the LIBTEST dynlink library by using the following command:

```
ICC TEST.C LIBTEST.LIB
```

In this small example, the benefits of using the IMPLIB utility are not apparent. Imagine that you need to create a definition file listing all the API functions you want to use. The task could get overwhelming, but using the IMPLIB utility allows you to link knowing just the name of the library.

THE DEFINITION FILE

To create dynlink libraries, it is necessary to write a definition file for each library. Depending on your programming needs, you may also need a definition file for application programs. As you have seen, the most common use for a definition file is to specify what functions a dynlink library exports or what functions an application file imports. However, there are several other pieces of information that can be included in a definition file.

The linker recognizes many definition file commands. Many of the commands are optional. When a command is not included in the definition file, the default setting is used. Let's take a look at some of these linker commands now.

CODE

The CODE command tells the linker how to handle the code of the associated program or library. It takes this general form,

CODE *option_list*

where *option_list* may be one of the following:

Option	Meaning
PRELOAD	The code is loaded when the program begins execution
LOADONCALL	The code is loaded when it is needed (Default)

DATA

The DATA command tells the linker how to handle the data in the associated program or library. It takes this general form,

DATA *option_list*

where *option_list* may be one or more of the following:

Option	Meaning
PRELOAD	The automatic data is loaded when the program begins execution
LOADONCALL	The data is not loaded until it is needed (Default)
SINGLE	The same data is used by all executing versions of the module

Option	Meaning
MULTIPLE	Each executing version of the module has its own data (Default)
READONLY	The automatic data may be read but not written to
READWRITE	The automatic data may be read and written to (Default)

LIBRARY

The LIBRARY command is used to name the library and to determine when the dynlink function will be initialized and terminated. The initialization and termination routines can be called each time a process uses a dynlink, or called just once, the first time any process loads the dynlink. The LIBRARY command takes this general form,

LIBRARY *lib_name option_list*

where *lib_name* is the name of the library and *option_list* may be one or more of the following:

Option	Meaning
INITGLOBAL	The initialization routine is called once, on the first access (Default)
INITINSTANCE	The initialization routine is called for each separate process access
TERMGLOBAL	The termination routine is called once, when all processes are finished with the library
TERMINSTANCE	The termination routine is called each time a process finishes with a library

DESCRIPTION

The DESCRIPTION command imbeds the string that follows it into the executable file or library. It takes this general form:

DESCRIPTION *'string'*

Notice that the string must be enclosed between single quotes.

The main use for DESCRIPTION is to add copyright information into a program or library prepared for distribution.

EXPORTS

The EXPORTS command tells the linker which functions in a module will be accessible by other modules. You can specify multiple exported functions in a single EXPORTS command, but each must go on a separate line. The EXPORTS command supports several options. However, in its simplest form, EXPORTS takes this general form,

> EXPORTS *func_name1*
> *func_name2*
> .
> .
> .
> *func_nameN*

where *func_name* is the name of an exported function.

The EXPORTS command supports some additional options, but they are for advanced programming situations that are beyond the scope of this book.

IMPORTS

The IMPORTS command tells the linker what functions are used by the module and what files these functions are in. This command is mainly employed when dynamic link library functions are called by the module. In its simplest form, IMPORTS takes the following general form,

> IMPORTS *filename.func_name1*
> *filename.func_name2*
> .
> .
> .
> *filename.func_nameN*

where *filename* is the name of the file that contains the function specified by *func_name*. For example, to import the function **test()** from the library LIBTEST.DLL, use this IMPORT statement:

```
IMPORT LIBTEST._test
```

The linker will automatically add the .DLL extension to the library filename. You may import any number of functions, but each one must be placed on a separate line.

NAME

The NAME command serves two purposes. First, it identifies the associated source file as a program rather than as a library. Second, it can be used to specify the name of the file. The command takes this form,

NAME *name*

where *name* is the name of the application. If no *name* parameter is present, the name of the executable application file is used.

ANOTHER DYNLINK EXAMPLE

For a slightly larger example of creating and using dynlink libraries, separate routines are put in a dynlink library that may be accessed by any program you write. The source code for each of the functions is shown here. Call this file MYLIB.C.

```c
/* A dynlink library of functions. */

#define INCL_DOS
#include <os2.h>
#include <stdio.h>
#include <stdlib.h>
#include <time.h>

#define STDOUT 1
CHAR str[256];
ULONG written;


/* A simple clear screen—let the system do it. */
VOID EXPENTRY clear_screen(VOID)
```

```
{
  system("cls");
  return;
}



/* Prompt for input after clearing the screen. */
VOID EXPENTRY prompt_user(VOID)
{
   strcpy(str, "\n\nEnter a string:");
   DosWrite(STDOUT, str, sizeof(str), &written);
   return;
}



/* Display the time. */
VOID EXPENTRY do_beep700(VOID)
{
   DosBeep(700,700);
   return;
}
```

In order to create a dynlink from this file, you will need to create the definition file MYLIB.DEF, as shown here:

```
LIBRARY mylib
EXPORTS clear_screen
        prompt_user
        do_beep700
```

Compile and link this file into a dynlink library using the following command:

```
ICC /Ge- MYLIB.C MYLIB.DEF
```

To try the library, use this short program called SCREEN.C:

```
/* A sample program that calls the example library. */

#include <os2.h>
#include <stdio.h>

VOID EXPENTRY clear_screen(VOID);
VOID EXPENTRY prompt_user(VOID);
```

```
VOID EXPENTRY do_beep700(VOID);


main()
{
CHAR str[256];

  clear_screen();
  prompt_user();
  gets(str);
  printf("You entered: %s \n", str);
  do_beep700();
  return 0;
}
```

Create the SCREEN.DEF definition file for the SCREEN program as follows:

```
NAME test WINDOWCOMPAT
IMPORTS mylib.clear_screen
        mylib.prompt_user
        mylib.do_beep700
```

Compile and link the program using the following commands:

```
ICC SCREEN.C SCREEN.DEF
```

As explained earlier in this chapter, you can skip creating the application definition file if the IMPLIB utility is used to create an import library. The following command will create an import library for MYLIB:

```
IMPLIB MYLIB.LIB MYLIB.DEF
```

Now, instead of entering the SCREEN.DEF application definition file, the library can be linked directly with the following command:

```
ICC SCREEN.C MYLIB.LIB
```

Either method of building and linking your programs results in the same executable file and functionality.

RUNTIME DYNAMIC LINKING

As flexible as loadtime dynamic linking is, it is not the answer for all situations because it requires the name of the module and the name of the functions within the module to be known at compile time. Some applications need the ability to access a dynlink routine that is defined at runtime. For example, a problem-solving AI-based program may access a collection of problem-solving routines in its attempt to find a solution to a given problem. Using runtime dynamic linking, the problem solver could try an arbitrarily long list of different problem-solving functions—even new ones added while it is running—in its attempt to find a solution. In general, runtime dynamic linking allows your program to handle changing situations easily.

To enable runtime dynamic linking, OS/2 provides the services shown in Table 12-1. In this section, these services are discussed and an example is developed.

Service	Function
DosLoadModule( )	Loads the specified dynlink library
DosQueryProcAddr( )	Returns the address of a specific function within a dynlink module
DosQueryProcType( )	Returns procedure type: 16- or 32-bit
DosQueryModuleHandle( )	Returns the handle of a previously loaded module
DosFreeModule( )	Disposes of a dynlink module and frees the memory used by it

TABLE 12-1

Runtime Dynamic Linking Services

LOADING THE DYNLINK LIBRARY

Before your program can access a function that is loaded dynamically at runtime, the module that contains the function must be loaded into memory using the **DosLoadModule()** service whose prototype is shown here:

```
APIRET APIENTRY DosLoadModule(PSZ failbuf,
                              ULONG failbuf_size,
                              PSZ name,
                              PHMODULE mhandle);
```

The region of memory pointed to by *failbuf* receives information about the cause of a failure should an error prevent **DosLoadModule()** from finishing its load operation. The size of the buffer is specified by *failbuf_size*. Generally, 128 bytes is sufficient. The filename of the dynlink library, including drive and path information, must be pointed to by *name*. If successful, **DosLoadModule()** returns a module handle in the variable pointed to by *mhandle*.

If the module has already been loaded by another program, it is not reloaded.

ACCESSING DYNAMICALLY LOADED FUNCTIONS

Once the module has been loaded, you must use **DosQueryProcAddr()** to obtain the address of each function in the library you want to call. **DosQueryProcAddr()** has this prototype:

```
APIRET APIENTRY DosQueryProcAddr(HMODULE mhandle,
                                 ULONG ord,
                                 PSZ func_name,
                                 PFN func_addr);
```

The *mhandle* parameter must have been acquired through a call to **DosLoadModule()**. The parameter *ord* is the ordinal value of the desired procedure. If *ord* is set to zero, then the following parameter, *func_name*, must provide the function name. The string pointed to by *func_name* contains the name of the function that you want to call. This parameter is ignored if the previous parameter, *ord*, is a non-zero value. A pointer to the requested function is returned in the function pointer pointed to by *func_addr*.

To see a simple example of runtime dynamic linking, try this program:

```
/* This program assumes that the dynlink library MYLIB.DLL,
   developed earlier in this chapter, is available.
   If it is not, you must create it before attempting to
   use this program.
*/

#define INCL_DOSMODULEMGR

#include <os2.h>

CHAR failbuf[128];
HMODULE mhandle;

PFN func;

main()
{
  if(DosLoadModule(failbuf,          /* name of fail buffer */
                   sizeof(failbuf), /* size of fail buffer */
                   "libtest",       /* name of dynlink lib */
                   &mhandle))        /* the module handle   */
  {
    printf("error loading dynlink module");
    exit(1);
  }

  if(DosQueryProcAddr(mhandle, 0, "my_write", &func))
  {
    printf("cannot find the specified function");
    exit(1);
  }

  func("runtime dynlink module loading works");
}
```

As the comment at the start of the program suggests, this program dynamically loads the LIBTEST.DLL dynlink library developed in the first part of this chapter and uses **my_write()** from that library to display a message. You should pay special attention to the declaration of the function pointer **func**. Remember that **func** is the name of a *pointer* to a function. It is not the name of a function.

UNLOADING A DYNLINK LIBRARY

In the preceding example, the program terminated immediately after calling the dynlink function. However, in a real application this will probably not be the case. Since a program may need to load, at different times, several different library modules, OS/2 provides the **DosFreeModule()** service that removes a module and frees the memory it used. The prototype for **DosFreeModule()** is shown here,

APIRET APIENTRY DosFreeModule(HMODULE *mhandle*);

where *mhandle* is the handle of the module that is being removed.

A RUNTIME DYNAMIC LINK EXAMPLE

To help give you a feeling for using runtime dynlink libraries, a short file utility dynlink library will be created, along with a program that uses it. The file utility library is a slightly modified collection of functions developed in Chapter 11 that allows you to list the directory, browse through a file, list the contents of a file, and display information about your hard disk. Although this example could have been written without using runtime dynamic linking, it does illustrate its use. (Programs that actually need runtime dynamic linking tend to be quite long and complex, making them unsuitable for examples.)

The file dynlink functions are shown here:

```
/* A sample file utility library containing four functions. */

#define INCL_DOS

#include <os2.h>
#include <stdio.h>

VOID EXPENTRY show_dir(VOID);
VOID EXPENTRY browse_file(PSZ fname);
VOID EXPENTRY display_file(PSZ fname);
VOID EXPENTRY disk_info(VOID);


/* This program lists a directory. */

VOID EXPENTRY show_dir(VOID)
{
  FILEFINDBUF3 f;
```

```
  HDIR hdir;
  ULONG count;

  hdir = HDIR_CREATE; /* cause a new handle to be returned */
  count = 1;  /* find the first match */
  DosFindFirst("*.*", &hdir, 0, &f, sizeof(f), &count, 1);
  do
  {
    printf("%-13s %d\n", f.achName, f.cbFile);
    DosFindNext(hdir, &f, sizeof(f), &count);
  } while(count);
  DosFindClose(hdir);
}


/* A file browse program. */

VOID EXPENTRY browse_file(PSZ fname)
{
  ULONG fh;
  ULONG action;
  ULONG num_bytes;
  CHAR buf[513], ch;
  ULONG pos;
  LONG p;

  /* open the file, no file sharing */
  if(DosOpen(fname,       /* the file to open */
             &fh,         /* pointer to handle */
             &action,     /* pointer to result */
             0,           /* initial length */
             FILE_NORMAL, /* normal file */
             OPEN_ACTION_FAIL_IF_NEW | /* do not create */
             OPEN_ACTION_OPEN_IF_EXISTS, /* open if exists */
             OPEN_ACCESS_READONLY |   /* read only with */
             OPEN_SHARE_DENYREADWRITE, /* no sharing allowed*/
             0))   /* no extended attributes */
  {
    printf("error in opening file");
    exit(1);
  }

  /* main loop */
  pos = 0;
```

```
    do
    {
      if(DosRead(fh, buf, 512, &num_bytes))
      {
        printf("error reading file");
        exit(1);
      }
      buf[num_bytes] = '\0'; /* null terminate the buffer */
      printf(buf); /* display the buffer */

      /* see what to do next */
      ch = tolower(getc(stdin));
      switch(ch)
      {
        case 'e': /* move to end, the last 512 bytes */
          DosSetFilePtr(fh, -512, FILE_END, &pos);
          break;
        case 's': /* move to start, the first 512 bytes */
          DosSetFilePtr(fh, 0, FILE_BEGIN, &pos);
          break;
        case 'f': /* move forward */
          /* forward is automatic, so no change is required */
          pos += num_bytes;
          break;
        case 'b': /* move backward */
          p = pos - 512;
          if(p < 0)
            p = 0;
          DosSetFilePtr(fh, p, FILE_BEGIN, &pos);
      }

    } while(ch != 'q');

    if(DosClose(fh))
      printf("error closing file");
}

/* This function lists the entire file. */

VOID EXPENTRY display_file(PSZ fname)
{
  ULONG fh;
  ULONG action;
  ULONG num_bytes;
  CHAR buf[513];
```

```
  /* open the file, no file sharing */
  if(DosOpen(fname,        /* the file to open */
             &fh,          /* pointer to handle */
             &action,      /* pointer to result */
             0,            /* initial length */
             FILE_NORMAL,  /* normal file */
             OPEN_ACTION_FAIL_IF_NEW | /* do not create */
             OPEN_ACTION_OPEN_IF_EXISTS, /* open if exists */
             OPEN_ACCESS_READONLY |   /* read only with */
             OPEN_SHARE_DENYREADWRITE, /* no sharing allowed */
             0))   /* no extended attributes */
  {
    printf("error in opening file");
    exit(1);
  }

  do
  {
    if(DosRead(fh, buf, 512, &num_bytes))
    {
      printf("error reading file");
      exit(1);
    }
    buf[num_bytes] = '\0'; /* null terminate the buffer */
    printf(buf);
  } while(num_bytes);

  if(DosClose(fh))
    printf("error closing file");
}


/* Display information about the hard disk. */

VOID EXPENTRY disk_info(VOID)
{
  FSALLOCATE f;

  DosQueryFSInfo(0, 1, &f, sizeof(f));

  printf("Bytes per sector: %ld\n", f.cbSector);
  printf("Sectors per cluster: %ld\n", f.cSectorUnit);
  printf("Total disk space: %ld\n",
         f.cbSector * f.cSectorUnit * f.cUnit);
```

```
  printf("Total available disk space: %ld\n",
          f.cbSector * f.cSectorUnit * f.cUnitAvail);
}
```

Call this file FILE.C. The definition file for the library is shown here:

```
LIBRARY FILE
EXPORTS show_dir
        display_file
        browse_file
        disk_info
```

Compile and link FILE.C using the following commands:

```
ICC /Ge- FILE.C FILE.DEF
```

The next sample program shown here loads FILE.DLL during runtime and calls the appropriate function chosen by the user from the menu. Notice that the function pointer **func** does not have a prototype parameter list declared. Since the file functions do not all take the same number of parameters, it is not possible to use a prototype.

```
/* A simple menu driven file manager program that uses
   a runtime dynlink library.
*/

#define INCL_DOS

#include <os2.h>
#include <stdio.h>
#include <process.h>

UCHAR EXPENTRY menu(VOID);

CHAR failbuf[128];
HMODULE mhandle;
PFN func;

main()
{
  UCHAR choice;
  UCHAR fname[80];

  /* Load the dynlink library module. */
```

```
if(DosLoadModule(failbuf,          /* name of fail buffer */
                 sizeof(failbuf),  /* size of fail buffer */
                 "file",           /* name of dynlink lib */
                 &mhandle))        /* module handle */
{
  printf("error loading dynlink module");
  exit(1);
}

/* Display a menu of choices and process the selection. */
do
{
  choice = menu();
  switch(choice)
  {

    case 1:
      /* Display a file. */
      if(DosQueryProcAddr(mhandle, 0,
                          "display_file",
                          &func))
      {
        printf("cannot find the specified function");
        exit(1);
      }

      /* Get the file name. */
      puts("\nEnter a filename: ");
      gets(fname);

      /* Call the library routine. */
      func(fname);
      break;

    case 2:
      /* Browse through a file. */
      if(DosQueryProcAddr(mhandle, 0,
                          "browse_file",
                          &func))
      {
        printf("cannot find the specified function");
        exit(1);
      }

      /* Get the file name. */
```

```
         puts("\nEnter a filename: ");
         gets(fname);

         /* Call the library routine. */
         func(fname);
         break;

       case 3:
         /* Display the directory list. */
         if(DosQueryProcAddr(mhandle, 0,
                             "show_dir",
                             &func))
         {
           printf("cannot find the specified function");
           exit(1);
         }

         /* Call the library routine. */
         func();
         break;

       case 4:
         /* Display disk information. */
         if(DosQueryProcAddr(mhandle, 0,
                             "disk_info",
                             &func))
         {
           printf("cannot find the specified function");
           exit(1);
         }

         /* Call the library routine. */
         func();
         break;
     }
  } while(choice!=5);
  DosFreeModule(mhandle);
  return 0;
}


/* Display a menu. */

UCHAR EXPENTRY menu(VOID)
{
```

```
UCHAR reply[256];
UCHAR choice;

do {
/* Display menu choices */
puts("1. list a file");
puts("2. browse through a file");
puts("3. directory");
puts("4. disk info");
puts("5. quit");

  /* Get choice from user */
  puts("Enter your selection: ");
  gets(reply);
  choice = reply[0];
} while (choice < '1' || choice > '5');
/* convert to an ASCII value, and return */
return(choice - '0');
}
```

As you can see, the example program displays a list of menu choices to select from. To quit the program, select **5** from the menu.

DYNAMIC LINKING IMPLICATIONS

The use of dynlink libraries at either loadtime or runtime not only expands the options available to you when you create an application, but their use implies a fundamental restructuring of the approach taken to a program's design. To take the best advantage of dynlinks, it is necessary to group the various functional elements of your program into separate dynlink libraries. While this step is fairly obvious, the next is not. You must decide what parts of your program are, more or less, fixed and what parts might change. While it is conceivable to have the main program consist simply of a **main( )** function that issues calls to dynlink routines, a more likely situation will involve a balance between dynlink code and statically linked program code. The proper mix will vary between applications, and achieving it requires both thought and experimentation. Remember: the flexibility and improved maintainability of your programs is worth the extra effort dynamic linking requires.

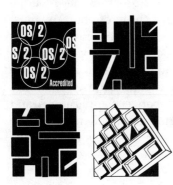

INDEX